D1370022

60 HIKES within 60 MILES
BIRMINGHAM
INCLUDING ANNISTON, GADSDEN, AND TUSCALOOSA

60 Hikes within 60 MILES

BIRMINGHAM

INCLUDING ANNISTON, GADSDEN, AND TUSCALOOSA

FIRST EDITION

Russell Helms

MENASHA RIDGE PRESS
Birmingham, Alabama

Library of Congress Cataloging-in-Publication Data
Helms, Russell, 1963–
60 Hikes within 60 miles, Birmingham (including Anniston, Gadsden, and Tuscaloosa)/
Russell Helms.—1st ed.
p.cm.
ISBN 0-89732-549-4
1. Hiking—Alabama—Birmingham Region—Guidebooks. 2. Trails—Alabama—Birmingham Region—Guidebooks. 3. Birmingham Region (Ala.)—Guidebooks. I. Title: Sixty hikes within sixty miles, Birmingham (including Anniston, Gadsden, and Tuscaloosa). II. Title

GV199.42.A22B574 2003
796.52'09761'781—dc22
2003058830
CIP

Cover design by Grant M. Tatum
Text design by Karen Ocker
Cover photo © Russell Helms
Author photo by Linda Frost
All other photos by Russell Helms
Maps by Steve Jones, Peggy Gordon, and Russell Helms

Menasha Ridge Press
P.O. Box 43673
Birmingham, AL 35243
www.menasharidge.com

For Granny—the toughest, kindest, most sensible
grandmother that has ever lived

TABLE OF CONTENTS

TABLE OF CONTENTS

ACKNOWLEDGMENTS

A special thanks to all of the hardworking men and women who created these trails and to those who maintain them. A special nod goes out to the staff of Ruffner Mountain Nature Preserve, Oak Mountain State Park, Cheaha State Park, Guntersville State Park, the Alabama Trails Association, and the American Hiking Society. The folks at Menasha Ridge Press are due their kudos, including Bob Sehlinger, Molly Merkle, Tricia Parks, Gabbie Oates, Nathan Lott, Steve Jones, Annie Long, Chris Mohney, Bud Zehmer, Marie Hillin, Marco Palmer, Travis Bryant, and Mopsy Gascon, my mysterious editor. I'd like to thank my wife and two daughters for accompanying me on many of these hikes, and for allowing me the many weekends I needed to knock these trails off one at a time. Last, but not least, I need to thank my feet for all of their hard work.

—*Russell Helms*

ABOUT THE AUTHOR

Russell Helms's lifelong interest in hiking and the outdoors has carried him along a variety of paths, from the mountains of the Appalachian Trail all the way to the remote highlands of Ethiopia. A graduate of Jefferson State, Auburn, and Yale, Helms lives in Birmingham. Happily, he reports, his wife and two children enjoy the outdoors, especially hiking and backpacking. Helms is an editor with Menasha Ridge Press of Birmingham, publishers of the *60 Hikes within 60 Miles* series. If you have any comments or discover any errors in the text or on the maps, please e-mail him at rhelms@menasharidge.com or write to Menasha Ridge Press, P.O. Box 43673, Birmingham, AL 35243.

FOREWORD

Welcome to Menasha Ridge Press's *60 Hikes within 60 Miles,* a series designed to provide hikers with the information they need to find and hike the very best trails surrounding metropolitan areas typically underserved by outdoor guidebooks.

Our strategy is simple: First, find a hiker who knows the area and loves to hike. Second, ask that person to spend a year researching the most popular and very best trails around. And third, have that person describe each trail in terms of difficulty, scenery, condition, elevation change, and other categories of information that are important to hikers. "Pretend you've just completed a hike and met up with other hikers at the trailhead," we told each author. "Imagine their questions, be clear in your answers."

An experienced hiker and writer, Russell Helms has selected 60 of the best hikes in and around the Birmingham metropolitan area. From the rugged wilds of the Cheaha wilderness to the urban gardens and green spaces of Birmingham, Helms provides hikers (and walkers) with a great variety of outings—and all within roughly 60 miles of Birmingham.

You'll get more out of this book if you take a moment to read the Introduction explaining how to read the trail listings. The "Topographic Maps" section will help you understand how useful topos are on a hike, and will also tell you where to get them. And though this is a "where-to," not a "how-to" guide, readers who have not hiked extensively will find the Introduction of particular value.

As much for the opportunity to free the spirit as well as to free the body, let these hikes elevate you above the urban hurry.

All the best,
The Editors at Menasha Ridge Press

PREFACE

Whether you need to clear the cobwebs, stretch your legs, hug a tree, or all of the above, the 60 hikes that follow guarantee a wealth of healthy walking (a.k.a. salubrious perambulation). Every third commercial on television touts a drug of some sort, but you'll never see hiking celebrated as the strong medicine it is. It may not come in a pill, but a vigorous hike is always good for what ails you.

For the hiker, Birmingham and the surrounding area, including Gadsden, Anniston, Tuscaloosa, Cullman, Blount County, St. Clair County, and Shelby County, host a surprising variety of trails. This book profiles day hikes, most of which can be hiked in a couple of hours. However, due to driving time and long trail length, some walks, such as the Sipsey River Trail or the Dugger Mountain Trail may require your entire day. But if you get to any trail in this book by noon, you'll never have to worry about the sun setting on you, unless you get lost (please don't do that).

Hiking is great sport and one that breaks with the conventions of many other sports. You don't have to wear a uniform (shorts and a T-shirt are fine). You can go alone if you want (it's usually safer to travel with another person, but a solitary hike can be a good thing). No one's timing you (you hope). And there's no official finish line (just don't get caught in the woods after dark).

Discovering and hiking the trails in my own backyard has been a real pleasure. Although I hiked most of them alone, I can't wait to revisit them with my family and friends. Most of the hikes proved to be not only great destinations for hiking but also great destinations for family recreation. For example, Hurricane Creek Park near Cullman has a cool trail and also has a scenic picnic area. Walk the trail and then eat a picnic lunch by the shaded creek. If you need more exercise, stop by the Ave Maria Grotto on your way back and round out your day with an unusual tour through Jerusalem in miniature.

Taken one at a time or packaged into a double-header, the hikes here provide a range of ways to fill an afternoon or a day with a healthy dose of breezy mind clearing and aerobic heart pumping.

A CITY MADE OF IRON

Birmingham is a city founded on coal, iron ore, and limestone. When blasted with fire exceeding 2,000 degrees, these minerals combine to form iron. Without iron, Birmingham as we know it would not exist. In fact, it would be a gas station (without

rest rooms) between Montgomery and Huntsville or a half-price fireworks stand between Atlanta and Tuscaloosa.

"Until the end of the nineteenth century, a bluff cap of fossil-bearing iron ore, 25 to 30 feet thick, rose from Red Mountain's Summit. Dozens of detached pieces, some 30 feet long, lay along its many ridges. Within the mountain, interspersed with shale and limestone, a red hematite ore formation spread in three seams from 3 to 50 feet thick. The seams extended 16 miles in an almost unbroken line from Ruffner Mountain, east of the city of Birmingham, to a point four miles south of the city of Bessemer. This mineral endowment gave the mountain its red hue, its name and, from 1864 until 1971, supported the growth of Birmingham's iron and steel industry."

—The Birmingham District: An Industrial History and Guide
by Marjorie White. Birmingham Historical Society, 1981.

The legacy of iron, and steel is all around us. Just look toward Red Mountain for the shiny new spear and freshly polished bottom of Vulcan, the Roman god of the forge. You certainly can't miss Sloss Furnaces looming above the First Avenue North viaduct. Drive through Tarrant City and you're sure to notice the quenching white smoke and yellow flames of the ABC plant where coke, an ingredient used to make steel, is still produced.

Travel away from the city in most any direction and the evidence continues. Take a trip out to Margaret in St. Clair County to see the old coal mines that helped feed the fires and purify the iron ore. Drive down to Tannehill State Park and see a Civil War–era furnace, located about a mile away from a cemetery where hundreds of slaves who worked the furnaces and mines are buried. Go southwest toward Tuscaloosa and you'll find more coal. Birmingham was, and still is, a city of iron.

PREFACE

The trails in this book are scattered across a wide area, but there are a few sites where trails are concentrated. The most accessible of these areas is Ruffner Mountain Nature Preserve, followed closely by Oak Mountain State Park. Which one is more accessible depends on what end of town you live in. The other area trail meccas, Cheaha State Park, Guntersville State Park, and the Sipsey Wilderness, are located east, northeast, and northwest of Birmingham. In a category of its own, located east of Birmingham, the 104-mile Pinhoti Trail traverses the Talladega National Forest, making for numerous day hike opportunities along its length.

RUFFNER MOUNTAIN

Ruffner Mountain is a 1,000-acre nature preserve, with 11 miles of marked trails, located in the East Lake/Eastwood area of Birmingham. The preserve is a public facility operated by the Ruffner Mountain Nature Coalition, which is a private not-for-profit corporation. Founded initially with only 20 acres back in 1977, Ruffner is now the second-largest urban nature preserve in the United States.

Numerous blazed paths crisscross the preserve, providing day hikers of all skill levels with something to appreciate. The preserve's main trail, the Quarry Trail, traverses the mountain, which is oriented in a general north-to-south direction. The Quarry Trail is a long ridge walk through a typical Southern upland forest.

The scenery within this forest gem is augmented with a rich history of iron-ore and limestone mining. From nearly all trails, ore pits and other remnants of mining from the late nineteenth century dot the forest. The most dramatic mine attraction is the abandoned limestone quarry located at the end of the Quarry Trail and its views from the top at Hawk's View Overlook and Sloss Peak (1,044 feet).

In addition to the 2.4-mile Quarry Trail (round-trip), the preserve hosts ten other marked trails, which generally travel up, down, and along the slopes of Ruffner Mountain, providing a variety of woodland scenery.

Not all there is to see on this mountain, though, is accessible from the marked trails. Ruffner boasts an active and energetic volunteer and nature education program, which includes guided hikes through unmarked portions of the preserve.

Trees blanket the mountain, including oaks, maples, pines, magnolia, cedar, elm, tulip poplar, persimmon, and many others. Wildflowers such as trillium, hydrangea, and black-eyed Susan abound in the warmer months. Due to its urban setting, visitors can also expect to see a variety of invasive ornamental plants. Russian olive, privet, mimosa, kudzu, and English ivy are among the non-native species that compete with and often overwhelm native species.

CHEAHA STATE PARK, THE CHEAHA WILDERNESS AREA, AND THE PINHOTI TRAIL

Located about 70 miles from Birmingham within the Talladega National Forest, Cheaha State Park and the Cheaha Wilderness are the premier rugged hiking venues in this area. Although located about 10 miles beyond the geographical scope of this book, Cheaha is simply too important and too much fun to bypass.

Cheaha State Park sits roughly in the middle of the surrounding Cheaha Wilderness, which is a rolling, steep collection of undulating ridge lines blanketed in pine and hardwood forests. The longer trails of Cheaha are not for the faint of heart (feet), but there is a hike here for everyone, including children.

At the top of Cheaha State Park is its namesake, and the highest point in Alabama, Cheaha Mountain. At 2,405 feet, it's not a very tall mountain. However, mountains in our part of the world are not characterized by height alone. Spend a few days hiking along the Pinhoti Trail, which passes over Cheaha Mountain, and you'll feel the raw power of these "hills" as some might call them.

Four of the hikes in this book incorporate different portions of the Pinhoti. Over 100 miles in length, the Pinhoti is Alabama's premier long trail. To read about a journey along its entire majestic length, find a copy of Johnny Molloy's *Long Trails of the Southeast* (2002). Often riding roughshod over sandstone outcroppings and plundering through gardens of quartzite, the Pinhoti offers a variety of challenging hikes.

The Pinhoti and other Talladega National Forest trails make beautiful walks, but can be unforgiving to an unwary hiker, especially where they cross the Cheaha and Dugger Mountain Wilderness Areas. In November 2002, two women and two children lost their way while on the Cave Creek Trail, just below Cheaha State Park. After three days, everyone feared the worst but fortunately the weary and cold hikers made it out safely, thanks to a massive search and rescue effort. Be prepared when you head to this neck of the woods. Study your map before you take off, and then don't forget to take it with you. Even without a compass, a map is very useful when faced with an unexpected trail fork. But don't fear the forest, just respect it.

One of the perks of a visit to Cheaha, in addition to the views, the trees, and the exercise, are the facilities. After a tromp around the Nubbin Creek Loop or a glute flex along the Pinhoti Trail: Blue Mountain Jaunt, head up to the Cheaha Lodge Restaurant and dig in to their expansive and tasty lunch buffet. Feel like spending a couple of nights in the woods to clear your head? Well, you can either do it by camping out on the trails or in one of the campgrounds. If you're feeling royal, you can stay in one of the park's lodge rooms. Cabins are available as well.

OAK MOUNTAIN STATE PARK

The most visited hiking destination near Birmingham, 9,000-acre Oak Mountain State Park sees over half a million visitors each year. Not only a hiking destination, Oak Mountain is home to a variety of other recreational opportunities such as trail running, mountain biking, horseback riding, swimming, camping, and canoeing.

It's a great place to spend the day. I like to picnic by the lake and then take the family on a short hike, usually along the Tree Top Nature Trail and then up through the woods to the Wildlife Rehabilitation Center. If I'm not with the family, I'm liable to break out the mountain bike and tear around the Red Trail or head straight up

Mushroom Rock at Horse Pens 40

Double Oak Mountain on the Peavine Falls Trail for a vigorous leg stretcher.

In 2003, Oak Mountain made the front page after details of a planned expansion of park services was unveiled. Especially provoking to many hikers and bikers was a plan to increase road penetration into the scenic areas of the park. The public controversy has brought a temporary halt to planned road construction, but what the master plan ultimately holds remains to be seen.

The largest of Alabama's state parks, Oak Mountain needs around $3 million a year in revenue to stay open. Golf greens fees and cart rentals have historically been the workhorse of the revenue stream, but golf revenues have been declining. Gate fees are now a much more significant component of revenue for Oak Mountain. Thus it's important to keep the people coming to the park, and hopefully that can be accomplished without compromising the solitude many seek along its slopes and ridges.

LAKE GUNTERSVILLE STATE PARK

A small but well-kept state park, Lake Guntersville contains quite a number of worthy trails, three of which have been profiled in this book. You'll occasionally spot deer in other state parks, but this park almost guarantees a sighting of one, if not many in a large group of white tails.

With a large lakeside campground, a spacious swim beach, a resort lodge, cottages, chalets, and a convention center, Lake Guntersville is a destination. But whether you visit for a day or a week, the park's 31 miles of wooded trails are worth the drive. Not only can you spot deer here, you can also join other visitors during the month of January for special eagle-watching programs. The Cutchenmine Trail (p.79) is an especially good area from which to watch for endangered American bald eagles.

TRAILS GALORE

If you think that these 60 hikes are all that the area has to offer, think again. As I finished the last trail for this book, I couldn't help but ponder the wealth of wooded paths that are not included. I constantly stumbled across new paths and promises of even newer paths.

Although the Talladega National Forest and the Sipsey Wilderness contain many trails not profiled here, the decommissioned military base at Fort McClellan and lands around the Anniston/Oxford area probably hold the greatest number and variety of previously inaccessible trails.

Wild and wooly Coldwater Mountain, located southwest of Anniston, has just recently been declared a state nature preserve and recreation area. Already trail construction has begun on the 3,900-acre tract, but the area is not yet open to the public.

When complete, a 40-mile network of multiuse trails will provide hikers, bikers, and runners with a new playground. The downside to this development is that current access points to the mountain are occupied by Solutia-owned hazardous waste landfills located along Highway 202.

Another boon to future trails is the Mountain Longleaf National Wildlife Refuge. Discovered only recently on lands occupied by Fort McClellan, the 9,000-acre site is home to the last old-growth stand of mountain longleaf pine in the state. The Nature Conservancy has identified 11 rare plant species and 21 rare animal species within the preserve. Look for both Coldwater Mountain and Mountain Longleaf to open to the public in 2004.

And that's just the tip of the iceberg. With all of the wild woodlands and urban green spaces available to us, it seems that hiking reality in Birmingham is catching up with hiking potential.

RECOMMENDED HIKES

BUSY HIKES

Aldridge Gardens Trail
Ave Maria Grotto Trail
(Doug Ghee) Bald Rock
 Boardwalk
Cahaba Lily Park Nature Trail
Chinnabee Silent Trail
 featuring Cheaha Falls

Civil Rights Trail
Hurricane Creek Park Loop
Jefferson State Combo
Jemison Park Nature Trail
Lakeshore Trail
Martin Wildlife Park Trail

Moss Rock Preserve Trail
Oak Hill Cemetery Walk
Oak Mountain: Tree Top
 Nature Trail
Ruffner Mountain:
 Quarry Trail
Sloss Furnaces Trail

HIKES FEATURING WATERFALLS

Chinnabee Silent Trail
 featuring Cheaha Falls
Hurricane Creek Park Loop
Moss Rock Preserve Trail

Noccalula Falls Historic
 Gorge Trail
Nubbin Creek Loop

Oak Mountain: Peavine Falls
 Combo
Sipsey River Trail
Swann Bridge Trail

HIKES FEATURING WILDFLOWERS

Aldridge Gardens Trail
Cheaha Lake Trail
Chinnabee Silent Trail
 featuring Talladega
 Mountain
Dugger Mountain
 from the East
Dugger Mountain
 from the South

Flint Creek White Loop
Guntersville State Park:
 Tom Bevill Trail
Horse Pens 40 Loop
Lake Chinnabee Loop
Martin Wildlife Park Trail
Pinhoti Trail: Pine Glen to
 Sweetwater Lake
Pulpit Rock Trail

Ruffner Mountain: Marian
 Harnach Nature Trail
Ruffner Mountain:
 Trillium/Hollow Tree Trail
Sumatanga Mountain Loop
Sumatanga Red Trail
University of Alabama
 Arboretum Trail

HIKES GOOD FOR CHILDREN

Aldridge Gardens Trail
Ave Maria Grotto Trail
(Doug Ghee) Bald Rock
 Boardwalk
Big Mountain Loop
Cahaba Lily Park Nature Trail
Chinnabee Silent Trail
 featuring Cheaha Falls
Civil Rights Trail
Coleman Lake Loop
Deerlick Creek Combo

East Lake Park Loop
Guntersville State Park:
 Cutchenmine Traill
Jemison Park Nature Trail
Lakeside Park Loop
Martin Wildlife Park Trail
Moss Rock Preserve Trail
Oak Hill Cemetery Walk
Palisades Park Nature Trail
Pinhoti Trail: Pine Glen to
 Sweetwater Lake

Pulpit Rock Trail
Ruffner Mountain:
 Geology Trail
Ruffner Mountain: Marian
 Harnach Nature Trail
Ruffner Mountain:
 Trillium/Hollow Tree Trail
Sloss Furnaces Trail
Tannehill Ironworks Trail
University of Alabama
 Arboretum Trail

RECOMMENDED HIKES

HIKES GOOD FOR SOLITUDE

Dugger Mountain
   from the East
Dugger Mountain
   from the South

Nubbin Creek Loop
Oak Mountain Loop
Oak Mountain: Lake
   Tranquility Loop

Pinhoti Trail: Cave Creek
   Loop
Sipsey River Trail
Sumatanga Mountain Loop

HIKES GOOD FOR WILDLIFE VIEWING

Cahaba River WMA Hike
Coleman Lake Loop
Dugger Mountain
   from the East
Dugger Mountain

from the South
Guntersville State Park:
   Cutchenmine Trail
Guntersville State Park:
   Lickskillet Trail

Horse Pens 40 Loop
Martin Wildlife Park Trail
   (waterfowl)
Sumatanga Mountain Loop

HIKES WITH STEEP SECTIONS

Cahaba River WMA Hike
Cheaha Lake Trail
Chinnabee Silent Trail
   featuring Talladega
   Mountain
Dugger Mountain
   from the East
Dugger Mountain
   from the South
Guntersville State Park:
   Lickskillet Trail

Noccalula Falls Historic
   Gorge Trail
Oak Mountain Hike and Bike
Oak Mountain Loop
Oak Mountain: Lake
   Tranquility Loop
Oak Mountain: Peavine Falls
   Combo
Pinhoti Trail: Adams Gap to
   Disaster
Pinhoti Trail: Blue Mountain
   Jaunt

Pinhoti Trail: Cave Creek
   Loop
Ruffner Mountain: Buckeye
   Trail
Ruffner Mountain:
   Mines Hike
Ruffner Mountain:
   Quarry Trail
Sumatanga Mountain Loop
Sumatanga Red Trail

HISTORIC TRAILS

Ave Maria Grotto Trail
Civil Rights Trail
Horse Pens 40 Loop
Noccalula Falls Historic
   Gorge Trail

Oak Hill Cemetery Walk
Ruffner Mountain:
   Geology Trail
Ruffner Mountain:
   Mines Hike

Ruffner Mountain: Quarry
   Walk
Sloss Furnaces Trail
Swann Bridge Trail
Tannehill Ironworks Trail

LAKE HIKES

Aldridge Gardens Trail
Cheaha Lake Trail
Coleman Lake Loop
Deerlick Creek Combo

East Lake Park Loop
Guntersville State Park:
   Cutchenmine Trail
Lake Chinnabee Loop
Lakeside Park Loop

Martin Wildlife Park Trail
Oak Mountain: Lake
   Tranquility Loop
Sumatanga Mountain Loop

RECOMMENDED HIKES

SCENIC HIKES

Aldridge Gardens Trail
Ave Maria Grotto Trail
(Doug Ghee) Bald Rock
  Boardwalk
Cheaha Lake Trail
Dugger Mountain
  from the East
Dugger Mountain
  from the South
Horse Pens 40 Loop

Hurrican Creek Park Loop
Noccalula Falls Historic
  Gorge Trail
Nubbin Creek Loop
Oak Hill Cemetery Walk
Oak Mountain Hike and Bike
Oak Mountain Loop
Oak Mountain: Lake
  Tranquility Loop

Pinhoti Trail: Cave Creek
  Loop
Pulpit Rock Trail
Ruffner Mountain:
  Mines Hike
Ruffner Mountain:
  Quarry Trail
Sumatanga Mountain Loop
Swann Bridge Trail

TRAILS GOOD FOR MOUNTAIN BIKES

Cahaba River WMA Hike
Flint Creek White Loop

Maplebridge–Horseshoe
  Ramble

Oak Mountain Hike and Bike
Munny Sokol Park Loop

TRAILS GOOD FOR RUNNERS

Cahaba Lily Park Nature Trail
Cahaba River WMA Hike
Deerlick Creek Combo
Flint Creek White Loop
Guntersville State Park:
  Cutchenmine Trail

Jefferson State Combo
Jemison Park Nature Trail
Lakeshore Trail
Lakeside Park Loop
Martin Wildlife Park Trail
Oak Hill Cemetery Walk

Oak Mountain Hike and Bike
Oak Mountain: Lake
  Tranquility Loop
University of Alabama
  Arboretum Trail

URBAN HIKES

Aldridge Gardens Trail
Ave Maria Grotto Trail
Cahaba Lily Park Nature Trail
Civil Rights Trail
Jefferson State Combo

Jemison Park Nature Trail
Lakeshore Trail
Lakeside Park Loop
Martin Wlidlife Park Trail

Moss Rock Preserve Trail
Oak Hill Cemetery Walk
Sloss Furnaces Trail
Vulcan Trail

HIKES LESS THAN 1 MILE

Ave Maria Grotto Trail
(Doug Ghee) Bald Rock
  Boardwalk

Big Mountain Loop
Oak Hill Cemetery Walk
Ruffner Mountain:
  Geology Trail

Ruffner Mountain: Marian
  Harnach Nature Trail

RECOMMENDED HIKES

HIKES 1 TO 3 MILES

Aldridge Gardens Trail
Cahaba Lily Park Nature Trail
Civil Rights Trail
Coleman Lake Loop
East Lake Park Loop
Fossil Mountain Trail
Guntersville State Park:
  Cutchenmine Trail
Horse Pens 40 Loop
Hurrican Creek Park Loop
Jefferson State Combo
Lake Chinnabee Loop

Lakeside Park Loop
Maplebridge–Horseshoe
  Ramble
Martin Wlidlife Park Trail
Moss Rock Preserve Trail
Noccalula Falls Historic
  Gorge Trail
Oak Mountain: Tree Top
  Nature Trail
Palisades Park Nature Trail
Pulpit Rock Trail
Ruffner Mountain:
  Buckeye Trail

Ruffner Mountain: Ridge and
  Valley Combo
Ruffner Mountain:
  Trillium/Hollow Tree Trail
Sloss Furnaces Trail
Munny Sokol Park Loop
Sumatanga Red Trail
Swann Bridge Trail
University of Alabama
  Arboretum Trail
Vulcan Trail

HIKES 3 TO 6 MILES

Cahaba River WMA Hike
Cheaha Lake Trail
Chinnabee Silent Trail
  featuring Cheaha Falls
Chinnabee Silent Trail
  featuring Talladega
  Mountain
Deerlick Creek Combo

Guntersville State Park:
  Tom Bevill Trail
Guntersville State Park:
  Lickskillet Trail
Jemison Park Nature Trail
Lakeshore Trail
Pinhoti Trail: Blue Mountain
  Jaunt

Pinhoti Trail: Pine Glen to
  Sweetwater Lake
Ruffner Mountain: Mines
  Hike
Ruffner Mountain:
  Quarry Trail
Sumatanga Mountain Loop
Tannehill Ironworks Trail

HIKES LONGER THAN 6 MILES

Dugger Mountain
  from the East
Dugger Mountain
  from the South
Flint Creek White Loop
Nubbin Creek Loop

Oak Mountain Hike and Bike
Oak Mountain Loop
Oak Mountain: Lake
  Tranquility Loop
Oak Mountain: Peavine Falls
  Combo

Pinhoti Trail: Adams Gap to
  Disaster
Pinhoti Trail: Cave Creek
  Loop
Sipsey River Trail

INTRODUCTION

Welcome to *60 Hikes within 60 Miles: Birmingham*. If you're new to hiking or even if you're a seasoned trail-smith, take a few minutes to read the following introduction. I'll explain how this book is organized and how best to use it.

HIKE DESCRIPTIONS

Each hike contains six key items: a locator map, an brief description of the trail, an at-a-glance information box, directions to the trail, a trail map, and a hike narrative. Combined, the maps and information provide a clear method to assess each trail from the comfort of your favorite chair.

LOCATOR MAP

After narrowing down the general area of the hike on the overview map (see p. 288–inside back cover), the locator map, along with driving directions given in the narrative, enable you to find the trailhead. Once at the trailhead, park only in designated areas.

IN BRIEF

A "taste of the trail." Think of this section as a snapshot focused on the historical landmarks, beautiful vistas, and other interesting sights you may encounter on the trail.

KEY AT-A-GLANCE INFORMATION

The information in the key at-a-glance boxes gives you a quick idea of the specifics of each hike. There are 12 basic elements covered.

LENGTH The length of the trail from start to finish. There may be options to shorten or extend the hikes, but the mileage corresponds to the described hike. Consult the hike description to help decide how to customize the hike for your ability or time constraints.

CONFIGURATION A description of what the trail might look like from overhead. Trails can be loops, out-and-backs (that is, along the same route), figure eights, or balloons.

DIFFICULTY The degree of effort an "average" hiker should expect on a given hike. For simplicity, difficulty is described as "easy," "moderate," or "difficult."

SCENERY Rates the overall environs of the hike and what to expect in terms of plant life, wildlife, streams, and historic buildings.

INTRODUCTION

EXPOSURE A quick check of how much sun you can expect on your shoulders during the hike. Descriptors used are self-explanatory and include terms such as shady, exposed, and sunny.

TRAFFIC Indicates how busy the trail might be on an average day, and if you might be able to find solitude out there. Trail traffic, of course, varies from day to day and season to season.

TRAIL SURFACE Indicates whether the trail is paved, rocky, smooth dirt, or a mixture of elements.

HIKING TIME How long it takes to hike the trail. A slow but steady hiker will average 2 to 3 miles an hour depending on the terrain.

ACCESS Notes fees or permits needed to access the trail. In most cases no fees or permits are required. Oak Mountain and Tannehill State Parks are the only places where you'll have to pay an entry fee to access a trail. Some trailhead parking, though, in the National Forest areas have self-pay boxes ($2–3) per day).

MAPS Which map is the best, or easiest, for this hike and where to get it.

FACILITIES What to expect in terms of rest rooms, phones, water, and other niceties available at the trailhead or nearby.

SPECIAL COMMENTS These comments cover little extra details that don't fit into any of the above categories. Here you'll find information on trail hiking options and facts such as whether or not to expect a lifeguard at a nearby swimming beach.

DIRECTIONS

Used with the locator map, the directions will help you locate each trailhead.

DESCRIPTIONS

The trail description is the heart of each hike. Here, I provide a summary of the trail's essence as well as highlight any special traits the hike offers. Ultimately, the hike description will help you choose which hikes are best for you.

NEARBY ACTIVITIES

Not every hike will have this listing. For those that do, look here for information on nearby sights of interest.

WEATHER

A nice thing about Birmingham is that the weather is generally pleasant. There are cold snaps and hot spells as the older folks say, but there is no time of the year when hiking is not an option due to weather.

Forested areas such as Ruffner Mountain, Oak Mountain, and Cheaha Wilderness generally maintain a cooler atmosphere in the summers, which can be very hot out in the open. Highs in July and August often exceed the high 90s. This kind of heat is dangerous if not prepared for, so it's best to hike in the morning or late afternoon. A wooded destination is a wise choice as well.

The coldest months in Birmingham are December, January, and February. Someone visiting Birmingham from further north would find the winters here very pleasant. The primary concern with these cold-weather months is rain. It rarely snows in Birmingham, maybe a light dusting or two each year, but when the temperature drops below freezing after or during a steady rain, watch out!

Within a few hours, a thin layer of ice can build up on area roads and completely paralyze the city and the surrounding area. It's not uncommon for school systems to close with just a threat of icy roads. Needless to say, this correlates with hiking in two ways. First, during road icing, it's impossible to drive because of road closures. Second, an icy trail can be hazardous to your health, especially your tailbone.

Ultimately Birmingham weather is optimal for year-round hiking. Just take the proper precautions during hot spells, cold snaps, and rain; and you're set.

TEMPERATURE AVERAGES BY MONTH

	JAN	FEB	MAR	APR	MAY	JUN
High	53	58	67	74	81	88
Low	32	35	42	48	58	65
Mean	43	47	55	61	69	76

	JUL	AUG	SEP	OCT	NOV	DEC
High	91	90	85	75	65	56
Low	70	69	63	51	42	35
Mean	80	80	74	63	53	46

MAPS

The maps in this book have been produced with great care and, used with the hiking directions, will help you stay on course. But as any experienced hiker knows, things can get tricky off the beaten path.

The maps in this book, when used with the route directions present in each chapter, are sufficient to direct you to the trail and guide you on it. However, you will find superior detail and valuable information in the United States Geological Survey's 7.5-minute series topographic maps. Locally an extensive selection of topo maps is available at Carto-Craft (see Appendix C). Topo maps are available online in many locations. The easiest single web resource is located at terraserver.microsoft.com. You can view and print topos of the entire Unites States there, and view aerial photographs of the entire Unites States, as well. The downside to topos is that most of them are outdated, having been created 20 to 30 years ago. But they still provide excellent topographic detail.

If you're new to hiking you might be wondering, "What's a topographic map?" In short, a topo indicates not only linear distance but elevation as well, using contour lines. Contour lines spread across the map like dozens of intricate spiderwebs. Each line represents a particular elevation and at the base of each topo a contour's interval designation is given. If the contour interval is 200 feet, then the distance between each contour line is 200 feet. Follow five contour lines up on a map and the elevation has increased by 1,000 feet.

In addition to outdoor shops and bike shops, you'll find topos at major universities and some public libraries, where you might try photocopying the ones you need to avoid the cost of buying them. But if you want your own and can't find them locally, contact the United States Geological Survey (see Appendix C).

TRAIL ETIQUETTE

Whether you're on a city, county, state, or national park trail, always remember that great care and resources (from Nature as well as from your tax dollars) have gone into creating these trails. Treat the trail, wildlife, and fellow hikers with respect.

Here are a few general ideas to keep in mind while on the trail.

1. Hike on open trails only. Respect trail and road closures (ask if not sure), avoid possible trespassing on private land, and obtain all permits and authorization as required. Also, leave gates as you found them or as marked.

2. Leave only footprints. Be sensitive to the ground beneath you. This also means staying on the trail and not creating any new ones. Be sure to pack out what you pack in. No one likes to see the trash someone else has left behind.

3. Never spook animals. An unannounced approach, a sudden movement, or a loud noise startles most animals. A surprised snake or skunk can be dangerous for you, for others, and to themselves. Give animals extra room and time to adjust to your presence.

4. Plan ahead. Know your equipment, your ability, and the area in which you are hiking—and prepare accordingly. Be self-sufficient at all times; carry necessary supplies for changes in weather or other conditions. A well-executed trip is a satisfaction to you and to others.

5. Be courteous to other hikers, or bikers, you meet on the trails.

WATER

"How much is enough? One bottle? Two? Three?! But think of all that extra weight!" Well, one simple physiological fact should convince you to err on the side of excess when it comes to deciding how much water to pack: A hiker working hard in 90-degree heat needs approximately ten quarts of fluid every day. That's two and a half gallons—12 large water bottles or 16 small ones. In other words, pack along one or two bottles even for short hikes.

Serious backpackers hit the trail prepared to purify water found along the route. This method, while less dangerous than drinking it untreated, comes with risks. Purifiers with ceramic filters are the safest, but are also the most expensive. Many hikers pack along the slightly distasteful tetraglycine hydroperiodide tablets (sold under the names Potable Aqua, Coughlan's, and others).

Probably the most common water-borne "bug" that hikers face is *Giardia,* which may not hit until one to four weeks after ingestion. It will have you passing noxious rotten-egg gas, vomiting, shivering with chills, and living in the bathroom. But there are other parasites to worry about, including *E. coli* and *Cryptosporidium* (that are harder to kill than *Giardia*).

For most people, the pleasures of hiking make carrying water a relatively minor price to pay to remain healthy. If you're tempted to drink "found water," do so only if you understand the risks involved. Better yet, hydrate prior to your hike, carry (and drink) six ounces of water for every mile you plan to hike, and hydrate after the hike.

FIRST-AID KIT

A typical kit may contain more items than you might think necessary. These are just the basics:

Sunscreen

Aspirin or acetaminophen

Butterfly-closure bandages

Band-Aids

Snakebite kit

Gauze (one roll)

Gauze compress pads
  (a half-dozen 4 in. x 4 in.)

Ace bandages or Spenco joint wraps

Benadryl or the generic equivalent—
  diphenhydramine (an antihistamine,
  in case of allergic reactions)

A prefilled syringe of epinephrine (for
  those known to have severe allergic
  reactions to such things as bee stings)

Water purification tablets or water filter
  (see note above)

Moleskin/Spenco "Second Skin"

Hydrogen peroxide or iodine

Antibiotic ointment (Neosporin or the
  generic equivalent)

Matches or pocket lighter

Whistle (more effective in signaling rescuers than your voice)

Pack the items in a waterproof bag such as a Ziploc bag or a similar product. You will also want to include a snack for hikes longer than a couple of miles. A bag full of GORP (Good Ol' Raisins and Peanuts) will quickly kick up your energy level.

HIKING WITH CHILDREN

No one is too young for a hike in the woods or through a city park. Be mindful, though. Flat, short trails are best with an infant. Toddlers who have not quite mastered walking can still tag along, riding on an adult's back in a child carrier. Use common sense to judge a child's capacity to hike a particular trail, and always rely on the possibility that the child will tire quickly and need to be carried.

INTRODUCTION

When packing for the hike, remember the needs of the child as well as your own. Make sure children are adequately clothed for the weather, have proper shoes, and are protected from the sun with sunscreen. Kids dehydrate quickly, so make sure you have plenty of fluids for them as well.

To determine which trails are suitable for children, a list of hike recommendations for children is provided on p. xvi.

Finally, when hiking with children, remember the trip will be a compromise. A child's energy and enthusiasm alternate between bursts of speed and long stops to examine snails, sticks, dirt, and other attractions.

THE BUSINESS HIKER

Whether in the Birmingham area on business as a resident or visitor, these 60 hikes offer perfect getaways from the busy demands of commerce. Many of the hikes are classified as urban and are easily accessible from downtown areas. For downtown workers, Oak Hill Cemetery, the Vulcan Trail, or one of the trails of Ruffner Mountain are good choices for a lunchtime meander. Check the overview map (p. 288–inside back cover) to locate hikes nearest your workplace.

A NOTE ABOUT HUNTING

Trails that pass through national forest land or state Wildlife Management Areas (WMA) are best avoided during the various hunting seasons. As a rule of thumb, avoid trails in the Choccolocco WMA and the Shelby County WMA from September 7 through April 30. For the Talladega National Forest, the primary concern to hikers is deer season, which runs from November 26 through January 31.

SNAKES

In summer while hiking, I almost always have a nonpoisonous snake sighting. Rarely do I come across a rattlesnake or other poisonous variety. If I do, I make a wide berth and leave it alone. The snakes I find are usually king snakes, rat snakes, or black racers. The best way to recognize a poisonous snake is to spend some time studying the subject before you head into the woods. As a simple rule of thumb, don't toy with any snake, especially ones with triangular-shaped heads. Of the approximately 40 species of snake in Alabama, only 6 are actually poisonous.

TICKS

Ticks like to hang out in the brush that grows along trails. I've noticed that July is the peak month for ticks in our area, but you should be tick-aware during all months of the spring, summer, and fall. Ticks, actually arthropods and not insects, are ectoparasites, which need a host for the majority of their life cycle in order to reproduce. The ticks that light onto you while hiking will be very small, sometimes so tiny that you won't be able to spot them. Primarily of two varieties, deer ticks and dog ticks, both need a few hours of actual attachment before they can transmit any disease they may harbor. I've found ticks in my socks and on my legs several hours after a hike that have not yet anchored. The best strategy is to visually check every half-hour or so while hiking, do a thorough check before you get in the car, and then, when you take a post-hike shower, do an even more thorough check of your entire body. Ticks that haven't latched on are easily removed, but not easily killed. If I pick off a tick in the woods, I just toss it aside. If I find one on my person at home, I make sure and dispatch it down the toilet. For ticks that have embedded, removal with tweezers is best.

POISON IVY/POISON OAK/POISON SUMAC

Recognizing and avoiding contact with poison ivy, oak, and sumac is the most effective way to prevent the painful, itchy rashes associated with these plants. In the South, poison ivy occurs as a vine or shrub, three leaflets to a leaf; poison oak occurs as either a vine or shrub, with three leaflets as well; and poison sumac flourishes in swampland, each leaf containing 7 to 13 leaflets. Urushiol, the oil in the sap of these plants, is responsible for the rash.

Within 12 to 24 hours of exposure, raised lines and/or blisters will appear, accompanied by a terrible itch. Refrain from scratching because bacteria under fingernails may cause infection. Wash and dry the rash thoroughly, applying a calamine lotion to help dry out the rash. If itching or blistering is severe, seek medical attention. If you do come into contact with one of these plants, remember that oil-contaminated clothes, pets, or hiking gear can easily inflict an irritating rash on you or someone else, so wash not only any exposed parts of your body but also clothes, gear, and pets if applicable.

ALDRIDGE GARDENS TRAIL

IN BRIEF

The walk at Aldridge Gardens is short, but it's free, it's gorgeous, and it's right in your own backyard.

DESCRIPTION

Formerly the Coxe Family Estate, horticulturalist Eddie Aldridge purchased the garden's 30 acres in 1977, planning to develop the land into a public garden. Aldridge, along with the City of Hoover, dedicated the land in 1997 to that purpose. In its first year of public operation (2003), the gardens are open to the public and are still expanding. One of the gardens' goals is to host the largest collection of hydrangeas in the world.

The bulk of this walk is the loop around the lake. After that, a route is profiled here that takes you past most of the gardens' highlights. You'll probably want to wander around to see it all, though. To begin, pass through an ornamental iron gate flanked by an abundance of flowers and shrubs, including elephant ear, holly, magnolia, and hydrangea. Tall white pines shade the landscaped areas.

Walk along a paved path, pass a manicured picnic area to your right and head toward the Aldridge House, which serves as a visitor center. Pass by an elegant gingko tree in the middle of a paved loop in front of the house and pick up a map and other brochures at kiosks there.

To reach the lake loop, head back toward the main gate and take a left on a paved path lined

KEY AT-A-GLANCE INFORMATION

LENGTH: 0.8 miles

CONFIGURATION: Loop around the lake; meander through the garden

DIFFICULTY: Easy

SCENERY: Small lake, beautifully landscaped flower-and-shrub garden featuring hydrangeas

EXPOSURE: About half shaded

TRAFFIC: Moderate

TRAIL SURFACE: Gravel path and paved walkways

HIKING TIME: 30 minutes to an hour

ACCESS: Open 8 a.m.–8 p.m., Monday–Saturday; 1–8 p.m., Sunday. Admission is free, but donations are welcome

MAPS: Available from an on-site kiosk

FACILITIES: Rest rooms, water, vending machine, picnic area; gardens are available for events such as weddings

SPECIAL COMMENTS: Inquire about classes with expert gardeners by calling (205) 682-8019.

DIRECTIONS

From I-459, exit onto US 31 North. At the first light, turn right onto Municipal Drive. In 0.6 miles, turn right onto Lorna Road. Drive 0.2 miles and turn left into Aldridge Gardens. Park in the large paved lot. The gated garden entrance is easy to spot.

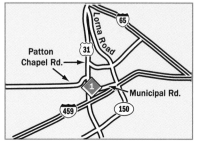

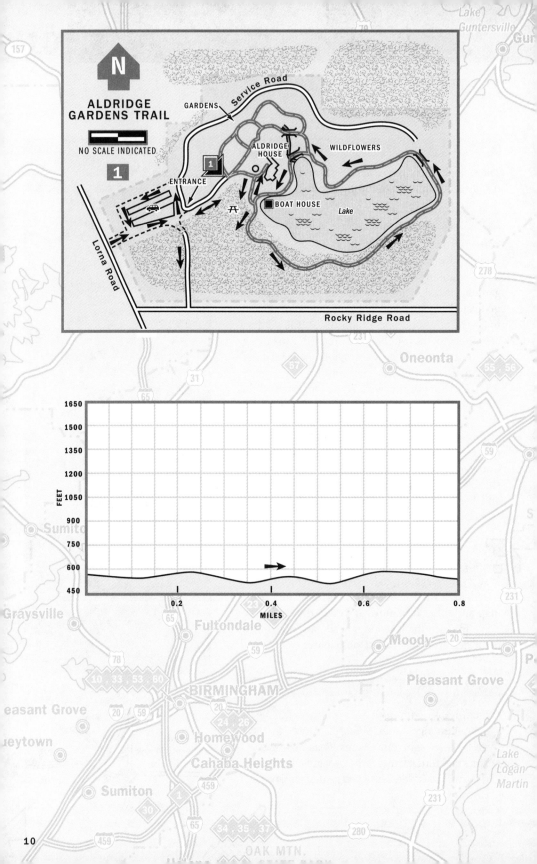

ALDRIDGE GARDENS TRAIL

N

NO SCALE INDICATED

1

GARDENS
Service Road
ALDRIDGE HOUSE
WILDFLOWERS
ENTRANCE
BOAT HOUSE
Lake
Lorna Road
Rocky Ridge Road

with bricks. Heading south initially, cross a small footbridge and walk onto a trail paved with crushed, iron-stained rock. Signature hydrangeas, both wild and domestic, and numerous tall magnolias lend a distinctly Southern feel to the walk.

Pass a gravel service road on your right and then bear left around the scenic lake, descending slightly into an area of pine-covered hillocks. Throughout the gardens understory brush has been cleared, but along the lake the forest scrub remains intact. The woods soon blend into a mix of pine and hardwoods such as maple, white oak, and hickory. With a rolling slope to your right, descend briefly as the lake begins to appear on your left.

Birds love it here, and numerous benches around the gardens provide ideal spots to sit and observe. Head east, passing one of these benches on your right. The path is nicely shaded through here. It's also quiet, but the dull drone of traffic on nearby I-459 prevents full-blown silence. At a quarter mile, pass a bench on your right and then another as the slope you're traversing on a level path steepens. Tick off another bench and then at 0.3 miles bear left heading northwest toward a bench on your left that has a clear view over the lake.

Walk across the earthen dam that creates the lake, occasionally glimpsing homes off to your right. At the end of the dam, cross over the spillway on an arched wooden footbridge with iron railings. Bear right after the bridge and circle around to the southwest—back toward the gardens and back into the shade. Off to your right is a large field planted with wildflowers, including Queen Anne's lace, bachelor's buttons, and green coneflowers.

At lake level, be sure and gaze back to your left. The reflection of the forested slope above the opposite bank shimmers in the pea-green lake. Now approaching a half-mile, pass three successive benches and then leave the gravel path to return to a paved walkway. Pass behind the Aldridge House, with another bench on your right, and soon cross a small footbridge over a stream that flows through a garden filled with ferns, shrubs, and other flora such as lambs ear and black-eyed Susans.

Walk beneath a large waterside magnolia on your left to reach a small boathouse and picnic pier. Inside are a vending machine and six picnic tables. After half a mile reach the intersection where you began the loop, bear right, and continue straight ahead into an area of labeled plants such as Japanese maple, azalea, and an endless variety of hydrangea. Pass a large cement pad on your right and reach a T in the path. Straight ahead is a grassy area with three benches. You can turn right here to the Aldridge House, but instead go left into a rich garden area filled with Japanese quince, Annabelle hydrangea, Georgia blue, Oriental fringe tree, blue billow hydrangea, wild blue phlox, sparkling burgundy, and purple coneflower. Staying to the outside by turning left whenever the opportunity arises, pass a bench on your right, and at another T, go left.

Following a small waterfall on your left that soon flows into the lake below, pass another bench and cross over a footbridge. Look for tall, straight tulip poplar and graceful, maroon-leafed Japanese maples, right before the trail Ts into the Lake Trail to complete the walk.

The lake at Aldridge Gardens

Just minutes away is another suburban Hoover gem, Moss Rock Preserve Trail (p. 123). Known as the Shades Crest boulder fields prior to the development of the land as a city of Hoover park, Moss Rock is popular with climbers but is also a great destination for hikers (and mountain bikers) as well.

AVE MARIA GROTTO TRAIL

Feel like a giant walking through one of Alabama's most unique outdoor attractions. Easily combined with other area hikes, this fascinating walk meanders through miniature replicas of buildings from the Holy Land and other historic places.

DESCRIPTION

In 1892, Brother Joseph Zoettl left his home in Landshut, Bavaria, came to Alabama, and joined the Benedectine brotherhood at Saint Bernard Abbey in Cullman. For over 40 years, Brother Joseph indulged his talent of creating miniature shrines from ordinary materials such as cold-cream jars, cement, and other odds and ends, until he completed his last model in 1958 at the age of 80.

The first replicas were erected on the monastery recreation grounds but proved so popular with visitors that in 1934 they were moved to the present location, land dedicated as the Ave Maria Grotto. The Grotto, located on the grounds of Alabama's only Benedictine Abbey, grew into a fantastic assemblage of over 125 miniatures, including replicas of Jerusalem, the Lourdes Basilica, churches, shrines, and other historic buildings. In 1984 the Grotto was added to the National Register of Historic Places.

To access the Ave Maria Grotto, enter the gift shop, pay the fee, and pick up a small interpretive brochure. The gift shop sells an amazing selection

KEY AT-A-GLANCE INFORMATION

LENGTH: 1 mile (0.4 miles for the grotto and cemetery; add 0.6 miles for a tour of the St. Bernard campus)

CONFIGURATION: Loop with out-and-back to cemetery

DIFFICULTY: Easy

SCENERY: The holy sites of Christianity in miniature

EXPOSURE: Partial shade

TRAFFIC: Light on weekdays

TRAIL SURFACE: Paved loop, gravelly path

HIKING TIME: 1 hour

ACCESS: Adults, $5; children ages 6-12, $3.50

MAPS: None

FACILITIES: Rest rooms, water, gift shop, picnic tables, phone

SPECIAL COMMENTS: For additional information, go to www.avemariagrotto.com.

DIRECTIONS

From Birmingham, travel north on I-65 and exit right on US 278. Go 1.5 miles and turn left onto Main Avenue (follow Ave Maria Grotto sign). In one block bear back right onto Third Street SW. At 1.6 miles turn right onto Saint Bernard Drive SE. Drive half a mile and pull into the Grotto parking lot.

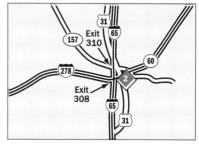

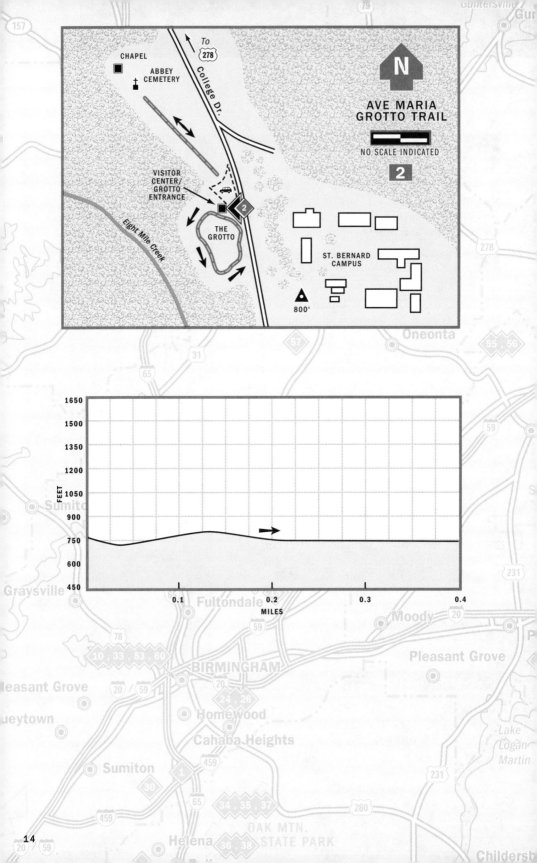

of rosaries, religious ephemera, and jewelry depicting Catholic saints. Located on only four acres of attractively landscaped ground, the Grotto may be small, but it's dense with the creations of Brother Joseph. It is planted with white pine, cedar, magnolia, dogwood, and a variety of ornamental shrubs that seems peaceful and cool even on a hot day. Following the sidewalk on its counterclockwise circuit, you'll find plenty of shaded benches lining the way.

Just hitting the highlights, walk down a paved ramp and view a re-creation of the city of Bethlehem, complete with a shrine to the birthplace of Jesus. Next, the Shrine of Peter, dating from 1938, is typically elaborate, meticulous, and faithful to Brother Joseph's use of ordinary objects, such as seashells, marble, and various stones. Numerous Spanish Missions are represented throughout the walk, including San Antonio, as well as Carmel and Mission Dolores in California. A miniature of the Alamo has been thrown in for good measure.

As evidenced by the Alamo replica, not all of the models depict holy places. Children will enjoy gazing at the Temple of the Faeries. Made from cold-cream jars, pumice, mortar, and other materials, the creation depicts Hansel and Gretel visiting a fairy castle. Look into a niche beneath the castle for an unpleasant surprise.

Continuing around to the left, encounter an entire hillside bustling with replicas of catacombs, mausoleums, shrines, and other structures. Peer into a large, cave-like room complete with stalactites hanging from the cave ceiling. The shrine, a replica of the Fortress of Antonia, depicts where Jesus is said to have spent the night in jail after his arrest at the Garden of Gethsemane.

Perhaps the topper for the Grotto experience is the presentation of the city of Jerusalem, one of the early works of Brother Joseph. As you near the end of this quarter-mile walk, pitch a coin into the Waldkapelle, a shrine to the Virgin Mary, located on the right. Pass a small stone building on the right and exit through the gift shop.

To round out the experience, take a short tour of the Abbey grounds and visit the cemetery where Brother Joseph is buried, and then walk over to the Abbey church, the largest handcut-stone church in North Alabama. From the gift shop, cross the parking lot to your left and take the gravel path to the cemetery. Pass a group of picnic tables on the right and visit the 14 stations of the cross as you approach a low stone wall. The circular cemetery holds the graves of Brothers who have died here over the year, each grave marked with a white stone cross. A large stone chapel with vaulted ceiling, tile floor, and elaborate door hinges stands at the end of the cemetery.

To visit the church, walk back to the gift shop and through the parking lot, with the Grotto on your right. Bear right and pass the Heidrich library. The grounds here are well groomed and shaded by magnolia and cedar. Pass the monastery on your left and then bear around left, where you'll see the light-tan stone church straight ahead, fronted with a carillon. Retrace your steps to your vehicle or take a longer stroll around the St. Bernard campus.

NEARBY ACTIVITIES

If you need an old iron skillet (expect to pay good money) or an old wardrobe (farmhouses in Cullman County had tiny closets), take US 278 across I-65 and turn right past the gas station to access the Cullman Flea Market. For a bite to eat, you can stop at Johnny's Barbecue on your way back to I-65. For a larger selection of eateries, from US 278 drive north on I-65 for about a mile and take the Highway 157 exit. Turn right and take your pick of the usual fast-food places.

(DOUG GHEE)
BALD ROCK BOARDWALK

IN BRIEF

Take an easy stroll down a unique boardwalk trail named after a long-time supporter of Alabama's state parks. Located in Cheaha State Park, the hike ends in a rock outcropping that offers magnificent views of the surrounding valley and mountains.

DESCRIPTION

Opened in June 2000, this elevated boardwalk trail was designed to be accessible to everyone regardless of physical ability. Named after former Democratic Senator Doug Ghee, a long-time supporter of Alabama's state parks and primary innovator of Alabama's Forever Wild land acquisition and conservation program, this 1,519-foot trail is short for a "trail" but long for a boardwalk, especially one located in such a remote area.

About six feet off the ground, the boardwalk is solidly constructed of 2x6 boards with tension-cable enforced sides. A handrail runs the entire length of the boardwalk. A cooperative effort

DIRECTIONS

From I-459 take I-20 East from Birmingham for 50 miles to Exit 191. Bear right onto US 431 South. Follow signs to Cheaha State Park. Drive 2 miles and turn right onto CR 131. In half a mile, turn left onto AL 281 South, the Talladega Scenic Drive. Two scenic overlooks are on the way up: at 1.5 miles and 6.5 miles from intersection of CR 131 and AL 281, both on right. At 11.5 miles from the same intersection, pass Cheaha Trailhead parking lot on the left. Continue on AL 281 to top of mountain and turn right into Cheaha State Park at the sign. Drive up to the gate (deposit $2 per person day-use fee in honor box), and gate automatically lifts. Drive straight up the hill for 1 mile and turn right at sign for Bald Rock Lodge. Pass lodge on right and park on left. Boardwalk is visible ahead.

KEY AT-A-GLANCE INFORMATION

LENGTH: 0.6 miles

CONFIGURATION: Out-and-back

DIFFICULTY: Easy

SCENERY: Extended vista from Bald Rock viewing area located at the end of the boardwalk

EXPOSURE: Shaded

TRAFFIC: This is one of the shortest and busiest trails in the park

TRAIL SURFACE: Well-crafted wooden boardwalk

HIKING TIME: 20 minutes

ACCESS: Park gate opens at sunup, closes nightly at 9 p.m.

MAPS: State park map and FS Pinhoti Trail Map 4 (The map will read "1" on the front but that's a typo. The real Map 1 is brown; Map 4 is purple) both available in country store.

FACILITIES: Rest rooms, country store, restaurant on site

SPECIAL COMMENTS: This trail is also known as the Doug Ghee Accessible Trail and is wheelchair traversable. The grade is a very slight downhill.

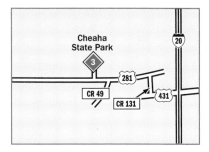

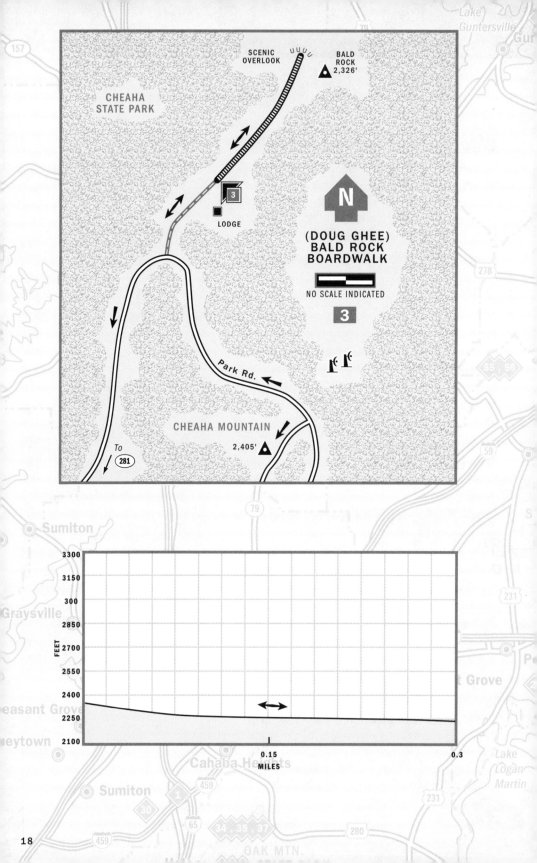

Beginning of the boardwalk

between the state's park system and the Environmental Policy and Information Center at Jacksonville State University, the trail is about five feet wide and suitable for strollers and wheelchairs. As you travel in a northeastern direction, you'll pass several information kiosks along the way.

The original trail to the Bald Rock overlook was cleared by Civilian Conservation Corps (CCC) workers back in the 1930s. Begun by Franklin D. Roosevelt in 1933, the CCC in Alabama built Cheaha's cabins, the Bald Rock Lodge, and the nearby stone observation tower that marks Alabama's highest elevation at 2,405 feet. Look to either side of the boardwalk to see the original CCC trails. At several points on the boardwalk, exits lead down to the ground via short sets of wooden stairs. Nearly level, the boardwalk also features covered resting areas, spaced every few hundred feet.

Nearing the overlook, the boardwalk takes a small zig to the left, then resumes its fairly straight course. Surrounding you on the walk is a fine hardwood/pine forest scattered with chestnut oaks, maples, and pines. Clumps of scattered ground rock, mostly sandstone, dressed in pale-green and bright-green mosses litter the leafy forest floor.

At the boardwalk's end is a magnificent viewing area. From this loftiest of Alabama heights, the sweeping vista includes (from left to right) Talladega, Munford, Coldwater Mountain, Lincoln, I-20, Oxford/Anniston, and the rugged wilds of Dugger Mountain. To assist your survey, there is a viewing scope located here. It's placed fairly low, which makes it accessible to kids and persons in wheelchairs. And, big surprise, it's absolutely free. No quarters required.

After gazing afar, look more closely at the weathered rocks and vegetation at the top of this windy bluff. Stunted Virginia pines keep a firm grip against exposure to strong winds and bitter cold, especially in winter. I've camped up here in January and, even in the shelter of a tent pitched in a calm spot, the cold is intense. Just take a long look at the gnarled Virginia pines. According to an interpretive sign at the lookout, a weather-ravaged tree found here, which is only six inches in diameter, was determined to be over 150 years old.

There are several short trails inside the park. To round out your day, try the Pulpit Rock Trail (p. 187) or take a stroll on the short Wildflower Garden Trail. To reach the Pulpit Rock Trail, after completing the Bald Rock Boardwalk drive back out past the lodge and continue around the one-way road. Pass a campground entrance on your left. A small pull-out parking area for the Pulpit Rock Trail (red blazes) will be ahead on your right near a group of stone cabins. The Wildflower Garden Trail is just a short walk downhill along the road from the Pulpit Rock parking area. This trail lies on both sides of the road and is best viewed in spring.

BIG MOUNTAIN LOOP

IN BRIEF

This easy, misnamed trail (it's a balloon and there is no big mountain) is a perfect hike for small children on which to cut their hiking teeth. Mountain bikes are allowed on all trails in the complex, but riders tend to stick with the longer paths.

DESCRIPTION

Established in 1820 and incorporated as a city in 1947, Trussville lures residents who mostly work in Birmingham but who want to live in a small-town environment. A fast-growing community just northeast of Birmingham, Trussville used to be known for its quiet main street lined with stately oaks. The tree-lined street is still there, but the popularity with families of this area has taken a bite out of the quiet.

To meet the recreational demands of its citizens, Trussville operates the 125-acre Trussville Sports Complex. Made up of eight baseball fields, six softball fields, four soccer fields, a football

DIRECTIONS

From I-59 North, take Exit 141. Go right onto Chalkville Road toward Trussville. Drive 1 mile and turn left onto Oak Street, which shortly becomes Cherokee Drive. Cross an old, stone bridge and see park entrance on left. Turn left and drive through park until you see the Trussville Racquet Club on your left. There, turn right into a large parking lot. The trailhead is in the northwest corner of the lot.

Alternate directions: From I-459 North, take Exit 32 (Trussville/US 11). Turn right onto Highway 11. Drive 2.8 miles and turn left onto Chalkville Road North. Drive 0.5 miles and turn right onto Oak Street, which shortly becomes Cherokee Drive. Cross an old, stone bridge and see park entrance on left. Turn left into park and follow directions above.

KEY AT-A-GLANCE INFORMATION

LENGTH: 0.8 miles

CONFIGURATION: Out-and-back or loop (if you walk back on road)

DIFFICULTY: Easy

SCENERY: Scruffy hardwood forest mixed with pines

EXPOSURE: None on the out-and-back; half exposed on the loop

TRAFFIC: Light

TRAIL SURFACE: Narrow dirt path, paved road

HIKING TIME: 40 minutes

ACCESS: Complex is opened 6 a.m.–11 p.m.

MAPS: None

FACILITIES: Water fountains near ball-field complexes, rest rooms available during games

SPECIAL COMMENTS: Call Trussville Park and Recreation at (205) 655-9486 for more information.

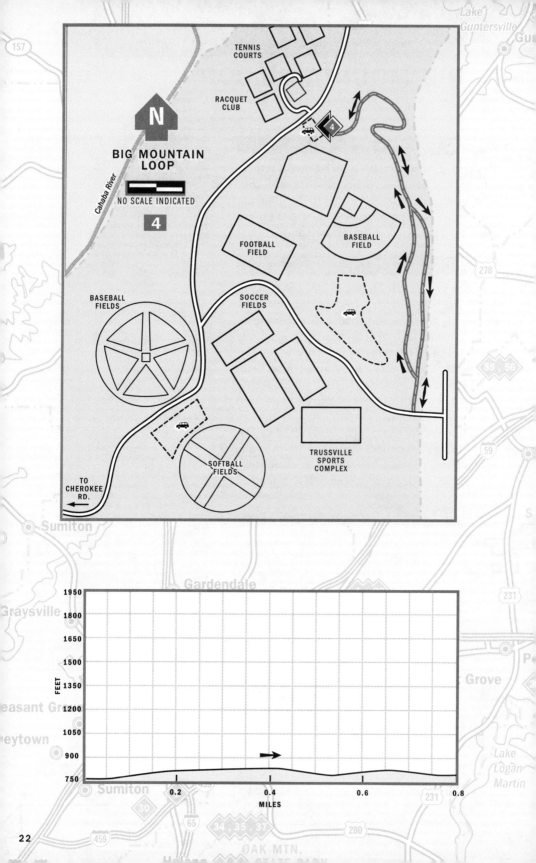

N

BIG MOUNTAIN
LOOP

NO SCALE INDICATED

4

TENNIS
COURTS

RACQUET
CLUB

4

FOOTBALL
FIELD

BASEBALL
FIELD

BASEBALL
FIELDS

SOCCER
FIELDS

SOFTBALL
FIELDS

TRUSSVILLE
SPORTS
COMPLEX

TO
CHEROKEE
RD.

Cahaba River

field, and twelve tennis courts, the complex seems to be all about hitting, kicking, throwing, and lobbing, but then there's the trails system.

Although the ball fields are the centerpiece of the complex, the city of Trussville and members of the Birmingham Urban Mountain Pedalers (BUMP) have done a nice job of constructing trails in the wooded areas that enclose the complex. The more than 4 miles of hiking/biking trails at the complex are not the slickest in town, but they are some of the most convenient.

Although called the Big Mountain Loop, this trail is neither a loop nor on a big mountain. It is an easy, winding balloon hike through a suburban strip of woods. The trail begins by rocketing steeply uphill, heading east along a rocky path. With a base-ball field complex to your right, enter the woods, which are primarily home to lots of small, two- and three-story oaks, small beeches, and a scattering of pines.

After the sharp climb, the trail slowly ascends along a narrow dirt path that winds and changes directions as often as a two-year-old asks, "What's that?" Head east, then bear back around right to the south, where you'll see houses to your left. The trail continues its winding ways as it begins to descend within sight of a ball field to your right.

The trail soon intersects a wider path. Turn right, heading south on a rocky path that is about six feet wide and muddy in places after a rain shower. The scrubby woods here are surprisingly quiet. Where the wide path continues right, go left to the east and pass a hiker sign as you wind uphill. The trail levels as you pass the end of gravel road to your right. At this point you've hiked about half a mile.

This short trail soon bears left toward a paved road. At the road, turn right and immediately turn right again to complete the balloon. This leg of the hike will wind back toward the hiker sign and the trail segment that leads back to the parking lot. Alternatively, you can turn right onto the paved road and follow it. As you walk along the road, pass soccer fields on the left and a gravel parking area on the right.

After you pass a football field on your right, the parking lot where you left your vehicle comes into view across the field. When you reach a three-way intersection, turn right and return to the parking lot.

NEARBY ACTIVITIES

If you're just getting warmed up and need more trail, turn left at the three-way stop and walk down to the Maplebridge-Horseshoe Ramble (p. 117). Your standard fast-food fare is available at many locations in Trussville. For more local flavor, try Joel's on Highway 11 in Trussville or Jim 'n' Nick's Barbecue in the Target shopping plaza along Highway 11.

CAHABA LILY PARK
NATURE TRAIL

KEY AT-A-GLANCE INFORMATION

LENGTH: 1.5 miles

CONFIGURATION: Out-and-back followed by a loop

DIFFICULTY: Easy

SCENERY: Mixed hardwood/pine forest, wildflowers

EXPOSURE: About 25% exposed

TRAFFIC: Moderate during week and on weekends

TRAIL SURFACE: Gravel path

HIKING TIME: 30–45 minutes

ACCESS: Park closes at 10 p.m.

MAPS: None

FACILITIES: Rest rooms, water, playground, picnic pavilions

SPECIAL COMMENTS: No alcoholic beverages, dogs on leash only

IN BRIEF

Set in a patch of woods surrounding a brand new playground and picnic area, this wide path is well marked and lit at intervals for night walks.

DESCRIPTION

This spiffy park near Helena is not on the Cahaba River, nor will you see the endangered Cahaba lily here. What you will find, though, is a neat picnic and playground area with a carefully marked gravel path that winds through a small patch of suburban woods off of CR 52.

The trail is wide and great for both walking and running. The hike is best described as a loop with an out-and-back to start. The out-and-back leads to a neighboring community, while the loop passes behind the park, heads toward Helena Intermediate School, and then returns to the park.

To begin, face the park from the parking lot, walk to your right past the rest rooms toward a marked gravel path. At a green trail sign, bear left and enter the woods. Within the balanced mix of hardwoods and pine, you'll see sugar maple, red oak, longleaf pine, white oak, water oak, hickory, and tulip poplar trees. Alabama's state wildflower, the oak-leaf hydrangea, is common here as well.

Where the trail forks, go right, heading south and downhill. The path is wide and clear, with streetlamp-type lights at regular intervals,

DIRECTIONS

Exit I-65 at Valleydale Road and head west on CR 17 toward US 31 for 1 mile. Upon crossing US 31, CR 17 becomes AL 261 South. From the intersection, drive 6 miles on AL 261 South, passing through Helena, to reach a junction with County Roads 52, 91, and 17. Turn right onto CR 52 West and drive 1.6 miles. At the sign for Cahaba Lily Park, turn left and follow the paved road into the adjacent parking area.

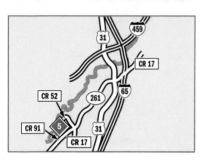

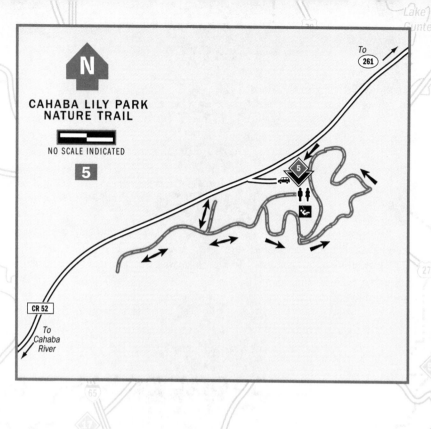

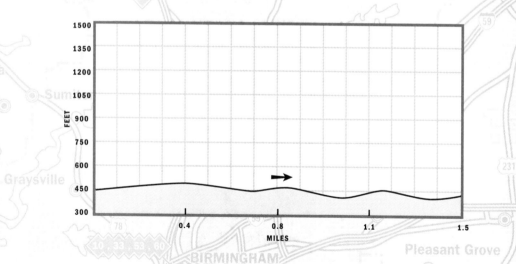

but the understory to the sides is thick and brushy. The trail is fairly shady as you pass a ravine down to your left. You can occasionally see homes through the trees here and may hear someone mowing their lawn. CR 52 is nearby, so you'll also hear the sounds of traffic over the cicadas and crickets.

A path soon comes in from the right, but continue straight and cross a thick-plank bridge that spans a tiny brook near several beech trees that have made this damp area home. Where the path joins a power-line swath, bear left and stick with the gravel trail to the left of the cut. It's not so pretty along this short stretch, but overall the trail is pleasant.

Heading west, the path leaves the swath and leads into a new housing area, giving the folks living there easy access to the park. Turn around here, retrace the power-line swath, turn right back into the woods, recross the footbridge, and then bear left at the first path coming in from the left. Loop around, rolling up and down along a short arm of trail that hits the power-line swath again. Turn on your hiking heels, bear left back at the T, and continue retracing your path back to the park.

At a signed Y in the trail, bear right, having covered 0.75 miles, and then bear sharp right. Judging from the size of the hardwoods here, it looks like it's been 20 or so years since this area was completely cleared. More recent harvesting of pines, by saw and by pine beetle, has left light gaps, and opportunistic trees such as Chinese sumac and mimosa have moved in, along with kudzu and honeysuckle. You'll also find quite a few very young longleaf pines here.

As the trail curves back toward the park, look and listen for a variety of common area birds, including cardinals, robins, towhees, and doves. Pass a sign on your right that indicates that the park is to your left and that the school is straight ahead. With a ravine down to the right, the trail dips up and down, but never steeply.

Take a sharp right at two tulip poplars beside a wet-weather drainage and soon reach the 1-mile mark. As you bear around left, you'll get your first glimpse of Helena Intermediate School off to the right. The trail is more open through here and in summer can be very hot if the sun is overhead. Shade from the sides is minimized by the height of the trees, which average less than 30 feet tall.

At 1.2 miles, the trail bends left, with the school directly off to the right about 300 feet away. Continue around left and see a sign that reads "Park Amenities." The park will soon come into view, and you'll emerge behind a covered picnic shelter to your right. Continue with the picnic/playground area on your right and loop back behind it again. Pass the swing set to your right, head back into the woods, crest a small hill, bear right, and then head back up toward the rest rooms to end the hike.

NEARBY ACTIVITIES

If you brought the kids, then spend some time on the jungle gym or toss a Frisbee in the park's open field. Otherwise, if you want a little more wilderness in your day, take a short drive to the Cahaba River Wildlife Management Area for a walk down to the Cahaba River (p. 27).

CAHABA RIVER WMA HIKE

IN BRIEF

Deep in the woods along the Bibb-Shelby county line, take a vigorous hike through a patchwork of forest types (some scenic, some barren) to reach a shoal that spans the wide and deep Cahaba River.

DESCRIPTION

Managed by Alabama Wildlife and Freshwater Fisheries in cooperation with USX and Cahaba Forest Management, the Cahaba Wildlife Management Area (WMA) is many things, but it is primarily a rough neck of the woods with endless exploration opportunities. The 40,000-plus acres, crisscrossed by logging and mining roads, ATV-tracks, and single-track, are best known to area hunters. Some sort of hunting goes on there from September through April each year. I would suggest avoiding this area during that time.

This hike is just shy of 5 miles, but I added a few miles extra by exploring. I forded the Cahaba River where this hike ends, but found that I

DIRECTIONS

Exit I-65 at Valleydale Road, and head west for 1 mile on CR 17 to US 31. Across US 31, CR 17 becomes AL 261 South. From US 31, drive 6 miles on AL 261 South, passing through Helena, to reach a junction with County Roads 52, 91, and 17. Follow AL 261 as it turns into CR 91. Drive 2.6 miles on CR 91 and the pavement turns to gravel. Soon after the pavement ends, see a sign for the Cahaba River Wildlife Management Area (WMA). The road splits; go left, following the hard-packed dirt/gravel road for 8 miles to a dead-end where rise of dirt blocks vehicular access to a condemned bridge just beyond. The last 200 feet or so down are fairly steep, so make sure that if you drive down, you can drive back up. I made the trip in a front-wheel drive Honda Civic, however, so you don't need four-wheel drive.

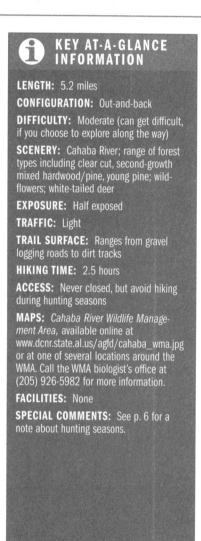

KEY AT-A-GLANCE INFORMATION

LENGTH: 5.2 miles

CONFIGURATION: Out-and-back

DIFFICULTY: Moderate (can get difficult, if you choose to explore along the way)

SCENERY: Cahaba River; range of forest types including clear cut, second-growth mixed hardwood/pine, young pine; wildflowers; white-tailed deer

EXPOSURE: Half exposed

TRAFFIC: Light

TRAIL SURFACE: Ranges from gravel logging roads to dirt tracks

HIKING TIME: 2.5 hours

ACCESS: Never closed, but avoid hiking during hunting seasons

MAPS: *Cahaba River Wildlife Management Area*, available online at www.dcnr.state.al.us/agfd/cahaba_wma.jpg or at one of several locations around the WMA. Call the WMA biologist's office at (205) 926-5982 for more information.

FACILITIES: None

SPECIAL COMMENTS: See p. 6 for a note about hunting seasons.

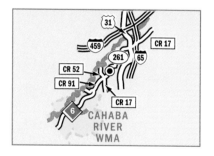

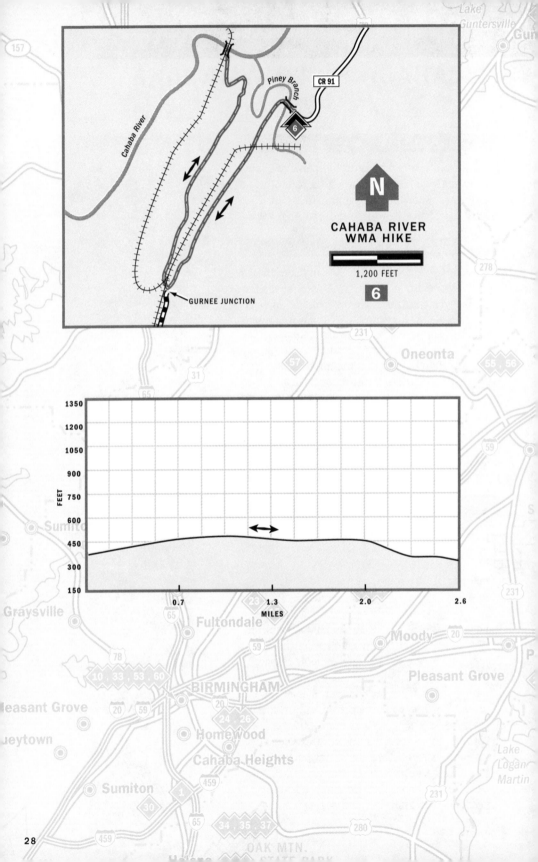

CAHABA RIVER
WMA HIKE

1,200 FEET

6

CR 91

Piney Branch

Cahaba River

GURNEE JUNCTION

had left the WMA and wandered onto private property. In fact, the entire WMA is pocketed with gated areas that are posted "No Trespassing." Heed these signs for your safety.

To start, walk up over a berm of dirt blocking access to a bridge that was condemned (for vehicular traffic) in 1999. Cross the bridge very carefully, since there are some gaps in the wood. The wide creek you pass over is Piney Branch, a slow-moving, sandy-bottomed tributary of the Cahaba River. Cross over another berm at the opposite end of the bridge and drop down onto a hard-packed dirt road.

The woods are scrubby through here and feature tulip poplar, white oak, hickory, longleaf pine, Virginia pine, and shortleaf pine. The brushy sides of the rough dirt track are home to morning glories, mimosa, and oak-leaf hydrangea. The path, which is colored with iron-tinged crushed rock, is a gently rolling affair with a ravine down to the right. At 0.3 miles, cross a railroad track and then parallel the railroad to your right. Look near the rails for chunks of coal, and also look in the mud for deer tracks.

The trail levels, but then begins its slow ups and downs again. A field of kudzu is located at 0.9 miles on trail-right, where you may spot lots of blue and yellow swallowtails in the summer. The further you walk, the prettier it gets. For example, the pines and hardwoods are much older and taller further back, giving the area more of a forest feel. You'll also pass through thick mimosa that have formed tunnels across the road.

At 1.1 miles, reach a road coming in from the right and turn right. This is Gurnee Junction, a mere spot in the road where two railroad tracks converge. Cross both sets of tracks just above the junction, and then pass a post on your right that has "One Bullet" written on it.

Begin your first real uphill walking, along a rocky, rusty gravel path littered with bits of coal. You could probably scoop the iron-colored rocks and coal into a furnace, add some limestone, and make a decent pig iron. The road soon changes color, becoming dark gray, sometimes nearly black. The forest mix also changes, with pines predominating.

It's quiet out here and deserted on weekends. On Saturday and Sunday mornings, you should have the place to yourself in summer and early fall. However, a lot of logging and mining still occurs in the WMA, and weekdays could find you sharing the road with a rusty log hauler.

The trail begins to descend at 1.3 miles and passes a series of pines blazed with blue paint. At 1.6 miles, an area of clearing begins off to the left, revealing a ravine, then a ridge, while the mixed pines continue on trail-right. At 1.9 miles, begin a downhill jaunt that soon levels, passing a bog on the left, and then climb again. Top out, descend, and at 2.1 miles follow the road sharply left. If you want a little extra exercise, go right here onto a wide dirt path into the woods. Follow it around to the left along what appears to be a weedy ridge built of mine tailings, with steep drops on either side. Look for a curiously large chunk of slag near the end of this spur trail.

Back on the packed-dirt road, veer left to enter a clearing that extends to trail-left; you may see stacks of scrap pine here. Soon, reach a crossroads at 2.4 miles to bear right and downhill. When you reach a point where the trail splits into three arms, you can head straight to the turnaround or you can take another side jaunt to see the confluence of Piney Branch and the Cahaba. To take the detour, go right, eventually following a steep narrow rut down to the confluence, a very scenic spot. Look downstream to glimpse the railroad trestle high above the Cahaba.

Return to the three-way split and take the middle path. You'll see lots of deer track through here, and you may glimpse a white tail like I did. The path approaches the railroad track just before it crosses the stone trestle some 50 feet above the river. Do not approach the tracks, and don't even think of walking out onto the trestle. Instead, follow a steep, dirt path leading down to the river on your right.

Paralleling the trestle across the river is a shoal of rock where the Cahaba shallows and forms a gentle river-wide riffle. This is a great spot to dangle your toes in the water.

NEARBY ACTIVITIES

There is an endless array of trails and dirt roads to explore in Cahaba River WMA. Just be mindful of the private sections interspersed with public-access lands. If you decide to take off and explore, a GPS unit is valuable help when navigating back to your vehicle.

CHEAHA LAKE TRAIL

IN BRIEF

This is a rocky hike (or slide if you're not careful) down through a healthy, mixed hardwood/pine forest. But don't gloat for long as you savor the flat walking around Cheaha Lake, because the best part of this hike is the thigh-burning climb back to the top.

DESCRIPTION

This hike, which links Cheaha Mountain with Cheaha Lake below, is by far the steepest sustained ascent/descent within Cheaha State Park. But, perhaps the hardest part of this mountain-side hike is finding the trail.

From your car, walk uphill, north, toward the park restaurant. Pass through the vehicle gate and take the fork to the left. You'll pass the restaurant on your left, but before pressing on, step down to a viewing area beside the restaurant for a gander at the sweeping valley vista and Cheaha Lake far below.

Continue uphill along the road, bearing left at the Y. The road here is lined with lush Virginia

KEY AT-A-GLANCE INFORMATION

LENGTH: 3.2 miles

CONFIGURATION: Out-and-back with loop in the middle

DIFFICULTY: Difficult

SCENERY: Long-distance views, mountain laurel slicks, streams, quartzite cliffs, Cheaha Lake

EXPOSURE: Mostly shaded, except for loop around lake

TRAFFIC: Light on trail, may be crowded around lake in summer

TRAIL SURFACE: Very rocky, steep path

HIKING TIME: 2 hours

ACCESS: Park gate opens at sunrise, closes nightly at 9 p.m.

MAPS: State park map and FS Pinhoti Trail Map 4 (The map will read "1" on the front but that's a typo. The real Map 1 is brown; Map 4 is purple) both available in country store.

FACILITIES: Rest rooms, country store, restaurant on site

SPECIAL COMMENTS: This trail is very steep and can be tricky to find.

DIRECTIONS

From I-459 take I-20 East from Birmingham for 50 miles to Exit 191. Bear right onto US 431 South. Follow the signs to Cheaha State Park. Drive 2 miles and turn right onto CR 131. In half a mile, turn left onto AL 281 South, the Talladega Scenic Drive. There are two scenic overlooks on the way up: at 1.5 miles and 6.5 miles from the intersection of CR 131 and AL 281, both on the right. Pass the lot signed "Cheaha Trailhead" on the left 11.5 miles from the CH 131/US 281 intersection and continue on 281 to top of mountain and turn right into Cheaha State Park at the sign. Drive past the country store (on left) and park above it on the left.

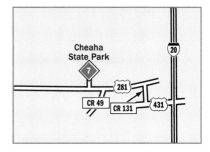

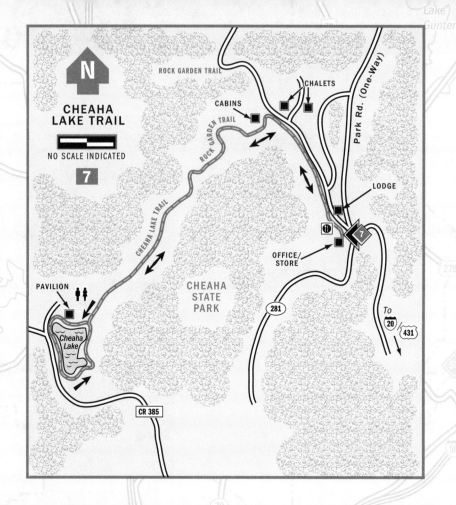

CHEAHA LAKE TRAIL

NO SCALE INDICATED

7

ROCK GARDEN TRAIL

CHALETS

CABINS

Rock Garden Trail

LODGE

CHEAHA LAKE TRAIL

Park Rd. (One-Way)

7

OFFICE/
STORE

PAVILION

Cheaha
Lake

CHEAHA
STATE
PARK

281

To
20

431

CR 385

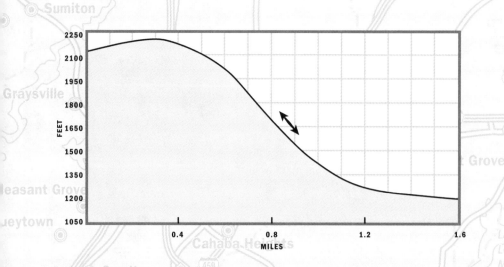

pines, with a hardwood/pine mix uphill to the right and downhill to the left. At the next Y in the road, stay left and watch for a group of stone cabins on your left. When you turn in toward the cabins, you've already covered half a mile. Pay close attention from here until you reach the Cheaha Lake trailhead.

Pass cabin 9 on your left and look for a sign that reads, "Rock Garden/Lake Trail." Go left and downhill onto the Rock Garden Trail, heading south/southwest. Right away the steep slope kicks in. House-sized chunks of quartzite, small holly trees, and wild azaleas line the trail as you travel roughly west. There may be a few downed trees to navigate around, but stay straight and head toward a small creek in front of you. Do not go left here.

Continuing west, cross the stream and, within 20 feet, turn right and look for a post (redwood in color) that looks like it should have a sign on top. This is the missing marker for the Lake Trail. Look downhill to locate a blue blaze, which marks the trail to the lake. You are about 1 mile from your vehicle at this point.

On the way down, the trail zigzags, making sharp turns as you descend through rock fields. Heading west, make a sharp left and continue south with a 30-foot rock wall to the left; do not continue along the rock wall, but turn right and look downhill for the blue blazes.

Listen and watch for large pileated woodpeckers through here. The trail stays steep as it pokes through magnificent slicks of mountain laurel. The elliptical leaves are green year round; in spring the mountain laurel flowers bright pink, adding a bold slash of color to the forest.

Heading down and west, make a sharp left, and walk south along another boulder face to your left. About 0.1 mile later, watch for a double-blue blaze that indicates another sharp left. The trail through here is well marked, mostly on the trees but also on the boulders.

Pass through a boulder garden with car-sized rocks and more mountain laurel. When it's not rocky through here, it's rooty. The trail, especially in winter, may also be slick with decaying leaves. Enter an area of the forest that opens slightly to the west. Here the decline lessens briefly as the open, rocky path jounces down through more boulder fields that soon yield once again to the steep mountainside.

Continue down a finger ridge, with ravines off to the right and left. Unlike many parts of the Talladega National Forest, the pines through here appear healthy with no evidence of pine beetles. You'll see and hear a small stream flowing 100 feet away and downhill from you. As you wade through another large patch of mountain laurel, level out in the ravine bottom, with the stream to your left. Approach a small branch feeding into the stream and look for a U.S. General Land Office survey marker on the left, just a small, easily overlooked bit of capped pipe in the ground.

The walking is easy and flat through here, with a packed-earth trail about five feet wide. Just after passing a green utility building on the left, the trail exits the forest into a clearing behind Cheaha Lake. Straight ahead is a stone building.

Walk toward the stone building as you begin a counterclockwise loop around the lake. Bearing right, you'll see covered pavilions, picnic tables, grills, and a playground with swings and slides. There are rest rooms here, but they are closed during winter. Walk along the swimming beach and look out toward the diving platform in the middle of the lake. The lake and its facilities are not exactly five-star, but it is a nice place to cool off in the summer. Be mindful, if you do visit the lake in season, that pets, glass bottles, and alcohol are not permitted.

Where the lake flows out over a short dam, cross the overflow and bear back left to continue around the lake. Here you'll be walking on the side of a paved road. Immediately to your right, across the road, is a set of stone steps that lead up to the lower Cheaha campground. Walking roughly south, cut across to the left through a wooded area as you bear back around east, following the lake.

Access a gravel road and turn left, following the lake back to the pavilion area. Off to your right is the steep climb back to the top of Cheaha Mountain. Go ahead and pull out your Power Bar. You're going to need the boost shortly.

Return to the trailhead at the forest entrance on your right. Relish the short level stretch, and, as the path begins to lift off, look ahead for blue blazes as the stream drops away steadily on your right. Keep an even, slow pace as you climb, resting whenever necessary. When you step up and see the signless redwood post, give yourself a high five, turn right, cross the stream, and follow the trail straight out to the cabin area. Walk out to the road, turn right, and take an easy downhill stroll to your vehicle.

NEARBY ACTIVITIES

From June through August, a lifeguard is on duty daily at Cheaha Lake. Bring your trunks and a few burgers and make a day of it. Paddleboats are rented at the lake for $5 per hour. The lake is open 9:30 a.m.–5 p.m. You can fish here, but you'll need a fishing license (available at the country store).

There are several short trails inside the park. To round out your day, try the Bald Rock Boardwalk (p. 17), the Pulpit Rock Trail (p. 187), or a stroll on the short Wildflower Garden Trail. To reach the Wildflower Garden Trail, turn left on the road as you exit the cabin area after completing the Lake Trail and walk uphill about a quarter-mile. The short trail lies on both sides of the road and is best viewed in spring.

CHINNABEE SILENT TRAIL
FEATURING CHEAHA FALLS

IN BRIEF

With a small falls and swimming holes at both ends, this is the perfect hike for a hot summer day.

DESCRIPTION

The Chinnabee Silent Trail was carved from the Talladega National Forest between 1973 and 1976 by members of Boy Scout Troop 39 based at The Alabama Institute for the Deaf and Blind in Talladega. An impressive undertaking, the 6-mile path begins at Lake Chinnabee and ends atop Talladega Mountain. The portion of trail profiled on this hike follows Cheaha Creek's cool waters from Lake Chinnabee Recreation Area to Cheaha Falls.

Cheaha Creek originates just south of Cheaha Lake and is fed by various small streams that drain Cheaha and Talladega Mountains. The creek was dammed in the 1930s, creating 17-acre Lake Chinnabee. The lake and the first half-mile of the trail are popular with area folks who like to cool off in the creek, canoe the lake, or fish from the banks. Beyond the first half-mile, though, traffic drops considerably, until you reach another popular swimming hole, Cheaha Falls.

To begin, pass the pit toilets on your left and head south along Cheaha Creek, walking against its flow. A paved path soon gives way to a wet,

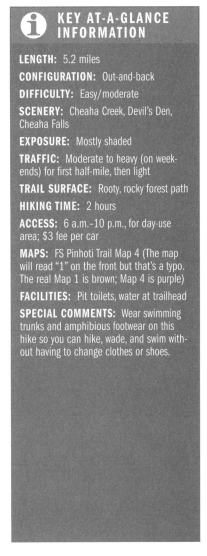

KEY AT-A-GLANCE INFORMATION

LENGTH: 5.2 miles

CONFIGURATION: Out-and-back

DIFFICULTY: Easy/moderate

SCENERY: Cheaha Creek, Devil's Den, Cheaha Falls

EXPOSURE: Mostly shaded

TRAFFIC: Moderate to heavy (on weekends) for first half-mile, then light

TRAIL SURFACE: Rooty, rocky forest path

HIKING TIME: 2 hours

ACCESS: 6 a.m.–10 p.m., for day-use area; $3 fee per car

MAPS: FS Pinhoti Trail Map 4 (The map will read "1" on the front but that's a typo. The real Map 1 is brown; Map 4 is purple)

FACILITIES: Pit toilets, water at trailhead

SPECIAL COMMENTS: Wear swimming trunks and amphibious footwear on this hike so you can hike, wade, and swim without having to change clothes or shoes.

DIRECTIONS

From the intersection of I-459 and I-20, head east toward Anniston. Drive 50 miles and take the first Anniston exit onto AL 21 South. At 13.8 miles, turn left onto CR 398 East. Drive 3.4 miles and turn right onto Cheaha Road. Pass through Camp Mac. Follow the Cheaha State Park signs along a narrow, twisting paved road. Drive 9 miles on Cheaha Road, then turn right onto FS 646. Drive 1.3 miles and enter the Lake Chinnabee Recreation Area. Park in the lot on your left. Walk toward the rest rooms to begin the hike.

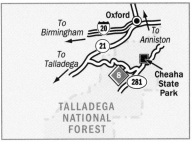

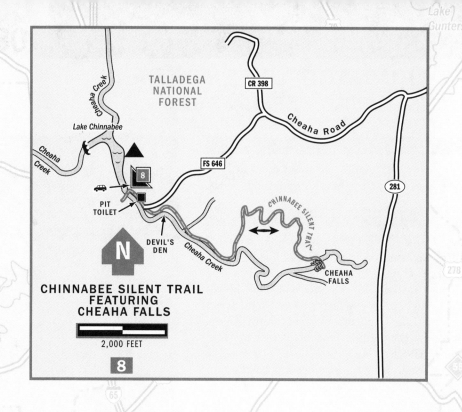

TALLADEGA NATIONAL FOREST

CR 398

Cheaha Creek

Lake Chinnabee

Cheaha Creek

Cheaha Road

FS 646

281

8

PIT TOILET

DEVIL'S DEN

Cheaha Creek

CHINNABEE SILENT TRAIL

CHEAHA FALLS

N

CHINNABEE SILENT TRAIL
FEATURING
CHEAHA FALLS

2,000 FEET

8

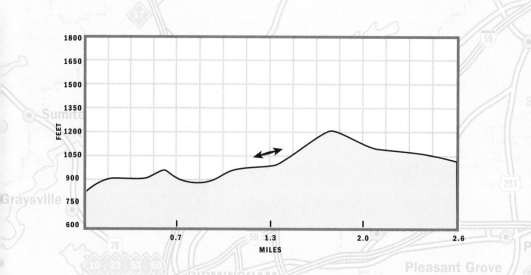

sandy, and rooty trail. Old loblolly pines grow right along the creek banks. In summertime, you'll see blue and yellow swallowtails flitting among the wildflowers and gathering in small clusters on the trail. The trail is blazed with blue rectangles.

Pass the turn for the Lake Chinnabee Loop on your right and continue walking, with pleasantly noisy Cheaha Creek burbling over stones on your right. The trail begins to climb, passing red maple and white oak trees along the way. Pass a posted trail on your right that leads to the Skyway Loop Trail and Adams Gap on the Pinhoti.

In July 1991, the slopes to your left were cut to help eliminate the infestation of the Southern pine beetle. Since then, scores of young hardwoods have taken advantage of the resulting light gaps. Cross a small feeder stream, keeping in mind the scenic, but steep, 90-foot drop to your right. After you cross a long boardwalk, take a set of stairs down to resume the trail. Soon you'll be able to hear the squeals and shouts of folks enjoying the falls and pool at Devil's Den downhill to your right.

At just under half a mile, the rooty winding path continues to trace the creek, passing more tall loblolly pines and their dead kin stretched out on the forest floor. Reach a small feeder stream, which you can cross on a log or by rock-hopping. Lots of wildflowers and shrubs grace the path, including oak-leaf hydrangea and mountain laurel. To your right, the creek alternates between relatively still pools and segments that gently break over and around boulders.

Just shy of 1 mile into the hike, the trail climbs steadily and veers away from the creek, heading north. Soon after, the rushing sounds of the creek fade away completely. The walking is easier here as you meander but stay fairly level along a hillside contour. Look for tulip poplar and chestnut oak trees as you work your way up a ravine that flattens as you climb. Cross the brook that runs down the ravine and bear right to trace the opposing hillside. Soon switchback left, tracing the heads of two more drainage ravines.

Emerge into a flat clearing with young hardwoods, including mulberry and sourwood. At 1.6 miles, drop down to cross another ravine at its head and bear right down toward a fern-lined stream. Cross the clear stream on rocks, accompanied by the roller-coaster cadence of cicadas in the trees above. Reach another flat at 1.7 miles, cross a logging road at 1.9 miles, and then cross a small brook. An easy, rolling path continues to trace successive ravines. Look for bits of pinkish marble in the sun-dappled trail through here.

At 2.1 miles, reach a three-sided shelter on your left. The 150-square-foot wooden structure is open in the front and has a nicely leveled "yard" area in addition to a picnic table, fire ring, food pole, and a small broom for tidying up. Sitting in front of the shelter, you'll have a nice view of Talladega Mountain to the southwest.

Resume the trail for the short walk to Cheaha Falls and, with a steep downhill to your right, back down to Cheaha Creek. To cross the creek or to reach a resting spot above the small yet scenic falls, you'll have to negotiate stones and large boulders. Before you head back, take a dip in the pool below the falls or at least take your boots off and cool your heels.

NEARBY ACTIVITIES

There's a 1.6-mile loop around Lake Chinnabee. See p. 105 for more information. From June through August, a lifeguard is on duty daily at Cheaha Lake in nearby Cheaha State Park. Paddleboats are rented at the lake for $5 per hour. The lake is open 9:30 a.m.–5 p.m. You can fish here, but you'll need a fishing license (available at the park store).

There are several short trails inside the park, including Cheaha Lake (p. 31), Bald Rock Boardwalk (p. 17), and the Pulpit Rock Trail (p. 187).

CHINNABEE SILENT TRAIL
FEATURING TALLADEGA MOUNTAIN

IN BRIEF

Reserve this thigh buster for a cool autumn or winter day. With the leaves off the trees, you'll also have better views from atop the mountain than in summertime.

DESCRIPTION

The Chinnabee Silent Trail was carved from Talladega National Forest between 1973 and 1976 by members of Boy Scout Troop 39 based at The Alabama Institute for the Deaf and Blind in Talladega. An impressive undertaking, the 6-mile, blue-blazed path begins at Lake Chinnabee and ends atop Talladega Mountain. The portion of the trail profiled on this hike begins near Turnipseed Hunter's Camp and proceeds straight up the mountain, gaining 800 feet in the process.

From the parking area, the Chinnabee Silent Trail enters the mixed hardwood/pine forest over to the left, near a brown carsonite hiker sign. If it's summer, run as fast as you can into the cooler forest and begin walking a needle-padded path. Trees

DIRECTIONS

From I-459, take I-20 East from Birmingham for 50 miles to Exit 191. Bear right onto US 431 South. Follow the signs to Cheaha State Park. Drive 2 miles and turn right onto CR 131. In half a mile, turn left onto AL 281 South, the Talla-dega Scenic Drive. There are two scenic overlooks on the way up: at 1.5 miles and 6.5 miles from the intersection of CR 131 and AL 281, both on the right. At 11.5 miles from the same intersection, pass a parking lot marked "Cheaha Trailhead" on the left. Continue on AL 281 to the mountaintop, passing the entrance to Cheaha State Park. Continue downhill, past a road that leads to Cheaha Lake, and look for a parking lot on the left side of the road. Pull in and park.

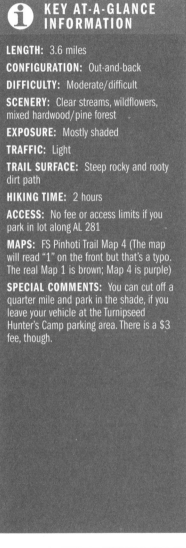

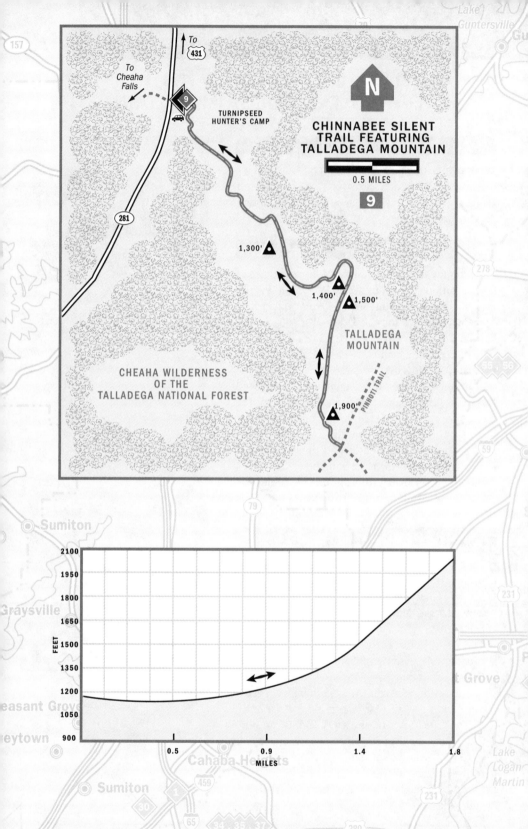

CHINNABEE SILENT
TRAIL FEATURING
TALLADEGA MOUNTAIN

0.5 MILES

9

To
431

To
Cheaha
Falls

TURNIPSEED
HUNTER'S CAMP

9

N

1,300'

1,400'

1,500'

TALLADEGA
MOUNTAIN

PINHOTI TRAIL

1,900'

CHEAHA WILDERNESS
OF THE
TALLADEGA NATIONAL FOREST

FEET

2100
1950
1800
1650
1500
1350
1200
1050
900

0.5   0.9   1.4   1.8
MILES

you'll see along the way include loblolly pine, white oak, and tulip poplar. Cross a stream and continue along a narrow, level woodland path. Reach a double-trunked white oak and bear right; don't be tempted to walk up a dry drainage to your left, which also looks like a trail.

At 0.15 miles, enter Turnipseed Hunter's Camp, cross the dirt road, and follow the level trail between two campsites. Reach a map board on your left, soon entering a thinly forested area littered with downed pines at 0.4 miles. The forest floor is very flat here and only a few tall pines remain standing amid frequent light gaps in the canopy.

Reach a pretty, clear stream at half a mile, crossing it on stones. Now at the bottom of the flank of Talladega Mountain, the trail begins to rise. You'll have good visibility through the forest and find lots of Alabama's state wildflower, oak-leaf hydrangea. Of the many trails in the Cheaha area, Chinnabee's wildflowers are notably prolific. The flowers attract monarchs, swallowtails, and other butterflies that feed on the yellow, white, and purple blooms of the many species growing here.

Hit an area of young, slender pines and 20-foot-high hardwoods and then follow a flat trail for awhile, heading east at 0.9 miles. Look for red oak and tulip poplar here and, in summer, lots of mushrooms, including the brilliant orange scarlet waxy cap.

At 1 mile, follow the trail as it dips down, noticing bits of pink and white marble in the trailbed. When it rains, this portion of trail likely doubles as a stream. With chunks of sandstone scattered about, steadily ascend to encounter a mild grade at 1.2 miles. Long mats of bright green bryophytes decorate the trail's edges. Soon reach a small spring in the trail and you'll begin to hear more water flowing in the distance. Pass a laurel slick on your left and bear right, now heading away from an unseen stream.

Reach a lichen-stained boulder garden, where the trail is less easy to follow. To stay on track, keep toward the middle of the rocks. With a slope down to your right and a hillside strewn with boulders above you to your left, continue to work your way up the mountain at an angle to the ridge.

At 1.5 miles, you begin to hear water flowing again. You'll notice some tall chestnut oaks on your right, but you won't be able to see the stream. By now the path has resumed its dirt track, although the area is still rocky. A boulder wall, composed of weathered, house-sized sandstone blocks, comes into view on your left.

Following along the rock face lined with galax, ferns, and an abundance of wildflowers, the trail maintains a constant uphill grade with a rocky sharp drop to your right. Reach a small spring in the trail that feeds a small jungle of tall ferns and bamboo at 1.7 miles. At this point your elevation will be right at 1,800 feet, with only 200 feet of gain to go. This is a good time to whip out your Power Bar, if you haven't already. Once again hear the tantalizing sounds of gurgling water ahead, but bear away to the left, leaving the stream for now. At a fork in the trail, 1.8 miles, you can go either way, since the extra path here is just a minor shortcut. Ascending and winding up through boulders and large oaks, begin to crest the mountain amid slabs of sandstone. The stream you heard earlier will finally appear to your right.

Just as you are about to reach the end, the path becomes hard to follow. Stay near the stream as you walk straight ahead. Soon you'll reach a posted trail crossroads, ending the Chinnabee Silent Trail. The Pinhoti Trail goes right and left, with the Odum Trail beginning and continuing straight ahead. This is your turnaround, at 2,005 feet on the ridge of rugged Talladega Mountain.

NEARBY ACTIVITIES

Once off the mountain, follow the Chinnabee Silent Trail across AL 281 and then hike a mile to scenic Cheaha Falls.

From June through August, a lifeguard is on duty daily at Cheaha Lake in nearby Cheaha State Park. Paddleboats are rented at the lake for $5 per hour. The lake is open 9:30 a.m.–5 p.m. You can fish here, but you'll need a fishing license (available at the park store).

There are several short trails inside the park, including Cheaha Lake (p. 31), Bald Rock Boardwalk (p. 17), and Pulpit Rock Trail (p. 187).

CIVIL RIGHTS TRAIL

KEY AT-A-GLANCE INFORMATION

LENGTH: 1.8 miles

CONFIGURATION: Loop

DIFFICULTY: Easy

SCENERY: Linn Park, Kelly Ingram Park, Civil Rights Institute, Sixteenth Street Baptist Church, 4th Avenue Historical and Business District, Eddie Kendricks Park

EXPOSURE: Open

TRAFFIC: Moderate to heavy during the day

TRAIL SURFACE: Asphalt and cement

HIKING TIME: Varies according to pace and stops

ACCESS: City parks closed 10 p.m. to 6 a.m.

MAPS: *Birmingham's Civil Rights Churches* by the Birmingham Historical Society

FACILITIES: Rest rooms, water, and phone available at points along the way, including City Hall, Civil Rights Institute (entry fee charged), and the AmSouth Plaza mall/food court.

SPECIAL COMMENTS: As with any downtown area, be alert for the rare opportunist. The downtown area is patrolled regularly by CAP personnel, who are highly visible on their mountain bikes.

IN BRIEF

No other city can top Birmingham for its historic role in the Civil Rights Movement of the 1960s. This walk visits a variety of major Civil Rights–era sites and passes through the heart of the 4th Avenue Historical and Business District.

DESCRIPTION

The words emblazoned on the cover of the December 1958 issue of *Time* magazine, "Birmingham: Integration's Hottest Crucible," accurately reflected the fight for basic civil and human rights that was spreading like wildfire through the city's African American community. A city known worldwide for its industrial strength, as well as its hardcore segregation policies, Birmingham in the 1950s and 1960s was challenged to overcome an entrenched system of organized racism.

This walk by no means tours all of the city's significant Civil Rights sites, but it manages to pack in a wealth of historic places that no person interested in Birmingham history should miss. Begin by walking toward Park Place, passing City Hall on your right with Linn Park to your left. You'll have a chance to wander through Linn Park

DIRECTIONS

From I-20/59, heading south, take Exit 125 to 22nd Street. At the bottom of the ramp, turn left onto 22nd Street. Go 1 block and turn right onto 8th Avenue North. Pass the Museum of Art on your right and then turn left onto 20th Street North. Park here, along Linn Park. If no spot is available, continue to Park Place, and turn left. If you haven't found a space by the time you reach 21st Street, turn left onto 21st and look for the parking garage on your right. Park in the garage or turn left onto 8th Avenue to make another loop around Linn Park.

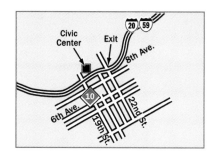

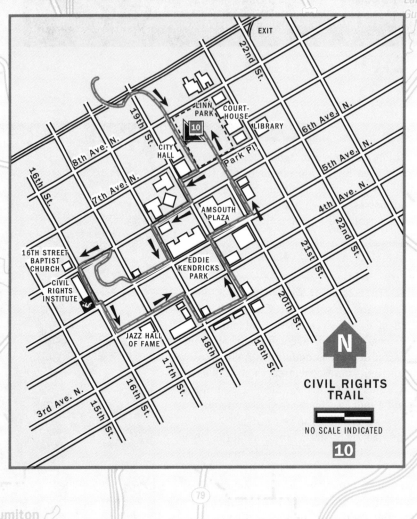

CIVIL RIGHTS
TRAIL

NO SCALE INDICATED

10

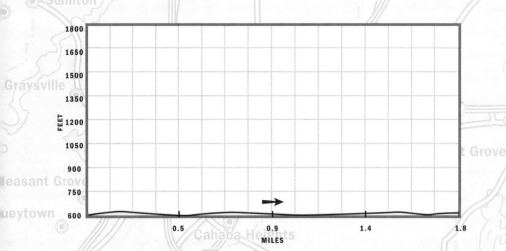

at the end of the walk, but even from this side of the street you can see the towering oaks and gingko trees.

Pass a stand of crape myrtle, cross Park Place and turn right, continuing straight across 19th Street North toward the BellSouth building. Turn left and walk toward Sixth Avenue Presbyterian Church, site of one of many kneel-ins where black worshipers knelt on the steps of white churches as a form of nonviolent demonstration.

At the church, turn right onto 6th Avenue North, walk a block, and then bear left onto 18th Street North. On your right, at the end of the block pass the Smith Building, which houses the Southern Christian Leadership Conference, also on your right. Cross 17th Street North and enter Kelly Ingram Park, a daily battleground in early 1963 now famous for its James Drake sculptures and Freedom Walk. Enter the park greeted by the words "Place of Revolution and Reconciliation" and a statue of three distraught men on their knees praying.

The park is nicely landscaped and sprinkled with tall oak, gingko, old magnolia, and large holly trees. A large fountain decorates the center of the park. Bear left to take a loop around the park along Freedom Walk. The first sculpture you'll encounter is "Police Dog Attack." The sculpture is designed so that you must pass through a narrow passage. From its walls, metal torsos of muscular police attack dogs, with fangs bared, lunge toward you.

The next sculpture is dedicated to the foot soldiers of the Civil Rights Movement, the ordinary young people who came out to demonstrate. On the right, a surly, helmeted policeman, restraining a frenzied attack dog, holds a young black man at bay. On the left is an upside-down jail with a sign that reads "Segregation is a Sin." To the side, a boy and girl proclaim, "I ain't afraid of your jail."

Continue around the loop and pass through a doorway to face replicas of two water cannons—a weapon often used to disperse demonstrations here. Behind you, two people knee with their backs to the water cannons, as if being blasted by them. Before leaving the park, bear left back onto the sidewalk, following 6th Avenue North toward the Civil Rights Institute.

At the corner of 6th Avenue and 16th Street, pass another entrance into the park on your left, this one home to a statue of Martin Luther King Jr. Directly across 16th Street is the Civil Rights Institute. To your right, across 16th Street, is the Sixteenth Street Baptist Church, a goldenrod-colored brick sanctuary decorated with stained-glass windows. A set of square towers in front flank a wide set of stairs leading to the entrance.

From a time of extreme violence, the seminal, most-remembered incident of the Civil Rights Movement remains the bombing of Sixteenth Baptist Church, in which four young girls were killed. One of those girls was the daughter of a black photographer, and future County Commissioner, named Chris McNair. Across the street from the infamous church stands the Civil Rights Institute, the most significant repository and public exhibit of Civil Rights–era artifacts and information in the nation.

Cross 16th Street and bear left to tour the Institute. A recent exhibit of photography at the Institute highlighted the varied complexity of perspectives that visitors find among the Institute's permanent and temporary exhibits. In one room hung poignant photographs of the often-violent demonstrations held in the city's streets, portraits of key Civil Rights leaders, including Martin Luther King Jr. and Rev. Fred Shuttlesworth, and a haunting photo of a black man who had been castrated and left for dead by members of the Ku Klux Klan.

Juxtaposed with those images were surreal and intimate photographs of Klansmen taken by white photographer Wayne Sides. Along with the expected witchy midnight cross burnings were candid home-style shots of Klansmen, including one image showing two robed Klansmen inside a mobile home, posing behind an ersatz Santa Claus.

Back outside, turn right and continue down 16th Street to 5th Avenue North. Cross over and walk down to 4th Avenue North, where the Metropolitan A.M.E. Zion Church stands on your right. Established in 1885, the church was a frequent meeting place for Civil Rights' leaders such as Reverend Shuttlesworth.

A sign that reads "Welcome to the 4th Avenue Historical and Business District" indicates you are entering what used to be known as the Black Business District. Turn left and follow 4th Avenue North to the Alabama Jazz Hall of Fame Museum/Carver Theatre on your right, passing Dawson's restaurant along the way. Across the street to your left is the Alabama F&AM (Free and Accepted Masons) Prince Hall Grand Lodge, long a hub of African-American business and social life.

Continue along 4th Avenue, cross 17th Street, and pass a series of historic businesses including the homestyle cookery Green Acres, the Civil Rights Activist Committee Headquarters, Backstreet Barbecue and Grill, and Magic City Barber Shop.

At the end of the block is a tiny but very cool space known as the Eddie Kendrick Memorial Park. Its sharply dressed statues are shaded with ornamental shrubs and trees. This tight corner park honors Eddie Kendrick, a founding member of the Temptations. Nicknamed "Cornbread," Kendricks was born in Union Springs, but attended school in nearby Ensley.

Leave the park and turn right onto 18th Street, passing the defunct Lyric Theater building across the street to your left. To your right, the stone historic building you see is the old Alabama Penny Savings Bank, the first black-owned bank in Alabama. Just around the corner is the Booker T. Washington Insurance building.

At the corner of 3rd Avenue North, turn left, cross 18th Street and continue straight down 3rd Avenue North. Pass the historic Alabama Theatre on your right. If you have time, step across to the theater and take a peek inside at the ornate lobby.

Reaching 19th Street, a former Woolworth's is to your right and the former Kress 5 & 10 is across from you. Cross 19th Street, turn left, cross 4th Avenue North and look to your right for the site of the old Trailways Bus Station, site of a brutal attack on Freedom Riders by civilians in 1961.

At 5th Avenue North, look to your left for the Vance Federal Building and then turn right to walk between the AmSouth and SouthTrust towers. At 20th Street, turn left. At the end of the block you can enter the AmSouth Plaza mall and food court (2nd floor) on your left to sample some fast food or use the rest rooms. Across 20th Street to your right is the Episcopal Cathedral of the Advent, another kneel-in site.

Cross 6th Avenue North and head straight toward Linn Park, where you can relax by the fountain, wander about and identify the trees, or if you have time, pay a visit to the Birmingham Museum of Art, which is across 8th Avenue North at the far end of the park.

The Birmingham Civil Rights Institute is located at 520 16th Street North. Hours are Tuesday–Saturday, 10 a.m.–5 p.m.; Sunday, 1–5 p.m.; closed on Monday and all major holidays except Martin Luther King Jr. Day (when admission is free). Institute fees are adults, $8; seniors (65+), $5; college students with ID, $4; and ages 17 and under, free of charge. Admission on Sunday is free to all visitors. For more information call (205) 328-9696; (866) 328-9696; or visit www.bcri.bham.al.us.

The Sixteenth Street Baptist Church is located at 1530 6th Avenue North. Worship services are held Sunday at 11 a.m. Tours are given by appointment only. Call (205) 251-9402 for more information.

The Alabama Jazz Hall of Fame, located at 1631 4th Avenue North, is open Tuesday–Saturday, 10 a.m.–5 p.m. and Sunday, 1–5 p.m.; closed on Monday. Call (205) 254-2731 for more information or visit www.jazzhall.com. Admission is free; donations are accepted.

The Birmingham Museum of Art is located at 2000 8th Avenue North. Hours are Tuesday–Saturday, 10 a.m.–5 p.m.; Sunday, 1–5 p.m.; closed on Monday. Admission is free; donations are accepted.

COLEMAN LAKE LOOP

 KEY AT-A-GLANCE INFORMATION

LENGTH: 1.9 miles

CONFIGURATION: Loop

DIFFICULTY: Easy

SCENERY: Coleman Lake, turtles, waterfowl, fern glens

EXPOSURE: Half shaded, half open

TRAFFIC: Light to moderate

TRAIL SURFACE: Sandy woodland path

HIKING TIME: 45 minutes

ACCESS: Pay your $3 day-use fee at any of the park's honor boxes; Coleman Lake Recreation Area is open 7 a.m–10 p.m.

MAPS: None

FACILITIES: 39-site campground with electric and water hookups, rest rooms, showers ($2 fee for non-campers), water, picnic area, swim beach

SPECIAL COMMENTS: No alcoholic beverages allowed; trolling motors only on lake. See p. 6 for a note about hunting seasons.

IN BRIEF

Located beside a well-kept campground within the Choccolocco Wildlife Management Area, 21-acre Coleman Lake is a lazy-day destination. Take your time on the trail that traces its perimeter, looking for painted wood ducks, kingfishers, lots of basking turtles, and maybe a surprise or two.

DESCRIPTION

A centerpiece for the Choccolocco Wildlife Management Area (WMA), Coleman Lake Recreation Area is a pleasant surprise, even though the ride to get there is a bit rough. Its namesake lake is an impoundment created by a small earthen dam. The small lake sends four slough-like arms into the ravines of the surrounding hills, tracing a lopsided watery X on the wooded landscape.

During the various hunting seasons, hunters frequent the rugged hills and hollows of the 46,550-acre Choccolocco WMA. Part of the Shoal Creek District of the Talladega National Forest,

DIRECTIONS

From the intersection of I-20 East and I-459, travel east on I-20 for 55 miles to Exit 191, US 431. Exit and turn left on US 431 North. In half a mile, turn right onto US 78 East. Drive 4 miles and turn left onto AL 9 North. Drive 4.6 miles and turn right onto Joseph Springs Motorway. Drive 3.3 miles and turn left onto FS 531 (not marked here). Drive 2.6 miles and turn left at a four-way intersection onto FS 500. Pass Pine Glen Recreation Area after driving 5.1 miles on FS 500. Turn left, still on 500, at a sign for Coleman Lake. Drive 0.3 miles and turn right at another Coleman Lake sign. Drive 1.7 miles and turn right into the Coleman Lake Recreation Area. Drive straight through until you reach a **Y**. Going left will take you down to the boat launch. Turn right and park in a large, paved lot.

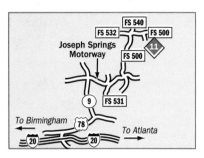

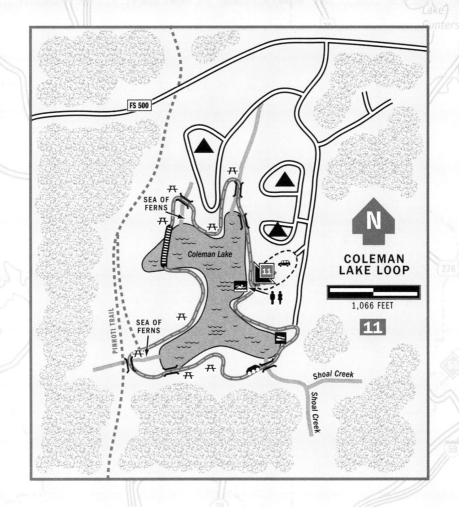

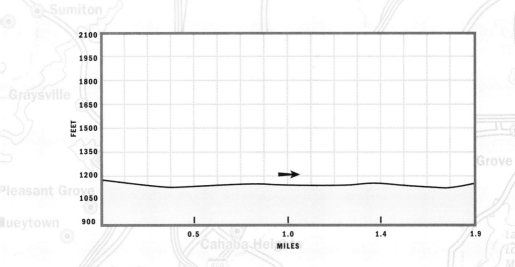

Coleman Lake

the Pinhoti Trail bisects the area and passes close by Coleman Lake. The trail around the lake is a pleasant, easy path that is great for kids. Benches placed along the trail encourage walkers to stop and take in the lake views. To begin, walk toward the swim beach from the parking lot, passing a modest, but clean, rest room facility. A picnic area with tables and grills is located over to the left of the rest rooms. Walking downhill, tall tulip poplars and other hardwoods shade the grounds.

With the 200-foot-long, sandy swim beach directly in front of you, bear right to begin a counterclockwise loop. There is no lifeguard here, so swim at your own risk. The lake water is a dark green, with two to three feet of visibility.

Walking north, pass the first of many tall loblolly pines that dot the forest. As with most other forested areas in north-central Alabama, the Southern pine beetle has been an unwelcome visitor, leaving many dead and dying pines in its wake. On this side of the lake, campsites are located off of loops nearby, and you'll be able to occasionally see an RV or tent through the trees to your right.

Pass a contemplation bench, the first of many that are beneath the shade of black cherry, sweetgum, and white oak trees. You'll also begin to see plentiful forest ferns. Bear away from the lake briefly on a wide, sandy path and cross a small clear stream on a footbridge. Right after you cross this bridge, look for some thick, old poison ivy vines clinging to a sweetgum tree on your right. Just beyond here I had a routine non-poisonous-snake sighting. This time, it was a gray rat snake playing dead in the middle of the trail. Black, with a pattern of mottled chainlike circles, the four-foot serpent came to life when I appoached. It fiercely coiled and managed to pull off a pretty good striking-cobra pose.

Pass a bench and bear around the first lake appendage, heading south. You should see lots of oak-leaf hydrangea here and rows of turtles sunning on logs in the lake. Pass another bench, strolling along a level path. To your left, there are several birdhouses next to the water. Though not birdhouse residents, I saw a couple of brilliant painted wood ducks here.

Pine beetle damage is very evident here, with many dead trees rotting on the ground. The path has been cleared, though, of pine trunks and debris. Head up into a swampy forest bottom, with a sea of bright green ferns growing on trail-left (a species of *dryopteris* is my best guess). Cross another footbridge over a small feeder stream that is alive with minnows, and then see a bench on your right. The trail bends around the fern glen at half a mile. Notice a clearing to your right, a large light gap left by fallen pines. In time, hardwoods such as sourwood, oak, and maple will fill the vacuum left by the evergreens.

After another bench on your right, you'll get to a long wooden boardwalk that crosses over the shallow lake appendage. Pass more birdhouses off to your right then bear left and head east toward the next bench. On your right, a scrubby hillside will emerge as you walk. I spied big-leaf magnolia, black-eyed Susans, and even a kingfisher along this stretch.

At 0.7 miles, you can look across the lake and see the swim beach as the trail meanders, passes a bench, and then dips back into the flat forest bottom. As you pass by in spring and summer, the sound of turtles sliding from rocks and logs will accompany you. Enter another fern-rich habitat, with thousands of the attractive plants. A bench is next, right before a footbridge.

With a myriad of songbirds and cicadas making music high above, pass over a wet-weather drainage and look for the peeling shagbark hickory. Here, as with most points along the trail, you'll be about 20 feet above the lake, with fairly clear views. Pass a bench on trail-right, and at 1.1 miles, reach a high point above the lake and head back into the woods. Walk on a sloping hillside, passing a pignut hickory, and then at 1.2 miles you'll emerge into a clearing. With a dirt road to your right, bear left and at the end of the clearing, downhill toward the lake. Look for blossoming mimosas as you bear right and back onto the trail.

Reach an earthen dam and approach a stone wall. The lake spills from left to right. You can go right to view the small spill cascading into a pool. Follow the trail back along the stone wall and continue to a plank placed across the spillway. The boat launch will be on your left as you walk uphill. Drift away from the lake, and at mile 1.4, cross the steep road that leads down to the boat launch.

You may find a few dragonflies zigzagging among purple clover and wild blackberries along the road. Back by the lake now, heading northwest, the trail returns to the swim beach. From there, head back uphill to the parking area.

NEARBY ACTIVITIES

The Frog Pond Wildlife Preserve and Observation Area makes an easy and interesting outdoor finale to the day. As you're driving back out to AL 9 from Pine Glen, 0.2 miles before you reach AL 9, look for a long, narrow, gravel parking area on your right. There will be a green sign about 100 feet distant that is visible from the road. The entire walk is 0.3 miles.

DEERLICK CREEK COMBO

KEY AT-A-GLANCE INFORMATION

LENGTH: 3.4 miles

CONFIGURATION: Jagged loop

DIFFICULTY: Easy/moderate

SCENERY: Holt Lake

EXPOSURE: Half exposed, half open

TRAFFIC: Light

TRAIL SURFACE: Winding woodland path, paved hiking path, and a grassy median alongside the park road

HIKING TIME: 1.5 hours

ACCESS: Park gate is open 7 a.m.–10 p.m.; campground is open March 1–November 15.

MAPS: Deerlick Creek Park Campground Map

FACILITIES: Rest rooms, water, phone, vending machines, swimming beach (day-use fee, 9 a.m.–dusk), picnic area, boat ramp, coin laundry, hot showers (for paid campers only)

SPECIAL COMMENTS: Call (205) 553-9373 for more information, including campground fees ($10–16 per night). There is no fee to hike the trails, but you must pick up a "walking" pass at the gate and display it in your vehicle.

IN BRIEF

Stitch together Deerlick Creek Park's short trails and wind up with a terrific day hike. Holt Lake is the feature here for campers, but the hilly hardwood forest that lines the shore is what makes the hike worthwhile.

DESCRIPTION

One of four US Army Corps of Engineers parks on Holt Lake, Deerlick Creek Park is cupped in the last bend of the lake before it meets Holt Lock and Dam, which holds back the Black Warrior River to create the 18-mile-long lake. The park is a very well kept facility with modern bathhouses and level campsites. It's a great place for RVers, but tent campers can escape the pop-ups and big rigs in a primitive camping area.

This hike will take you down to Holt Lake to trace the shoreline, gaining nice views of the lake and the dam. You'll have a steep hill or two to

DIRECTIONS

From the intersection of I-459 South and I-65, take I-459 South for 16 miles and merge with I-59 South/I-20 West. Drive another 32 miles, take Exit 73, and turn right onto US 82/McFarland Boulevard. Drive across the Black Warrior River and see a Holt Lake sign. Turn right onto Rice Mine Road and then left at the next light (still on Rice Mine). Drive 2.9 miles and turn right onto New Watermelon Road/CR 87. Drive 3.4 miles, passing Lake Tuscaloosa, and turn right onto CR 42. Drive 3.2 miles, passing Lake Nichol, and turn right onto CR 89. Drive 1.9 miles, and at the Y, bear left. Drive another 3.2 miles and enter the park. Stop at the gate, pick up your courtesy walking pass, then take your first right. Drive to the end of the road and park at the small loop at the end. The trailhead is directly in front of you.

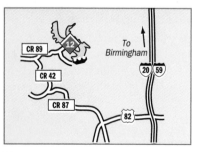

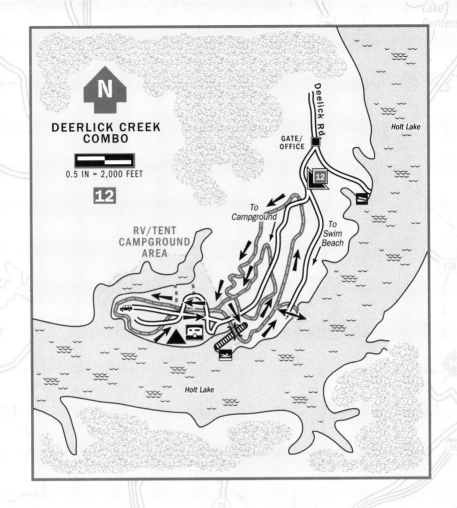

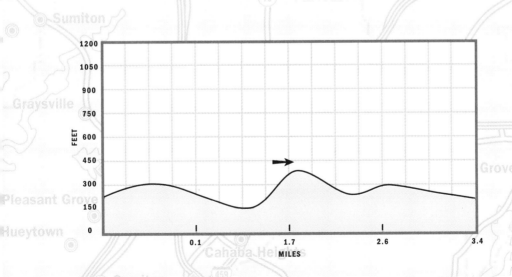

Holt Lake

climb on the way, but long level stretches will keep you from getting winded. You'll break up the woodland hiking with a couple of sections of easy walking in the grassy median alongside the park's quiet roads.

To begin, head down a series of steep wooden steps through a healthy stand of shortleaf pine. The deep green waters of Holt Lake appear as you wind down the rooty dirt path. The slough running back to your right is Deerlick Creek. Bear left, taking rocky steps down with a handrail by your side. Directly in front of you on the water is a fishing/swimming platform. Continue to follow the shore as the trail goes left, passing flaky, lichen-stained sandstone outcroppings on trail-left. The lake itself is very scenic, minus the ski boats and personal watercraft.

Look to the south for a good view of the dam, where a wooden rail keeps you from potentially pitching over into the lake. Pass a side trail from the left at 0.2 miles, go straight, and continue past another swim platform. You'll find pine, hickory, magnolia, and white oak through here. Reach yet another swimming pier, and after passing a bench and a marked pipeline crossing, bear away from the lake to trudge uphill on a steep rocky path lightly flanked with bamboo.

At the top, exit the woods at a picnic pavilion. Pass a bathhouse and rest room on the right, then pass a playground and basketball court. After the RV dumping station, access the shoulder of the quiet campground road. Follow the road and encounter the Settlers Camp primitive area at half a mile. On your right you'll see a sign for a swimming beach. Walk down the path to a large, clean swim beach across the slough. Cross the slough via a footbridge, turn right, and then walk up along the edge of the white, sandy beach. The beach is completely unshaded, and it can get pretty hot out there. One of the nice features of this hike is that there are water fountains and rest rooms scattered along the way, including at the beach area.

Above the beach, go right up the stairs, passing flowering yuccas on the hillside in summer. Bear left and continue up more stairs to the loop-shaped parking area;

rest rooms and showers are on the right. Go right, pass the entrance to the loop, and look for a day-use parking area to the right. You'll find another water fountain here and a short out-and-back trail that you'll take down to the lake. There are four level picnic sites near the road and another five sites down by the lake, along with a set of pit toilets.

What goes down must come up, so hike back up the steep hill to the road and turn right. Look for yellow buttercups growing at the edge of the woods and pass a gated service road on your right. Pass through the gate that closes the swim beach after hours, then walk beside a weedy clearing off to the left that is rife with wild blackberry. Pass a couple of bluebird nesting boxes to see the park entrance station ahead. Before reaching the entrance area, turn left onto the campground road and look for the Gobbler Ridge Trail, which forms a loop that is bisected by the road.

At the first trail entrance on the right, go right and step onto a nice boardwalk that leads to a wide macadam path. Hikers and bikers are welcome on this trail, but I met neither on my weekend walk. This trail is designed as a nature walk, so some trees are labeled. One of the most interesting trees in the area is the devil's walking stick. Look for a prime specimen of this thorny, rod-like tree growing on trail-right near a bench. The trail is flat as it wanders along easily. You'll notice some poison ivy to the sides, but the trail is very wide so no need to worry. Pass a food plot planted for wildlife on your right, and then come to and cross the campground road again, continuing on the Gobbler Ridge Trail. After a short stroll on this side of the road, turn right onto a narrow woodland trail at a sign for the Beech Tree Hollow Trail. The blue-blazed path is steep here as it descends among tall loblolly pines. You'll see many downed pines, but the trail is well maintained and the debris has been pushed to the side. Watch for a sharp left at a double-blue blaze and reach the tip of the slough that leads to the swim beach. A stream enters the slough here, flanked by the trail's namesake beech trees.

Roughly follow a stream uphill and note several big seeps in the ground. This stream ravine is the most pleasant section of the hike. Cross a footbridge, pass a dead beech and bench, and then pass between two large live beeches. Bear left and begin to ascend. Pass a simple wooden bench to meet the Gobbler Ridge Trail. Go left and look for a tree scarred with seven successive galls. Native Indians often scarred trees to mark a significant place.

Pass the entrance to the Beech Tree Hollow Trail on your left before turning back left onto the campground road. Follow the grassy road shoulder southwest to the far end of the campground where you parked.

As a note, I stopped briefly to do a quick tick check of my arms and legs. I plucked six spotted deer ticks off of my socks and lower legs. It takes them awhile to find a spot to burrow in, so it's always good to check for ticks during and right after a hike through any wooded area, as well as to wear long pants and sleeves.

NEARBY ACTIVITIES

On the way down, stop at the Mercedes plant near Vance and take the industrial tour. Visit www.mbusi.com for all of the information, including dress code and visitor restrictions (children under 12 years of age are not permitted to take the tour).

DUGGER MOUNTAIN
FROM THE EAST

 KEY AT-A-GLANCE INFORMATION

LENGTH: 6.8 miles

CONFIGURATION: Out-and-back

DIFFICULTY: Difficult

SCENERY: Meandering stream, gorgeous mixed hardwood/pine forest, wildflowers, white-tailed deer

EXPOSURE: Mostly shaded

TRAFFIC: Very light

TRAIL SURFACE: Narrow dirt path, often rocky and occasionally vague

HIKING TIME: 3.5 hours

ACCESS: Always open, but consider whether or not you want to hike here during deer hunting season, which runs from November 16 through January 31.

MAPS: FS Pinhoti Trail Map 1

FACILITIES: None

SPECIAL COMMENTS: Check for ticks after this woodland hike. The wilderness area is closed to bicycles, motorized equipment, motor vehicles, and hang gliders. See p. 6 for a note about hunting season.

IN BRIEF

Travel along the least visited portion of the Pinhoti Trail as you climb Dugger Mountain from the east. On this little-used trail, you'll most likely hike in complete solitude, but on a path that seems to disappear in places.

DESCRIPTION

Declared a Wilderness Area in 1999, Dugger Mountain's wilds were first protected by a man named Taylor Dugger, who owned large tracts of land along and on the mountain. To his neighbors' consternation he set aside the steep slopes as a wildlife refuge. His conservation efforts with oversight by the U.S. Forest Service and efforts of then

DIRECTIONS

From the intersection of I-20 East and I-459, travel east on I-20 for 55 miles to Exit 191/US 431. Exit and turn left on US 431 North. In half a mile turn right onto US 78 East. Drive 4 miles and turn left onto AL 9 North. Follow AL 9 for 9 miles and turn right onto Rabbittown Road. Follow Rabbittown Road/CR 55 for 5.5 miles and turn left onto unmarked FS 500. On this dirt and gravel road the only sign is small, tacked to a tree, and reads "Triple Creek Club No Trespassing." This warning applies only to the land, not the road. On FS 500, drive 1.1 miles and pass FS 500K on your left. Continue on FS 500 for another 0.6 miles and cross a small bridge. Turn left at the intersection that follows the bridge and drive for 0.2 miles. Look for a small pull-in on the left side of the road and park there. From the car, walk forward about 50 feet to where the Pinhoti crosses the road. There is a posted sign that reads "USA National Recreation Trail" on the right side of the road. Turn left on the Pinhoti, into the forest, to begin the hike.

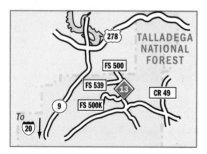

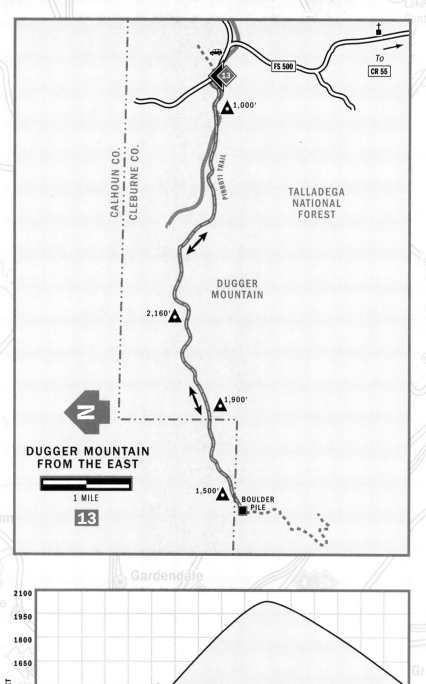

TALLADEGA
NATIONAL
FOREST

DUGGER
MOUNTAIN

PINHOTI TRAIL

CALHOUN CO.
CLEBURNE CO.

FS 500

To
CR 55

1,000'

2,160'

1,900'

1,500'

BOULDER
PILE

N

**DUGGER MOUNTAIN
FROM THE EAST**

1 MILE

13

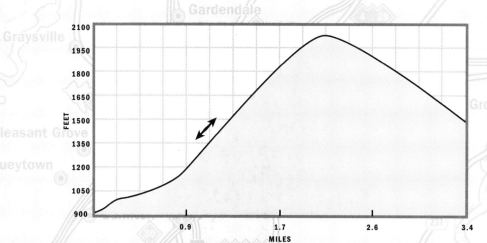

U.S. Rep. Bob Riley and Sen. Jeff Sessions preserved a nice slice of woolly Alabama woodlands for public enjoyment.

Initially, dip down into the woods to see your first blue blaze, painted on a large pine tree. You'll head roughly west, crossing a small stream several times before working your way up the southern flank of Dugger Mountain. At 2,104 feet, Dugger is second only to Cheaha Mountain as loftiest in the state. You'll top out at around 2,100 feet and then head slightly downhill to your turnaround, a strange jumble of boulders and trees. The "Dugger Mountain from the South" (p. 60) hike also ends at this boulder pile.

Just off the forest road, pass a small, neat campsite and wander along a flat forest bottom rich with red maple, loblolly pine, red oak, hickory, white oak, mountain laurel, and a variety of wildflowers. A small, clear stream meanders alongside the rooty, needled trail. A common sight, pines downed by the tiny-but-deadly Southern pine beetle lie rotting on the ground.

Surrounded by oak-leaf hydrangea and mountain laurel, use the stones to cross the six-foot-wide stream and walk against its flow. The narrow woodland path, covered with hickory nuts in summer, is bounded by a flat off to the right and steep uphill slope on the other side of the stream. Cross the stream again, now heading south, and look for spears of liatrus and groups of black-eyed Susans scattered along the trail.

You'll cross the stream three more times before the 0.75-mile mark. It was here that I spotted a young white-tailed deer leaping away through the trees. I couldn't see him, but a buck distinctly snorted in the distance. It's estimated that there are at least 15 deer per square mile in this area.

Due to light use, brush frequently encroaches on the trail, scratching your ankles. I like to feel the trail grabbing at me, so it's not a bother; just dress accordingly. Young hardwoods grow thick here as well, having taken advantage of the light gaps left when dead pines fell.

At 0.7 miles, a slope climbs to your left as you head west and uphill at a slight angle to the slope. Lots of sandstone rocks lie about, with the occasional chipmunk or granddaddy longlegs scampering over them. At 0.8 miles, enter a cooler pine thicket, which has a few hardwoods, including mulberries. Again walking a needled path, break onto a wide slope at 1 mile, then head north and more directly uphill, across a rounded slope. The trail soon levels and enters the first area of trail vagary at 1.25 miles—an area thick with vegetation. To help yourself navigate, look for blue blazes both in front of and behind you.

At 1.5 miles, the trail begins to ascend again toward the west, with a slope down to your right. The higher you get, the more you'll notice chestnut oak and mats of bright-green bryophytes. Soon, reach a sub-ridge of Dugger and look for a jumble of rocks with trees growing from it at 1.7 miles, followed by another long jumble that runs on your left. You can get a glimpse of the vistas beyond, but the trees block the views.

Pass a steep bouldered slope up to your right along a westbound trail that is clear and easy to follow here. However, at 2 miles, the trail thins again, often obscured by thick growths of wildflowers. To stay on track when the trail seems to disappear, walk a straight and level line for about 100 feet, look for a double-trunked chestnut oak on the right, and a blue blaze ahead.

Two and a half miles into the hike, the rocky slope continues up to your right, with a wooded forest slope down to your left. Roughly following a contour, with partial views to your left, soon top out on the ridge, but not at the mountain's highest point, which the Pinhoti Trail bypasses by less than 1,000 feet. The highest point is near a fire tower, which unfortunately I was never able to spot from the Pinhoti.

Work back to the right side of the ridge now, heading happily downhill for awhile. Once again, near the turnaround, the trail becomes very thin. To keep on track, when you reach a downed tree, hug the tree and don't wander to the right, then cross a second downed tree. Cross a third fallen tree, and look up-woods to your left for the big boulder pile, the turnaround.

Walk uphill, scramble up the rocks, sit a spell, and go ahead and eat that apple you've been saving. The boulder pile is roughly 100 feet long, 20 feet wide, and 30 feet high. There are several trees growing from it, including Virginia pines and chestnut oaks. Up on top, next to a tall pine, is a tiny foot-high pine growing in a small pocket of debris. Elevation on top is 1,580 feet.

To complete the hike, work your way carefully back to the trail. Due to the path's disappearing act, it's probably wise to plan your hike so that you do not risk having to walk out in the dark. Although many people balk (I once did) at toting a GPS unit in the woods, one comes in handy when you're backtracking along a path that is hard to follow. Finish the trail by taking the long, sometimes-fast hike back down the mountain to the parking lot at 877 feet.

NEARBY ACTIVITIES

Built in 1994, The Frog Pond Wildlife Preserve and Observation Area makes an easy and interesting outdoor finale to the day. As you're driving back to US 78 on AL 9 turn left onto Joseph Springs Motorway. Drive 0.2 miles and turn left into a long narrow gravel parking area on your right. There will be a green sign about 100 feet distant that is visible from the road. Pull in, park, and walk toward the sign, which will indicate that you are headed toward the Frog Pond. Walk in and turn left onto a wide woodland trail (just before a piled berm of dirt). Follow the trail to the pond, where you'll find a boardwalk and an observation tower that you can sit in to spot wildlife—or just listen to the frogs. The small marshy preserve is a joint project between Jacksonville State University and the Alabama Forestry Commission. There is neither running water nor a rest room here. The entire walk is 0.3 miles.

DUGGER MOUNTAIN
FROM THE SOUTH

KEY AT-A-GLANCE INFORMATION

LENGTH: 8.4 miles

CONFIGURATION: Out-and-back

DIFFICULTY: Moderate/hard

SCENERY: Pinky's cabin, mixed hardwood/pine forest, wild turkeys

EXPOSURE: Mostly shaded

TRAFFIC: Light

TRAIL SURFACE: Dirt woodland path, rocky and rooty in places

HIKING TIME: 3.5 hours

ACCESS: Open 24 hours, 7 days per week. Consider whether or not you want to hike through here during deer hunting season, which runs November 16–January 31. See p. 6 for more information

MAPS: FS Pinhoti Trail Map 1

FACILITIES: None

SPECIAL COMMENTS: Check for ticks after this hike. The wilderness area is closed to bicycles, motorized equipment and vehicles, and hang gliders.

IN BRIEF

Introduce yourself to the Dugger Mountain Wilderness Area with this moderately strenuous hike. You'll begin by climbing and working your way around Red Mountain, then hiking your way up the side of Dugger Mountain to a mysterious jumble of ridge-top boulders.

DESCRIPTION

Designated as a wilderness area by Congress in 1999, Dugger Mountain's 9,200 acres are part of a nationwide 106-million-acre wilderness preservation system. One unique public law for wilderness areas is that no motorized equipment or mechanical transport is allowed. The point of creating wilderness areas like Dugger Mountain is to protect roadless wilds and to create a resource for hikers and others who seek to explore in solitude.

The mountain itself is named for pioneer settler Taylor Dugger, who filed a homestead on the land and, to the surprise of many, declared the steep slopes of the mountain a wildlife refuge. His scheme was not received well at first, but his generosity and commitment to his idea gradually won his neighbors over. They even named the mountain after him.

DIRECTIONS

From the intersection of I-20 East and I-459, travel east on I-20 for 55 miles to Exit 191, US 431. Exit and turn left on US 431 North. In half a mile turn right onto US 78 East. Drive 4 miles and turn left onto AL 9 North. Follow AL 9 for 9 miles and turn right onto Rabbittown Road. Bear left at a country store, pass King Gap Road on your left, and watch for an old dog-trot cabin, known as Pinky Burns' Cabin, on the left side of the road. Pull in at the cabin and park. At the back of the vacant property you'll find a Dugger Mountain Wilderness plaque embedded in a large stone.

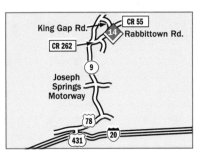

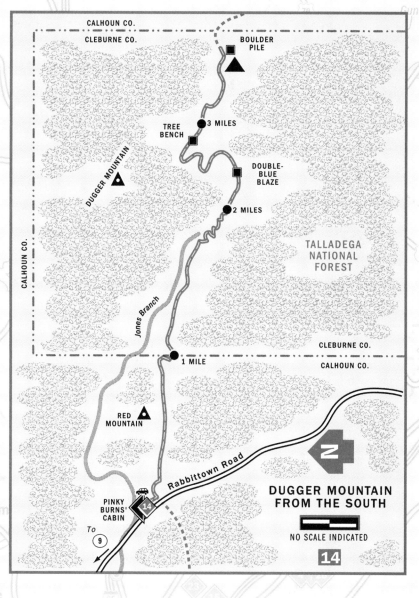

CALHOUN CO.
CLEBURNE CO.

BOULDER PILE

3 MILES

TREE BENCH

DOUBLE-BLUE BLAZE

DUGGER MOUNTAIN

2 MILES

CALHOUN CO.

TALLADEGA NATIONAL FOREST

Jones Branch

CLEBURNE CO.
CALHOUN CO.

1 MILE

RED MOUNTAIN

Rabbittown Road

N

DUGGER MOUNTAIN FROM THE SOUTH

NO SCALE INDICATED

14

PINKY BURNS' CABIN

14

To 9

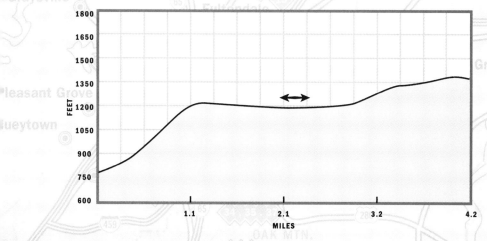

| | 1800 | 1650 | 1500 | 1350 | 1200 | 1050 | 900 | 750 | 600 |

FEET

1.1   2.1   3.2   4.2
MILES

The hike's turnaround

One of two Wilderness Areas in the Talladega National Forest (Cheaha Wilderness is the other), Dugger Mountain is a rugged day-hike destination. This hike does not traverse the entire mountain, nor does it include the entire 7.2-mile length of the Pinhoti Trail that passes through the wilderness. The hike takes you more than 4 miles deep into the wilderness area via Red Mountain, for a total of 8.3 miles—the perfect dayhike, especially considering the steady climb as you hike in. At around 1 mile, as you go north, you'll cross into Cleburne County from Calhoun County, then follow a contour line that runs between 1,200 and 1,300 feet for the next 2 miles. After turning west and descending into a narrow cleft valley, you'll begin to climb steadily up the side of Dugger Mountain to reach a turnaround point on its ridge.

At Pinky's cabin, you'll be tempted to browse around the old homeplace, peek inside the log structure, and poke around the old shed. Be respectful, though, of preservation efforts and look but don't touch. If you want to learn more about Pinky, visit the Alabama Trails Association website (www.alabamatrailsasso.org) and look up a short piece by Robby Bendall called "The Day I Met Pinky Burns." After you whet your curiosity at the cabin, take off for the trailhead, which is just down the road. Facing the road, you'll turn left and walk 0.2 miles to reach the point where the Pinhoti crosses Rabbittown Road from the right and re-enters the forest on your left.

You can also go through the woods beside the cabin and, heading east/northeast, scramble through the brush until you run into the narrow dirt path. Keep the road in sight to your right and you can't get lost. You'll cross an old logging road along the way before hitting the Pinhoti Trail at 0.2 miles. Once on the trail, look for blue blazes and an occasional faded, white blaze shaped like a turkey footprint. There are none of the familiar diamond-shaped Pinhoti turkey-foot tags through this wilderness area.

As you work your way up the side of Red Mountain, the forested slope hosts a mix of Southern hardwoods and pines. Without the approval of Congress, the Southern pine beetle has passed through, killing off many pines. Growing up, though, through a forest floor scattered with pale-green, lichen-stained rocks are red oak, mulberry, red maple, chestnut oak, and many other healthy hardwoods. Oak-leaf hydrangea and mats of bryophytes add to the solid woodsy flavor of Dugger.

At a quarter mile, work your way up at an angle to a slight slope that drops away to the right, passing many small hardwoods that have emerged in light gaps left by fallen pines. The path levels briefly at 0.4 miles then drops down and begins to meander at roughly 1,250 feet. Intermittent, very steep drainage ravines peel down to your right.

As I headed northwest, at 0.8 miles, a brief rain shower wet the trail, but left the forest very still and calm. At this point, as the up-slope on the right fades and a slope begins to build on your left, you should begin to see the ridge of Dugger Mountain as it looms above you to the northeast. Briefly trace a contour eastward to reach the 1-mile mark. As you develop a rhythm, the vastness of the forest, rolling mile after mile, is all the more impressive.

You'll encounter an occasional steep dip down and up drainage cuts, and you might notice the fragrant essence of the polecat. The forest gives the sun-dappled trail plenty of breathing room, and teases you with partially obstructed views of Dugger to the left. Pass through the occasional mountain laurel slick as you head north, and be careful not to step on those iridescent green beetles that occasionally scramble across the trail.

There's not a lot of water on top of the ridges through here, but you'll pass a few places along the way where you can slap some cold water on your face or filter a quart or two of everclear (the non-alcoholic version). Prior to the 2-mile mark, reach one of these tiny brooks, which flows down from the right.

Dip down slightly into some rolling ravines and then resume the winding contour. At 2 miles, a deep, narrow ravine to the northwest, which separates you from the ridge of Dugger, becomes evident. Dropping down and rolling over finger ridges, reach a double-blaze blaze and a sharp left at 2.1 miles. You'll quickly reach the bottom of the ravine and see a brown hiker sign. Continuing forward, turn a corner (left) at 2.3 miles to hear water flowing downhill on your right. Bear away from the creek to the southwest. It was here that I plowed into a big spider web with a bumblebee flapping in the silk. I didn't mean to, but I freed the bee. Happy bee, sad spider.

In half a mile, now heading west, you'll again hear the steady rush of water below. If you need to, you can always leave the trail to take a look, but the slope down is really steep. It probably won't take you long to get down, but getting back up is another story. If you're thirsty, there's another tiny brook running down from the left just ahead. And just beyond that, you'll pass through a rocky area and then cross a cool, clear, fern-lined stream.

If you need a place to sit and rest, wait until just before the 3-mile mark, where you'll find a natural tree bench. Continuing, walk along the smooth, rolling ridge that is thick with oaks: red, white, and chestnut. At 3.5 miles, walk into a flat area with a campsite and fire ring. Just ahead through the trees, you'll see a big jumble of large boulders with red oaks and Virginia pines growing out of it. That's the turnaround point.

The Pinhoti continues, but there is a segment through an area of storm damage that is difficult to navigate. Head up to the boulder pile that is roughly 100 feet long and 30 feet high and enjoy an apple and a long drink of water before the walk back.

Built in 1994, The Frog Pond Wildlife Preserve and Observation Area makes an easy and interesting outdoor finale to the day. As you're driving back to US 78 on AL 9 turn left onto Joseph Springs Motorway. Drive 0.2 miles and turn left into a long narrow gravel parking area on your right. There will be a green sign about 100 feet distant that is visible from the road. Pull in, park, and walk toward the sign, which will indicate that you are headed toward the Frog Pond. Walk in a short way and turn left onto a wide woodland trail (just before a piled berm of dirt). Follow the trail to the pond, where you'll find a boardwalk and an observation tower that you can sit in to spot wildlife—or just listen to the frogs. The small marshy preserve is a joint project between Jacksonville State University and the Alabama Forestry Commission. There is neither running water nor a rest room here. The entire walk is 0.3 miles.

EAST LAKE PARK LOOP

IN BRIEF

Once a gathering place for the employees of Birmingham's many steel-related industries, East Lake Park now provides numerous outdoor opportunities, including a hike around one of Birmingham's oldest parks. In addition to a vigorous walk, visitors can fish, soak up the sun, or play golf at nearby Don Hawkins Golf Course. Lots of geese and ducks wait for bread-crumb handouts, making this a great weekend walk with kids.

DESCRIPTION

In 1886, the East Lake Land Company created this 100-acre urban park for steel-industry laborers moving to Birmingham. Many of these laborers were Italian immigrants who helped build a vibrant East Lake community. The centerpiece of the neighborhood, the park's 45-acre lake, was first named Como, after the resort lake in the Italian Alps. Since 1917, when the City of Birmingham purchased the park, it has hosted various amusements, including a Ferris wheel, a shooting gallery, and water skiing. Today, the park provides welcome recreation to walkers and anglers alike. Keep in mind that the trail is completely unshaded, though shade can be found in areas to the side. The sparkling water of East Lake can also reflect a mean glare, so bring your shades and sunscreen on a bright day.

To start the hike, ease between the football and baseball fields, follow the sidewalk around to

KEY AT-A-GLANCE INFORMATION

LENGTH: 1 mile

CONFIGURATION: Loop

DIFFICULTY: Easy

SCENERY: Lake views, ducks, geese

EXPOSURE: Open

TRAFFIC: Light in cool weather, heavier in warm weather

TRAIL SURFACE: Fine gravel, sidewalks

HIKING TIME: 30 minutes

ACCESS: Park is closed 10 p.m.–6 a.m.

MAPS: None

FACILITIES: Picnic area with tables and grills, 2 covered pavilions with tables and a grill, rest rooms, football and baseball fields, water fountains, handicap accessible fishing piers.

SPECIAL COMMENTS: The park's future is being challenged by the nearby Birmingham International Airport, which wants to eliminate it to make room for an 8,650-foot runway.

DIRECTIONS

Access First Avenue North and drive to the intersection with 84th Street North. If heading south, turn right. If heading north, turn left. Pass a police station on your right and pull into the park's parking area, which is on the left next to the Shepherd Recreational Center; rest rooms are located here.

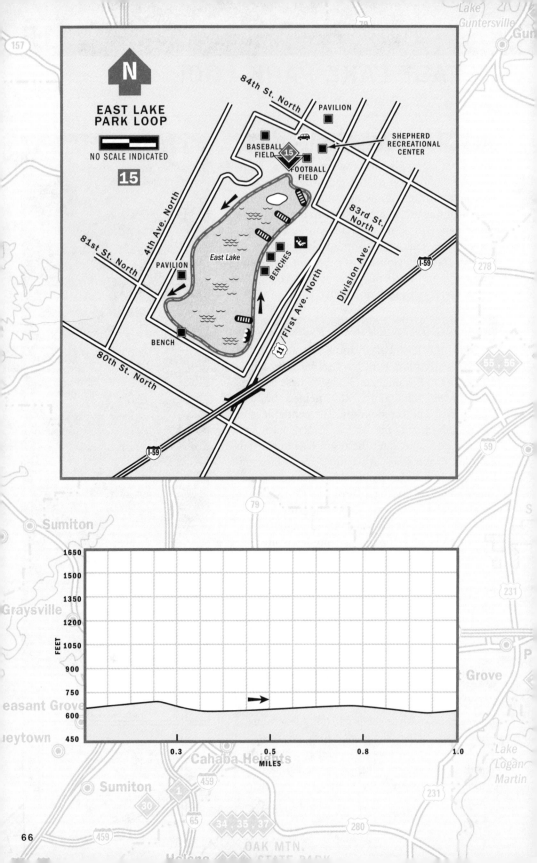

the gravel path that circles East Lake, and go to your right. Soon after you join the gravel path that circles the lake, ducks and pigeons flock to investigate. If you stand still long enough, even the more dignified geese will waddle down, creating quite a circus of birds. Children may be fascinated or terrified. If you want the birds to leave you alone, don't feed them. Otherwise they'll be your constant companions.

About a quarter mile around the loop, Lynn Park comes into view on the right, with the sparkling water of East Lake to your left. In the middle of the lake is a small wooded island that begs for exploration. However, swimming and boating are not allowed, so you'll have to be satisfied with gazing. Fishing is allowed in the lake, but you'll need an Alabama fishing license.

A covered pavilion with tables and a grill are to your right. Another pavilion is located across 84th Street North, the street from which you entered the park. The pavilions are first come, first served, unless a party has reserved the facility.

The lake scenery is peaceful, but there can be a lot of ambient noise. Traffic is always thick on nearby First Avenue North, and planes from the Birmingham International Airport fly overhead frequently. On a windy day, though, the breeze is sufficient to drown out most of the noise clutter, except for the planes.

Several simple fitness stations are strategically placed around the lake, but these seem to be rarely used. You can stop and stretch or do simple exercises like pull-ups and push-ups. At night the path is well lit, but it's best not to be out here walking after dark, especially if you are alone.

The open trail bends around the end of the lake, curving to the left. On your right, a bank of small trees and brush mark the park's boundary, obscuring the houses beyond. A lonely contemplation bench is near an old willow tree that leans into the lake. The trail continues around the lake, where it roughly parallels First Avenue North, which is separated from the park by Village Creek and a narrow band of trees.

The first of several railed piers that venture out over the water appear on your immediate left. Step out onto the pier and relax on one of the benches and catch the breeze, which is often blowing over the water. Return to the trail, and walk across a small dam that drains excess water into Village Creek. Just beyond, a small finger of land juts out into the water, a great place to cast a plastic worm or work a remote-controlled boat.

Moving on, reach another pier that extends left over the lake waters. Here, the path comes closer to the lake, following a brick-and-iron-rail barrier. To the right are numerous benches and a large open field. Shortly, reach a flagpole and a marker that details the park's history. A third pier with a covered gazebo appears next on your left. Walk out to the end of this pier to get your best look at the small, inaccessible island.

Back on the trail, look to the right for a well-kept playground area. A swing set and a jungle gym with a slide and swinging bridge will soak up a lot of excess toddler energy. Not far past the playground, the walk comes to an end. The path then turns left, crosses a bridge, and reaches to the sidewalk where you started. Take another jaunt around the lake if you wish, or turn right and head back to the parking lot and your vehicle.

FLINT CREEK WHITE LOOP

KEY AT-A-GLANCE INFORMATION

LENGTH: 9.6 miles (Bankhead literature cites the trail's length as 11 miles, but I clocked it with my GPS at 9.6 miles.)

CONFIGURATION: Loop

DIFFICULTY: Moderate

SCENERY: Big-leaf magnolia, lots of wild blackberries, rolling Southern hardwood forest

EXPOSURE: Half exposed

TRAFFIC: A weekday morning is the best time to hike. This is a multiuse trail, so you may encounter horses, mountain bikers, and four-wheelers.

TRAIL SURFACE: Wide, rocky, dirt track with occasional mud holes

HIKING TIME: 3 hours

ACCESS: Day-use parking area open 7 a.m.–10 p.m. A $3 day-use fee is required.

MAPS: *Sipsey Wilderness & Black Warrior Wildlife Management Area of the William B. Bankhead National Forest* by Carto-Craft of Birmingham

FACILITIES: Pit toilet at trailhead, map board

SPECIAL COMMENTS: At the map board, where you self register, place your $3 fee in the provided envelopes, tear off the receipt, slip the envelope into the metal box, and place the receipt tag on your dashboard.

IN BRIEF

Take a relatively easy but long and wavy hike through the Bankhead National Forest. You'll probably share this wide multiuse trail with some nonhiker company.

DESCRIPTION

It's nice to bushwhack your way along a wild path such as the nearby Sipsey River Trail (p. 220) or the Sumatanga Mountain Loop near Asheville (p. 234), but that's just one way to enjoy a walk in the woods. I hesitated to include the Flint Creek loop, knowing that four-wheelers and motorcyclists share the trail. But after hiking the loop on a hot and busy Sunday afternoon, I decided the contact with riders made the walk an interesting affair. I still experienced relative silence for most of the hike, and everyone I encountered was congenial. General politeness, an open mind, and stepping to the side of the trail when you hear an engine revving is the best way to approach this trail—or its 5.3-mile companion loop, which spurs off the route described here after the first mile.

After passing two cemeteries en route to the Flint Creek trailhead, you'll be glad to see a few warm bodies circulating in the large gravel parking

DIRECTIONS

From Birmingham, take I-65 North 46.5 miles to Cullman Exit 308 (a rest area is located at 40 miles). Exit and turn left onto US 278 West. Drive 20.7 miles and turn right onto CR 41. Drive 11 miles and turn left onto FS 249. You won't be able to see the marker from CR 41, but FS 249 is just past Cave Springs Cemetery on the left. Turn left onto the gravel road and drive 4.4 miles to an intersection with FS 268. Turn right, pass through a gate, and pull into the Flint Creek day-use parking area. Walk to the far end of the parking lot toward the pit toilet to begin the hike.

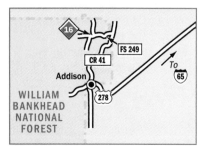

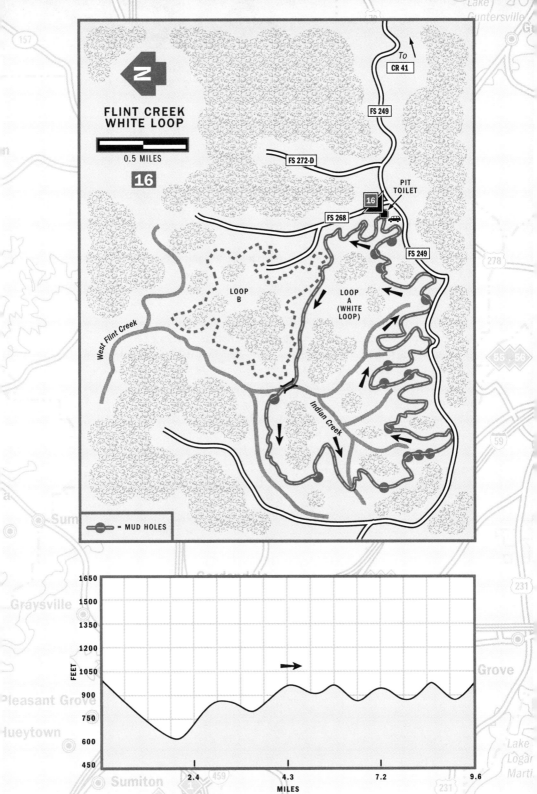

FLINT CREEK WHITE LOOP

0.5 MILES

16

To CR 41

FS 249

FS 272-D

PIT TOILET

16

FS 268

FS 249

LOOP B

LOOP A (WHITE LOOP)

West Flint Creek

Indian Creek

= MUD HOLES

1650
1500
1350
1200
1050
FEET 900
750
600
450

2.4   4.3   7.2   9.6
MILES

lot. At a stop sign, bear right onto the loop (Loop A), generously blazed with white diamond-shaped tags. The dirt path is wide enough to accommodate four-wheelers and is sandy in places. There are a few mud holes along the way, which are easily circumvented, but they should be dry unless it's rained in the past few days. I hiked this loop a couple of days after a week of heavy rain, so I was able to identify the tank traps.

The trail is fairly open, with occasional stretches in direct sunlight. The forest surrounding the trail is healthy, with hardwoods such as shagbark hickory, maple, white pine, persimmon, tulip poplar, and chestnut oak. An abundance of light gaps and pines rotting on the ground are a sure sign that the Southern pine beetle has been here. Other flora you'll encounter include black-eyed Susans, mimosa, wild muscadines, and wild blackberries.

Initially enjoy a slow meandering path that gently rises and falls. In warmer weather, cicadas buzz in the trees seemingly oblivious to the heat, big black ants zigzag frantically across the dirt, and blue-nosed dragonflies zip precisely along their flight paths.

At half a mile, cross a power-line clearing and quickly re-enter the forest. Here I saw a beautiful specimen of rat snake. About four feet long, coppery stripes and spots ran the length of its slender black body. At first it played dead, but as I squatted down for a closer look, the narrow tip of its tail began to quiver in the sand—an admirable but unimpressive rattlesnake rendition. Next, it tried a more aggressive move, coiling wickedly into a serious striking pose.

The trail soon begins to snake itself, following a woodland contour that varies between 800 and 1,000 feet in height. At the first fork in the trail, where the red-blazed 5.3-mile loop begins, stick with the white blazes, heading downhill along a steep ravine down to your left. At 1.2 miles, bear left to reach a Y intersection and veer left.

I saw rare patches of poison ivy, but the wide trail requires minimal contact with the understory flora. Compare this trail to the narrow, often choked Sipsey River Trail, which seems to constantly touch and grab at you. Without splintered beech trunks to straddle or bamboo to push aside, you move along at a rapid clip.

At 2.2 miles, wooden railings flank the trail down to a wooden bridge that spans 15-foot-wide Indian Creek, which flows north and empties into Flint Creek. Not surprisingly, you'll see the first major mud hole shortly after crossing the bridge. At 2.4 miles encounter another Y. The white trail goes straight, and the trail to the left, which is marked for hike/bike only, soon rejoins the white-blazed trail. Keeping to the multi-use loop the entire distance, look for thorny patches of wild blackberries growing along the trail. In summer, you'll see lots of red unripe berries and a few ripe berries. Purple, seed-laden scat along the trail indicates why there are so few ripe berries.

At 2.65 miles, pass under the power lines again and soon pass a clear-cut area on your right. Perhaps encouraged by the extra light afforded by the clearing, a tiny jungle of bright-green bryophytes carpets trailside rock ledges. Where you approach two steel posts, a stop sign, and a T in the trail, venture to the right to pick up the white-blazed trail. You'll soon stumble across (and around) a super rut, three feet deep and swimming in creamy mud after a rain, which would be a real kick to plow through on a bike.

For the next mile or so the trail opens up to sun and encounters a series of small mud traps. You'll notice run-offs dug at angles to the trail that divert water flow off the path, minimizing somewhat the development of really nasty mud pots.

Although you may get your boots a little muddy, you won't find many trees blocking the path. On the entire loop I only had to leave the trail twice to jag around downed trees. Pass a small mud hole, and at 5.5 miles, pass a hike/bike-only trail that comes in from your right. Winding along an increasingly wavy track, take a hairpin turn up a steep boulder-padded trail.

Here I met three easygoing moto-cross riders taking a break. They had already passed me a few times on the trail, nodding or waving each time they carefully cranked by. "You forgot your ride," quipped one. "Well I guess that's why I'm so tired," I replied, feigning a puzzled look.

Not far from the end at mile 8, stroll through a big patch of thriving kudzu, pass a stop sign, three yellow poles, and another stop sign. Bear left, pass a trail coming in from the left and bear around right to stay on the white-blazed trail. After skirting by three successive mud holes, just before a sharp left turn at mile 9, look for a nice specimen of devil's walking stick. It really looks like a walking stick growing out of the ground, and it's covered with devilish, prickly thorns. After 9.2 miles of easy forest strolling, bear right to the parking area to end your hike.

NEARBY ACTIVITIES

A policeman from Addison told me that Smith's Barbecue on US 278 serves up some good victuals. I didn't have time to stop by, but I'll take his word for it. Smith's is on your right about a mile before the turn onto CR 41. Two miles north of Exit 308, at I-65 North Exit 310, are several fast food restaurants and a Cracker Barrel. If you finish this hike by 2 or 3 p.m, you'll have time to drive out to Hurricane Creek Park for a rugged, short hike (p. 92).

FOSSIL MOUNTAIN TRAIL

KEY AT-A-GLANCE INFORMATION

LENGTH: 1.2 miles

CONFIGURATION: Loop

DIFFICULTY: Easy

SCENERY: Hardwood forest with lots of tall cedars, shagbark hickories, and acres of jumbled surface rock

EXPOSURE: Minimal

TRAFFIC: Light in cold weather, moderate to heavy in months when the caverns are open

TRAIL SURFACE: Limestone, sandstone, and dirt

HIKING TIME: 45 minutes

ACCESS: Open year-round, 8 a.m. to dark; $1 per person to enter park for ages 6 and up

MAPS: Trail map available at park office

FACILITIES: Rest rooms, vending machines, phone, playground (monkey bars, merry-go-round, slides, swings), picnic area with multiple tables and grills, one pavilion, air-conditioned snack bar by the caverns.

SPECIAL COMMENTS: Snack bar, pool, and mini-train ride open seasonally. Call (256) 647-9692 for details.

IN BRIEF

Definitely a geologist's dream, this hike leads visitors through an amazing rock garden amid a dominant forest of cedar in one of Alabama's remarkable state parks.

DESCRIPTION

With its "miracle mile" of caverns and limestone formations, Rickwood is unique among Alabama's state parks. Formed over 260 million years ago, the caverns, part of an ancient, dry seabed, were carved through the action of flowing water. The cave is still "active"; dripping water accumulates residue that continues to slowly build cave structures. This easy, short trail rises and falls gently, but is extremely rocky—a sturdy pair of shoes is a must.

To reach the trail, walk toward the office along the main road. With the office to your left, bear right onto a short trail, which leads to the loop through a boulder field. Right away, you get the sneaking suspicion that there are caves below. But don't forget to gaze at the forest as you walk; look for shagbark hickories peeling long strips of bark, aromatic green cedars, and a variety of healthy hardwoods.

When you the reach the loop and the trailhead sign, turn right to begin following the loop in a counterclockwise manner.

DIRECTIONS

From its intersection with I-59, take I-65 North 23.5 miles to Exit 284. Exit and turn left onto AL 160 West. Drive 0.2 miles and turn right on CR 8, following signs to the park. Drive 2.5 miles and turn right onto Campbell Road. Continue for 1.25 miles and turn right into Rickwood Caverns State Park. Drive into the park, pass the Park Office on the right, and park in the large lot on your left.

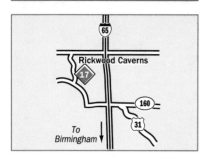

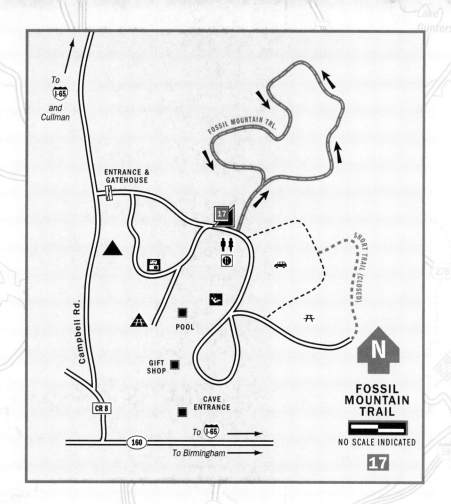

Fossil Mountain Trail — Map

To I-65 and Cullman

ENTRANCE & GATEHOUSE

FOSSIL MOUNTAIN TRL.

SHORT TRAIL (CLOSED)

Campbell Rd.

CR 8

160

To I-65

To Birmingham

POOL

GIFT SHOP

CAVE ENTRANCE

17

N

FOSSIL MOUNTAIN TRAIL

NO SCALE INDICATED

17

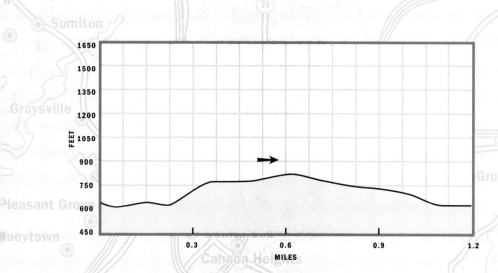

Immediately duck into a forest littered with carbonate rocks such as limestone and dolomite. Ascend past numerous large cedars as you head initially east. A relentless garden of boulders, ranging in size from a bowling ball to a large car, surrounds the trail. There will be a few downed trees in the area, but no pines. The soil here favors cedars.

Through breaks in the canopy, look for red-tailed hawks soaring high above this very quiet wood. Unless others are on the trail, only the titter of songbirds, the hammering of woodpeckers, and the whistle of wind will accompany you.

The trail is thin in places, so pay attention. At half a mile in, the trail appears to run straight, but you should bear left, heading northwest. Pass between large house-sized rocks and begin meandering along the trail. If you haven't noticed any blue blazes after the last turn, turn around and look for them behind you to make certain you're on the trail before continuing forward. The trail will gradually turn southwest, then south, then bear right to the north/northwest before the twisting trail descends in a zigzag fashion. Look for occasional blue blazes painted on rocks.

At 1 mile along the trail, reach a pit 10 feet across and 6 feet deep that is surrounded by rock. A shaft at the bottom appears to go into the ground. Next, veer left and down into a very rocky area with numerous sinks that funnel water into the ground.

As the trail begins to bear left, heading south, the trail thins again. Here, at 1.2 miles, the path begins to head east toward the loop's start. In 0.1 mile, the trail appears to go straight, but go right and downhill, passing a moss-covered rock wall to your left; a cedar on your right has a blue blaze on it. Soon you'll glimpse the park's maintenance shed as you continue bearing left. Emerge at the trailhead sign and walk out toward the office

Back in your vehicle, be careful as you leave the park. It's easy to make a wrong turn. Coming out of the park, turn left, then turn left again at the T. Turn left onto 160 at the I-65/US 31 sign.

NEARBY ACTIVITIES

Rickwood Caverns is the obvious must-do. Located inside the park grounds, the caverns are open 10 a.m.–5 p.m.: March–Memorial Day on weekends only, Memorial Day–Labor Day every day, and September–October on weekends only. Admission is $8 for ages 12 and older, $4 for ages 6–11. Group tours of 20 or more can be arranged by appointment. Call (205) 647-9692 for more information.

The park also has an Olympic-size pool, which is open during the summer, 10 a.m.–6 p.m. The fee is $2.50 per person.

GUNTERSVILLE STATE PARK:
TOM BEVILL TRAIL WITH THE CAVE TRAIL

IN BRIEF

Take a tour of Ellenberg Mountain and, along the way, take a side trip to visit a small cave.

DESCRIPTION

Named after former U.S. Congressman Tom Bevill, this orange-blazed trail mixes a little history with a lot of exercise. The first half of the hike circles around west, north, and then east to a junction with the Cave Trail. Take the Cave Trail to a small cave, where you may want to get down on your hands and knees and explore. Be sure to bring a flashlight, though. Finish the Cave Trail where it ends at a T with the Loop Trail. Return to the junction with the Bevill Trail and finish the interpretive trail by heading east, south, and then west.

Although there is an interpretive brochure that illuminates various sites along the trail, many of the numbered posts have been knocked over or are no longer visible. But don't let that stop you from exploring this small mountain, which is surrounded to the south and west by the waters of Lake Guntersville.

Cross the road, head into the woods, and begin the hike headed northeast up a hillside covered with pine trees. In summer, the air seems to cool immediately beneath the shade of the forest canopy. The path is moderately steep at first, rocky and rooty. An abundance of blue-green

KEY AT-A-GLANCE INFORMATION

LENGTH: 4.5 miles

CONFIGURATION: An out-and-back spur with a loop

DIFFICULTY: Moderate

SCENERY: Ellenberg Mountain, hardwood and pine forest, deeply lichen-stained boulders, small cave

EXPOSURE: Mostly shaded

TRAFFIC: Moderate on weekends, light on weekdays

TRAIL SURFACE: Sometimes rocky dirt trail that varies from narrow path to old two-track road

HIKING TIME: 2.5 hours

ACCESS: Trailhead never closed

MAPS: Lake Guntersville State Park Trail System

FACILITIES: Rest rooms and water at park office near trailhead

SPECIAL COMMENTS: Pick up an interpretive brochure at the park office

DIRECTIONS

Take the Tallapoosa Street exit off of I-59 North onto AL 79 North. At 11.7 miles, turn right onto AL 75 North—you'll actually be on AL 151 North briefly, but it runs directly into AL 75. At 51.3 miles, turn left onto US 431 North, then turn right onto AL 227 South at 60.7 miles. At 66.5 miles, reach the Lake Guntersville State Park office on your right. Pull in and park there. The trailhead is across the road.

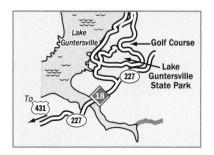

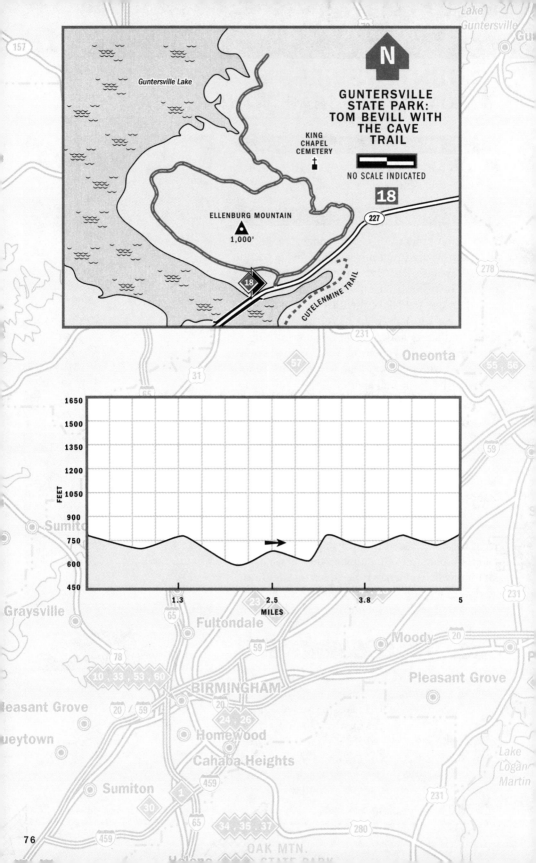

GUNTERSVILLE
STATE PARK:
TOM BEVILL WITH
THE CAVE
TRAIL

NO SCALE INDICATED

Guntersville Lake

KING
CHAPEL
CEMETERY

ELLENBURG MOUNTAIN
1,000'

CUTELENMINE TRAIL

lichen-stained stones and boulders catches your eye right away—not just a patch here and there, but consistent full coverage of nearly all exposed stone.

Mixed with the shortleaf and loblolly pines is a wide variety of hardwoods, including red oak, white oak, hickory, tulip poplar, mulberry, and persimmon. Along the way you'll also see oak-leaf hydrangeas, wild azaleas, and muscadine vines.

To begin the hike, follow a short spur to the loop that encircles Ellenburg Mountain, turning at an arrow pointing right. The trail levels briefly before reaching a T intersection, where you'll go left. You'll probably see hickory nuts on the ground, as you walk along a level path with a rocky slope up to your right. Chances are good that you will see a deer, but chances are better that you will see lots of chipmunks and gray squirrels.

The path follows what used to be a pioneer road. The established path was revamped and tooled into an interpretive nature trail in 1980 by youth volunteers working with the U.S. Youth Conservation Corps. The trail varies in width from a narrow walking path to a wider, two-wheel track. Occasionally you'll see a tree that has established itself in the middle of the wider track, indicating that there's been no vehicular traffic here for many years.

Continuing with a rocky slope up to your right, the path is fairly clear of debris, with only a couple of downed trees blocking the trail. Except for the faint buzz of boats in the distance, off to your left, the mountain is quiet and peaceful. The major disturbance you'll notice here, as in so many other wooded areas in Alabama, is the damage inflicted by the ubiquitous Southern pine beetle.

At 0.7 miles, you'll come upon one of the few remaining markers for items discussed in the interpretive brochure. The landmark is a hollowed century tree, now fallen, that harbored small mammals such as raccoons and squirrels. The hardwood presence seems to increase here, with many large white oaks and some chestnut oak. The path soon narrows again and begins to ascend steeply north, but then flattens after a 0.1-mile hump. One nice aspect of the walk is that spare underbrush allows for easy forest gazing and less trail watching (to avoid tripping).

At 0.9 miles, the lake comes into view on your left. Shortly afterwards, descend steeply between two large red oaks, known as the Twin Oaks. Look for more red oaks and black walnuts as well. The area that you're now passing through used to be a small community known as King's Chapel, settled in 1814. If you have a sharp eye, you may be able to flesh out old homesites by locating a single, large oak standing in an area that may have ornamental bulb flowers such as daffodils growing nearby.

You'll have a nice stretch of easy woodland meandering until you reach a trail crossroads at 1.75 miles, where the Cave Trail goes left. The Bevill Trail continues right, and the Terrell Trail begins straight ahead. Here, depart the Bevill Trail and turn left onto the red-blazed Cave Trail and descend Ellenberg Mountain on a narrow footpath that heads northwest. Look for orange-flowering trumpeter vine and poison ivy through here.

Descend into a verdant glen filled with vibrant forest grasses. Pass the rusty iron remains of an old still on your left and then, at 2 miles, cross a small footbridge. With a slough of Lake Guntersville visible to your left, push through a tangle of vines and walk toward a narrow paved road. Look for wildflowers here, including Queen Anne's lace, cross a small paved road, and then head northeast back into the woods. Soon, cross a footbridge over a still stream, with a water-loving beech tree standing nearby.

Wind uphill toward small, green boulders, and work up into a clearing to cross a small, flat ridge. This scruffy area has been cleared in the recent past, with small hardwoods such as sweetgum and Chinese sumac (considered an invasive species), taking over the light gaps left by felled pines. Briefly parallel a road to your left, then go down, left, and cross over to a tight, boulder-strewn hillside on your right. Pass an intersection with the yellow-blazed Terrell Trail, and then see the tunnel-like cave off the trail to your right. You'll need a flashlight to explore the cave, which is about four feet high. Without a flashlight, you can only see in about 15 feet.

To finish off the Cave Trail, continue past the cave, cross a small footbridge and head up the rocky face of a slope. At 2.6 miles, bear right at a Y and intersect the blue-blazed Loop Trail, which is the turnaround.

Back at the trail crossroads, continue straight onto the Bevill Trail, heading uphill on the Spring Trail, which connects the two ends of the Bevill Trail. Heading east, you'll encounter a small spring at 3.6 miles; it flows from an eroded area beneath a large beech tree. Since the flow continues year-round, even during dry weather, the spring was used by natives and settlers who lived in the area.

The trail then begins to meander up and down, approaching a summit ridge of Ellenberg Mountain at 3.9 miles. Descend a boulder-studded hillside, and at 4.25 miles, descending southeast, begin to hear sounds of traffic buzzing along AL 227. A quarter mile later, bear left, and then at a Y go left to reach and cross AL 227 back to your vehicle.

NEARBY ACTIVITIES

There's a fabulous swim beach and play area for kids inside the park. There are also numerous short trails, if you want to add some mileage. Visit www.dcnr.state. al.us/parks/lake_guntersville_1a.html for more information, or call the park at (256) 571-5444.

GUNTERSVILLE STATE PARK:
CUTCHENMINE TRAIL

IN BRIEF

Take this pleasant walk in winter, after the leaves have fallen, to get the best look at the lake and perhaps glimpse a bald eagle.

DESCRIPTION

This flat walk along the banks of Lake Guntersville runs just beyond the state park boundary on land that belongs to the Tennessee Valley Authority (TVA). The 76-mile-long lake, with about 900 miles of shoreline, is actually a TVA reservoir created by the damming of the Tennessee River. The dam, one of a series along the Tennessee that creates a 650-mile-long river highway, was completed in 1939.

This level, orange-blazed trail is easy to follow and would be great for trail running. The trail traces an old road that once led to a coal-mining venture along Short Creek. As you walk south and then east, you'll first follow a swampy finger of a lake slough, then pick up the slough and follow it as it necks down into Short Creek at the other end.

In the summer, stepping into the woods abutting Lake Guntersville provides instant relief from the heat, but not from the humidity. If it's a hot day, you'll sweat like there's no tomorrow on this trail. The pine-needled path is generally wide,

DIRECTIONS

Take the Tallapoosa Street exit off of 1-59 North onto AL 79 North. At 11.7 miles, turn right onto AL 75 North. You'll actually be on AL 151 North briefly, but it runs directly into AL 75. At 51.3 miles, turn left onto US 431 North. Then at 60.7 miles, turn right onto AL 227 South. At 66.5 miles, reach the Lake Guntersville State Park office on your right. Slow down, continue straight for 0.4 miles, and look for a small pull-in on the right that precedes the posted Cutchenmine trailhead. Pull in and park.

KEY AT-A-GLANCE INFORMATION

LENGTH: 4 miles

CONFIGURATION: Out-and-back

DIFFICULTY: Easy

SCENERY: Lake Guntersville, mixed hardwood and pine forest

EXPOSURE: Nearly completely shaded

TRAFFIC: Light

TRAIL SURFACE: Wide dirt track, rocky in places

HIKING TIME: 1.5 hours

ACCESS: Trailhead never closed

MAPS: Lake Guntersville State Park Trail System

FACILITIES: Rest rooms and water at park office near trailhead

SPECIAL COMMENTS: Hike this one during the week to minimize boat noise. There's only room for a couple of cars in the pull-in parking area near the trailhead.

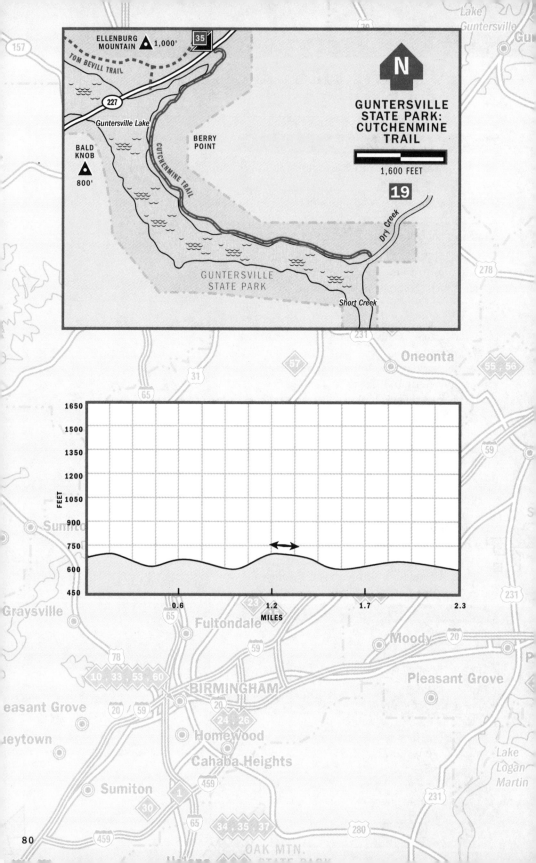

ELLENBURG
MOUNTAIN ▲ 1,000'

[35]

TOM BEVILL TRAIL

227

Guntersville Lake

BERRY
POINT

BALD
KNOB
▲
800'

CUTCHENMINE TRAIL

N

GUNTERSVILLE
STATE PARK:
CUTCHENMINE
TRAIL

1,600 FEET

[19]

Dry Creek

GUNTERSVILLE
STATE PARK

Short Creek

FEET

1650
1500
1350
1200
1050
900
750
600
450

0.6   1.2   1.7   2.3
MILES

but occasionally narrows to a footpath. You'll see loblolly pines here, but hardwoods predominate, especially tulip poplar and sweetgum. Alabama's state wildflower, oak-leaf hydrangea, also makes frequent appearances. In fact, the hydrangea here are some of the tallest I've ever seen, averaging six to eight feet in height.

Reach a newly-constructed footbridge that crosses a very slow-moving drainage, then begin to ascend, heading south. The path is straight and slowly curves southwest to follow the lake and creek. You'll notice right away the legacy of the Southern pine beetle—numerous pines decaying on the forest floor. At 0.1 mile, though, one hardy pine on trail-right continues to grow even though a large rock is embedded in its trunk.

As a swampy slough develops on your right, gradually widening and deepening, you may run through a succession of neatly woven spiderwebs, each with a small, black, spiny-bellied orb weaver tending the middle. The months of July through September are the worst. During those months, it's best to hike this with a small group and pull up the rear. While the lead hiker is cursing, you can keep an eye out for waterfowl.

With frequent birdsong echoing through the trees, the path rises 30 to 40 feet above the lake at a distance of 30 feet from its banks. Look for examples of the smooth and silvery bark of the beech, the bleached gray and peeling bark of the white oak, the deep brown bark of the red oak, the coffee-colored, evenly textured bark of the mulberry, and an occasional wispy cedar. At half a mile, the lake opens up to the northwest, and you should be able to see the small rounded peak of Bald Knob across the slough.

During warmer weather, a sustained breeze from the lake is strong enough to penetrate the narrow band of trees that separate you from the water. Along with the breeze comes the familiar warm and slightly fishy smell of lake water. It's not unpleasant, though, and if you've spent a lot of time around freshwater lakes, it's a familiar and memory-provoking scent.

On your left at 0.7 miles, pass layered stacks of sandstone and some boulders that could provide a rock climber with an afternoon's worth of stony puzzles. At 0.9 miles, cross a wet-weather drainage into the lake and pass through a thicket of young hickories that have taken advantage of large light gaps here. Continue tracing the lake to your right, along a path that cuts across a steepening slope. If the trees are in leaf, you'll only have occasional clear views of the lake to your right.

At 1 mile, bear east and away from the lake briefly, passing a Southern catalpa tree along the way. After 0.4 miles more, the trail draws close to the lake again. Look for a clearing on your right, which is a small bank-fishing area complete with log section "chairs" to sit on.

In summertime, you won't have a good view of the waterfowl, which often includes blue heron, white egrets, and other species. However, if you're wearing shorts, keep a close eye on your legs and you should have no trouble spotting any ticks that try to hitch a ride. They like to hang out in the tops of damp, sweaty socks, or just inside your boots, waiting for an opportunity to latch on, which usually takes several hours.

Cross another wet-weather drainage at 1.6 miles and relish the increasing quiet as you head toward the narrowing of the slough into Short Creek. The water grows clogged with vegetation, discouraging powerboats from venturing back this way.

Passing magnolia and black-eyed Susans at 1.8 miles, the trail heads down slightly to the east, and the slough begins to narrow even more. At 2 miles, reach Dry Creek, a wide, rocky-bottomed creek that only flows when it rains. Here you'll see "The End" painted in orange on a downed tree. An older white-blazed trail used to continue further on to the other side of the creek. To your right the lake water backs up into the creek bed about 40 feet. Before you head back, rest on a rock and soak in the stillness and birdsong.

NEARBY ACTIVITIES

There's a fabulous swim beach and play area for kids inside the park. There are also numerous short trails, if you want to add some mileage. Visit www.dcnr.state.al.us/parks/lake_guntersville_1a.html for more information, or call the park at (256) 571-5444.

GUNTERSVILLE STATE PARK:
LICKSKILLET TRAIL

IN BRIEF

Throughout the hike, you'll probably hear an occasional deer crashing through the woods around you. If you're lucky, you'll see one or, like I did, several.

DESCRIPTION

If you're licking the skillet after dinner it either means the food was mighty good or that the portions were mighty small. In the case of the orange-blazed Lickskillet Trail, the walk is scenic and the length is just right for an afternoon hike.

You can hike the trail from either end, but I describe the trail as an out-and-back beginning inside the park near the campground. You can also create a variety of trail options using the Meredith Trail, the Seales Trail, and the Old Lickskillet Trail, but I've stuck with the classic out-and-back method, keeping with Lickskillet the entire way.

DIRECTIONS

Take the Tallapoosa Street exit off of 1-59 North onto AL 79 North. At 11.7 miles, turn right onto AL 75 North—you'll be on AL 151 North briefly, but it runs directly into AL 75. At 51.3 miles turn left onto US 431 North, then turn right onto AL 227 South at 60.7 miles. At 66.5 miles, reach the Lake Guntersville State Park office on your right. Drive 1.7 miles and turn left into the park, just before a small country store and gas station on your right. Turn left at a sign that reads "Campground, Country Store and Beach Areas." In 0.8 miles, turn left again toward the beaches. Pass the Lakeshore Recreation Area on your left, the campground store, and then reach a sign for the Lickskillet Trail on your right. Pull off onto the grassy shoulder. Alternately, park back at the campground store and walk to the trailhead.

KEY AT-A-GLANCE INFORMATION

LENGTH: 4.4 miles

CONFIGURATION: Out-and-back

DIFFICULTY: Moderate

SCENERY: Taylor Mountain, white-tailed deer, mixed hardwood/pine forest

EXPOSURE: Mostly shaded, except for a couple of areas cleared due to pine-beetle damage.

TRAFFIC: Light on weekdays, moderate on weekends

TRAIL SURFACE: Dirt forest path interrupted with rocky section

HIKING TIME: 2 hours

ACCESS: Trailhead never closed

MAPS: Lake Guntersville State Park Trail System

FACILITIES: Rest rooms, water, food, drinks available at campground store

SPECIAL COMMENTS: If you want, you can start from the other end of this trail on AL 227.

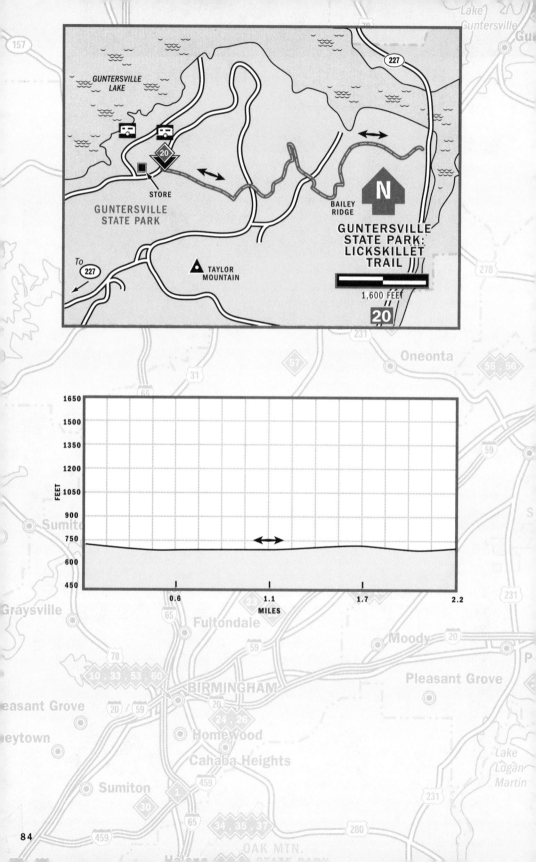

GUNTERSVILLE LAKE

157

227

GUNTERSVILLE STATE PARK

STORE

20

To 227

TAYLOR MOUNTAIN

BAILEY RIDGE

N

GUNTERSVILLE STATE PARK: LICKSKILLET TRAIL

1,600 FEET

20

FEET

1650
1500
1350
1200
1050
900
750
600
450

0.6   1.1   1.7   2.2
MILES

The trail, which follows an old pioneer road that in turn followed an older Native American path, traverses the northern slope and ridges of Taylor Mountain. You'll begin the hike by climbing from 600 to 800 feet, descending back to 600 feet, and then climbing steadily over the course of a mile or so to around 1,100 feet. The turnaround is within sight of Hurricane Branch, which, if followed northeast, narrows down into Town Creek.

Across the road from a busy campground, head into the cooler woods to encounter shortleaf pine, sweetgum, beech, hickory, maple, red oak, and tulip poplar. The path is generally wide but slims to a footpath in a few places. The forest is serene and fairly quiet, interrupted occasionally by the crashing of unseen deer. The relatively thin understory and widely spaced trees allow for extended forest gazing.

Heading east, you'll see pines downed by the Southern pine beetle, with telltale trunks snapped off six feet up.

The path is relatively flat, with a slope up to your right littered with large sandstone boulders. At a trail crossroads, the park lodge is accessed to your right; to your left is the Old Lickskillet Trail, while the Lickskillet Trail continues straight ahead. While cicadas and woodpeckers join together for an afternoon jam, begin climbing at an angle to a hillside on your right scattered with ferns, lichen-stained rocks, and tall hardwoods. Cross a dry streambed at 0.2 miles, and steadily ascending, pass by some large specimens of oak-leaf hydrangea. In another 0.1 mile, the Shannon Trail goes left, but continue forward, working your way up to a ridge on your right. The trail switches back sharply right, becomes rocky, and beelines for the ridge.

Cross a small footbridge, pass a few cedars, and emerge into a scruffy clearing. Cross a paved road (that leads, right, to the park golf course and lodge) and fall back into the woods. Head northeast and downhill at 0.7 miles on a needle and cone covered path when the trail widens from a footpath to a two-wheel track, with the slope down to your right.

Cross a gravel road at 1.2 miles, and after a section of level trail, take a steep downhill walk into a small valley that has another dry streambed running through it. Follow the ravine uphill, and if it's summer, wave away the sweat-seeking gnats as you step over green hickory nuts lying on the ground. At the top of the snaking ravine, intersect the Meredith Trail but continue on the Lickskillet.

The trail next heads north and downhill, then bears east approaching the 2-mile mark. You'll begin to see the slough that works into Town Creek and Hurricane Branch off to the left, along with AL 227. Pass a large beech on your left, descend toward a dirt bluff, and then bear left at another big beech, walking down toward AL 227. Reach a pull-in parking area, with the Town Creek Bridge just around the bend to your left and Hurricane Branch beyond the road.

At this point on my hike, I had heard but not seen deer bounding through the forest around me. I turned back repeatedly in hopes of spying at least one of these amazing runners, but as I got near my car the thought of deer completely left me, replaced by thoughts of cold sweet tea and hot pizza. Suddenly, three does ran across the trail in front of me, plunged down a ravine, hurdled up the opposing slope about 75 feet away from me, then just stopped. All three stood stockstill, gazing back at me as if I were supposed to give them permission to continue. While I contemplated the scenario, five more yearlings tumbled down the hillside and sped across the trail, each spaced about 30 feet apart. They too stopped, but only briefly, to turn and stare.

Although the sighting only lasted a couple of minutes, it seemed more like half an hour. I mopped my brow one last time, turned to continue, and along came another one. This straggler was obviously playing catch-up, because it did not slow down once across the ravine. With amazing speed and agility, the lone deer disappeared as quickly as it had arrived.

NEARBY ACTIVITIES

There's a fabulous swim beach and play area for kids inside the park. Visit www.dcnr.state.al.us/parks/lake_guntersville_1a.html for more information, or call the park at (256) 571-5444.

HORSE PENS 40 LOOP

This trail is short but tough. Be prepared to squeeze through cracks, negotiate slick rocks, and pick your way through a fantastic maze of house-sized boulders. If you like to boulder, don't forget your crash pad.

DESCRIPTION

With some of the oldest above-ground rocks in Alabama, Horse Pens 40 is a unique geological treasure. The park is situated on the southwestern end of flat-topped Chandler Mountain. From a satellite view, 1,500-foot Chandler Mountain looks like a raised shoe print. Roughly 2 miles wide and 9 miles long, it's strikingly out of place and completely different from the surrounding topography. Owner Mike Schultz describes it as a big fist punched straight up into the sky.

According to Schultz, who purchased the 120-acre park in 2002 to prevent it from being turned into a gated community, the name "Horse Pens 40" refers to an original deed, which dates back to 1900, given to John Hyatt. Written on sheepskin and signed by Pres. Benjamin Harrison, the deed divides the 120 acres into the "home 40, farming 40, and the horsepens 40." The latter boasts an unusual mix of huge, weathered boulders, which formed natural corrals for horses and

DIRECTIONS

From the intersection of I-459 and I-59, travel north on I-59 for 30 miles. Take the Asheville/US 231 exit and turn left onto US 231. Drive 3.3 miles and turn right at the large Horse Pens 40 sign onto CR 35. Continue 1.7 miles and turn right on CR 42. Wind uphill for 1.2 miles and the Horse Pens 40 entrance will be on your right. Turn in and drive to a small parking area across from the country store. The trailhead is on the other side of the store.

KEY AT-A-GLANCE INFORMATION

LENGTH: 1 mile

CONFIGURATION: Loop, with lots of short side ventures

DIFFICULTY: Moderate

SCENERY: Mammoth wind- and rain-carved boulders, valley overlook, mixed-hardwood forest, streams

EXPOSURE: Mostly shaded

TRAFFIC: Light to moderate on non-festival days, heavy otherwise

TRAIL SURFACE: Rocks, slick boulders, and dirt

HIKING TIME: 1 hour, including time to stop and gaze

ACCESS: Open year-round, but closed Christmas Eve and Christmas Day; entry fee is $3 for ages 10 and older; campsites are $8 per night.

MAPS: None

FACILITIES: Country store, restaurant, rest rooms, campground (water, electricity, hot showers), phone

SPECIAL COMMENTS: Trail is slick after a rain, so bring a walking stick and wear lightweight hiking boots or cross-trainers with a good tread. Visit www.hp40.com for more information.

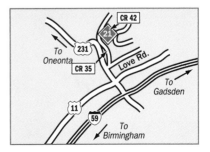

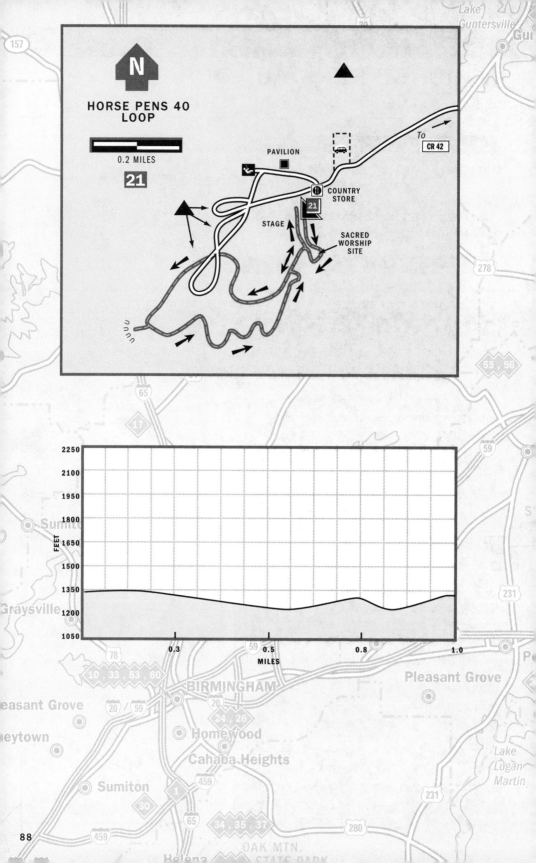

HORSE PENS 40 LOOP

0.2 MILES

21

PAVILION

To CR 42

COUNTRY STORE

21

STAGE

SACRED WORSHIP SITE

cattle. During the Civil War (or War of Northern Aggression as it's more popularly known on Chandler Mountain), citizens hid cattle and horses here from marauding Yankee soldiers. The remoteness of the area and inaccessibility of the mountaintop also attracted outlaws and moonshiners to the area.

Some years later, the Hyatt family went to the bank for a loan, and their deed to the land wasn't honored. The bank could not establish title to the land, and the Hyatts were forced to file for title under the Homestead Act. The Homestead Act was no longer in effect for the area, but fortunately the Hyatts received another presidential favor, this time from Woodrow Wilson, who signed a land patent for them in 1917.

Before you start the hike, head into the country store and restaurant to register and pay your day-use fee. Whether you're here to hike and/or boulder, the fee is a flat $3 per day. Horse Pens 40 is a family operation, so nearly everyone you see working here is a member of the Schultz family.

Negotiating a rocky grotto

Step out of the store and onto a large wooden deck. Look over to your left toward a natural outdoor amphitheater backed by a stolid fortress of 30-foot high boulders. The entrance through the rocks and into the "horse pens" is clearly marked. Animals you might see here include badgers, raccoons, gray fox, white-tailed deer, and maybe even a bear (a small black bear was spotted here in June 2003). Do not harm or harass the animals, including any snakes, which include the nonpoisonous king snake, rat snake, and corn snake.

Facing a large wall of house-sized boulders that appear to be stacked in layers, and with the aptly named Mushroom Rock on your left, walk beneath an overhang. Pass through a narrow cleft in the rock, following the red arrows. The cleft where horses entered the rocky grotto is further right before you enter. The rocks can be slick here, so be careful.

Pass into the amazing interior of this rock fortress, where a few trees now grow. According to Schultz, this enclosure is a sacred Native American site. Used to celebrate the rebirth of spring following the symbolic death of winter, this sacred enclosure resembles a stone temple. Beneath a ledge here, there is a large rock shaped like a thunderbird, a symbol central to the rebirth ceremony. Today, Native Americans still visit the sacred area for worship, prayer, and singing.

Follow the red arrows through another narrow passage, where you may have to turn sideways, and pass into an area known as the Big Horse Pens. As you bear left, inspect the rock walls that surround you. They are filled with jugs (hand holds) and are rife with enough excellent knobs to make rock climbers drool. Continue forward, and, on your right, pass a rock called the Headless Hen. Now on a wide dirt and sand path, pass another excellent bouldering site, Little Elephant Rock. Towering oaks and hickories punctuate the rocky stillness.

Following yellow arrows, walk downhill, looking along the boulder sides for granddaddy longlegs scampering to and fro across patches of reindeer moss and rock paper. Meander through ten-foot-high weathered boulders and walk up onto a boulder platform, with the rocks continuing on your right and a mixed hardwood forest picking up on your left.

Follow the yellow arrows into another stone enclosure, then bear left and emerge into a lush, green forest, alive with singing birds in spring. Zig and zag easily down flat stones in the path to head towards a boulder set called the Big Slipper. Continue straight ahead into an area thick with oak-leaf hydrangea. Reach and cross a small arched footbridge that, if it's wet, will be very slick. If you're afraid you might fall, you can do like my trooper, 94-year-old grandfather, and carefully crawl across on your hands and knees.

After negotiating the footbridge, you'll come face-to-face with a 20-by-20-foot boulder. Go right onto a sandy path; look down, and in other sandy areas, for animal footprints. You will probably be able to find some fox tracks, but don't expect to see deer tracks here. According to Schultz, there are mountain lions living in the area. Deer instinctively avoid passing beneath rocks from which a mountain lion can pounce.

Pass hawthorns, poplars, and other hardwoods as you bear left onto a wide path, with a double-trunked chestnut oak on the left. Emerge into a camping area, with an outbuilding up to the right. You can turn right here and walk back to the store along the dirt road. Otherwise, bear around left into an open area and walk toward a sign for Lookout Point. Back into relative shade on a rooty, rocky path, hardy Virginia pines, wild blackberries, and purple spiderwort appear as you approach the bluff edge.

Pass through a boulder field to emerge into a clearing with southwest views out over the valley and US 231 in the distance. If you want to get right out to the edge, cross a shingle-covered footbridge that leads out onto a large boulder. After admiring the view, turn back and bear to the right, following a stepped path down (ignore a white arrow here) and around to the left, heading east. Follow the trail marked with a red arrow so that the arrow points backward, keeping boulders on your left and the forest on your right

Meander down, with a small creek in the ravine to your right. Walking against the red arrows, you'll be overwhelmed with the white blooms and sweet perfume of the oak-leaf hydrangea in the spring. The green leaves turn red in fall and the blooms develop a rosy color. In spring though, you can't mistake the large, hand-like, five-lobed leaves and spikes of four-petal white flowers. With boulders on all sides, bear right onto a sandy path. Prior to crossing a small stream, you'll see a huge tree with a giant gall scarring it about 20 feet up its trunk.

Although galls, which look kind of like a goiter, will form as a result of fungal infections, this particular gall and others in the area are manmade. Schultz notes that Native Indians refer to these galled trees as marker trees that delineate boundaries and mark sacred sites. The galls are created by tightly wrapping honeysuckle vines around the tree. Two small sticks between the tree and the vines prevents complete encirclement, which would kill the tree.

Walking uphill against the creek's flow on your left, the path is a bit vague. Following white arrows now, going east/northeast, pass over seeps where the small stream disappears into the ground. I saw an adult gray fox here, trotting ahead about 20 feet. It also disappeared quickly but did not seem alarmed. Continue between two large boulders as the creek flows down the middle of the widened path. This section will be wet. If you can, walk in the stream to prevent disturbing any animal tracks that may have been left in the sandy areas to the side. As I walked toward the white arrow up ahead to the left of a large boulder on the right side of creek, a gray fox kit with large ears and a bushy tail walked easily across the creek on a log. After crossing, and seeing me, it sat in a narrow, den-like area, watching with its catlike face. Cautious but not alarmed, the kit lingered for nearly a minute then trotted away over a rise of boulders.

Cross the creek and head uphill, walking with the white arrows. Heading north, wend through the maze-like rocks that provide endless opportunities for exploration. When you reach a tall sweetgum tree growing up between two boulders, scramble up using its root. Emerge into a grassy field sprinkled with wild azaleas and spiderwort and look across it for the next white arrow.

Bear left onto a dirt path that T-bones into the Yellow Trail. Turn right and work your way back out to the signed "horse pens" entrance. When you emerge, take the wooden stairs up on top of the boulder wall for a scenic view of the area.

NEARBY ACTIVITIES

If there's a festival, you'll want to listen to music or, if you brought your guitar, you might want to join a group in one of the many picking sessions that seem to spontaneously happen around the campsites. The best way to enjoy the curious geology of this area is to tackle some of the park's boulders. If you don't know what you're doing, see if you can find a group who does and just watch. Anyone, though, who wants to give it a shot, can test some of the easier boulders. If you're serious about bouldering, you'll want to bring along a crash pad (available at outdoor stores in the area or rent one here). A simple pair of sticky-soled climbing shoes will give you a distinct edge, but a tough pair of sneakers works just as well for the novice. After you've worked up an appetite, you can drop in the Horse Pens 40 restaurant. The food's good and reasonably priced.

HURRICANE CREEK PARK LOOP

**KEY AT-A-GLANCE
INFORMATION**

LENGTH: 1.2 miles

CONFIGURATION: Loop

DIFFICULTY: Easy, with moderate moments

SCENERY: Scenic Hurricane Creek

EXPOSURE: Mostly shaded

TRAFFIC: Moderate to heavy on weekends, light on weekdays

TRAIL SURFACE: Rocky path, suspension bridge across creek

HIKING TIME: About 45 minutes

ACCESS: Open everyday (usually 8 a.m. –10 p.m., but hours may vary); $3 day-use fee

MAPS: Trail map on board at park

FACILITIES: Rest rooms, vending machines, deck area, picnic area by creek

SPECIAL COMMENTS: There is a short incline ride at the park, but it is currently out of service.

IN BRIEF

You'll break a furious sweat enjoying the rugged scenery of this steep creek valley, lined with dripping overhangs, small waterfalls, vertical rock, and giant boulders.

DESCRIPTION

According to John McCrary, parks manager for the City of Cullman, WWII fighter pilot Buddy Rogers started Hurricane Creek park 41 years ago as a private venture. Rogers had flown above the area and was intrigued by the steep, rugged valley. After his flying days were over, he purchased the land and made most of the park's improvements himself. A mere 67 acres, Hurricane Creek Park is small in area but rich in biodiversity and impressive rock formations. McCrary, who is an avid hiker, mountain biker, and certified mountain guide, is excited about future plans to construct mountain bike and horse trails at the park.

The trail described here roughly walks the perimeter of the park's land. The trail begins by paralleling the north ridge of Hurricane Creek Valley, heading northeast 50 feet below the ridgetop. The trail then switchbacks down to the creek, climbs to the south ridge of the valley, goes through a very interesting cavelike passage, and moves southwest on its second steep descent to the creek below. The hike ends with a short, steep ascent back to the trailhead

DIRECTIONS

From Birmingham, take I-65 North 48.5 miles to Cullman, Exit 310, (there's a rest area 40 miles en route). Turn right onto AL 157 and drive 1.5 miles. Turn left on US 31 North and drive 6 miles. The park will be on your right. Drive through an open fence gate into an unmarked gravel parking area. The park office is directly ahead.

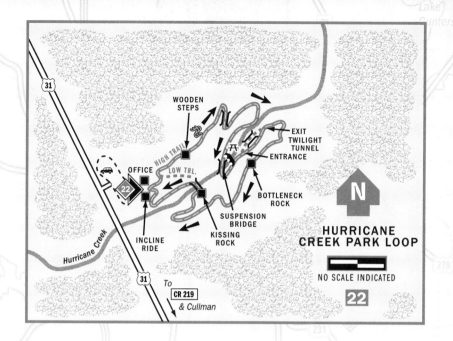

WOODEN STEPS

HIGH TRAIL

LOW TRL.

OFFICE

EXIT
TWILIGHT
TUNNEL

ENTRANCE

BOTTLENECK
ROCK

SUSPENSION
BRIDGE

KISSING
ROCK

INCLINE
RIDE

Hurricane Creek

31

157

31

22

To
CR 219
& Cullman

N

**HURRICANE
CREEK PARK LOOP**

NO SCALE INDICATED

22

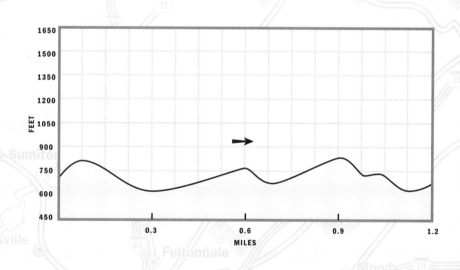

The cool, clear water of Hurricane Creek

After reviewing the map board, head east/northeast to begin the trail. You'll cross a wooden footbridge over a wet-weather falls into a cool mixed forest laced with mountain laurel, sweetbay magnolia, and oak-leaf hydrangea. With a steep slope dropping on your right, reach a Y in the path. Bear left to follow the yellow arrow for the High Trail, bypassing the Low Trail. Suspended overhangs of layered sandstone rise to your left.

Hike up a few wooden steps and bear right with the yellow blazes, passing more magnificent rock shelves on your left. Here you'll begin the first steep downhill section on a narrow, rocky sand path. The steep slope supports tall, straight tulip poplars, rugged chestnut oaks, and the eye-catching big-leaf magnolia. The bright green leaves are over a foot long and resemble blades from a ceiling fan.

Pass a 20-foot-high rock outcropping on trail-left; a tiny trickle of water spilling over its top echoes loudly in the damp rock hollow beneath. As the trail levels, take a sharp right at 0.2 miles, stairstepping down on large, flat stones. A cable handrail begins shortly thereafter, primarily to keep visitors from venturing too far out and taking an unhealthy plunge. Continue steeply downward to reach another wooden footbridge, then cross over the 30-foot span.

Taking a sharp left after the bridge, trace a rock face and overhang 30 feet high. Soon the burbling of Hurricane Creek grows audible up the boulder-strewn hillside. As the shallow creek comes into view directly in front of you, bear right to parallel and walk against its steady but patient flow. Peer into the water to see small bream and other fish darting to and fro. Meandering along the scenic bank, look for the labeled sweetbay magnolia at 0.4 miles.

Bear away slightly from the creek and enter a picnic area that sits near a low stone dam, which pools the creek's water to two or three feet. Small but cozy, the picnic area consists of a covered pavilion and two picnic tables. The Low Trail, which you bypassed earlier, enters here from the right.

To begin the climb out of the valley, bear left and cross an old rope suspension bridge that swings and bounces. Walk up a few steps and, at the sign for Twilight Tunnel, turn left to reach the cavelike tunnel that slices through a 50-foot rock bluff. You have the option of detouring around, but if you can stand the darkness and don't mind feeling your way through, why not take the more direct route?

The natural tunnel is actually a contained crack formed when a monolithic chunk of the 50-foot-high bluff broke away. The path through is about 3 feet wide and 100 feet long. It's dark inside, but the stray light that filters down from chinks and cracks above gives just enough visibility to enable you to navigate through. You'll want to move slowly and deliberately through the tunnel to avoid slipping or hitting your head on unseen protuberances.

Scramble up a bit at the end to exit back out into the bright sunlight. Go right, tracing an undercut rock ledge on your right to a trail junction. You can turn left to return to the picnic area. Instead, to get the most out of this hike, bear right at a sign that reads "To Hidden Valley, A Long Mile" and walk uphill through a lush forest area, ripe with green ferns and forest grasses.

Bottleneck Rock (the fun never ends) is next. Another crack, but open to the sky above, it's an easy squeeze for most hikers. But the narrow passage is easily bypassed, if you prefer. Either way, you'll find yourself on top of the ridge with the creek valley down below. Mirroring the walk on the opposite ridge, trace a rock face and dripping overhangs on your left. Where you spot a bench at 0.7 miles, with lots of big-leaf magnolia shading the forest floor, the trail begins its second steep descent toward Hurricane Creek.

Switchback down, stopping for a moment at Kissing Rock. If you're with your sweetie, plant a big one on her or him. However, if you're alone, tradition dictates you kiss the rock.

After passing a labeled patch of poison ivy to the left of the trail, reach three benches, then cross the creek over two wooden footbridges that are connected by a flat rock. With a weathered rock face looming over your right shoulder, immediately tackle the final uphill push. Hugging the rock face, reach a junction with the currently disabled, cable-hoisted incline ride and go right, trudging up the slope to a pair of switchbacks, which will bring you to the path that leads back to the main office.

You'll likely have worked up a glistening sweat in the humid, still, creek valley, especially if it's a muggy summer day.

NEARBY ACTIVITIES

While you're in Cullman, visit the world-famous Ave Maria Grotto (p. 13), a collection of miniature landscapes of cities and places considered holy by Christians. If you have time, follow that up with a visit to the opulent Shrine of the Most Blessed Sacrament. Visit www.olamshrine.com or call (256) 352-6267 for more information.

JEFFERSON STATE COMBO

KEY AT-A-GLANCE INFORMATION

LENGTH: 2.5 miles

CONFIGURATION: Out-and-back plus balloon

DIFFICULTY: Easy/moderate

SCENERY: Old hardwood forest, college campus

EXPOSURE: Half shaded

TRAFFIC: Mixed heavy on track (especially in early evening), lighter on trail

TRAIL SURFACE: Pavement, dirt trail

HIKING TIME: 1 hour

ACCESS: Open year-round

MAPS: None

FACILITIES: Water at track; rest rooms and pay phones in campus buildings (when open); rest rooms, pavilion, picnic tables at park by AL 79

SPECIAL COMMENTS: The out-and-back at the end of this hike is home to the best echo in Birmingham

IN BRIEF

The walking track at Jefferson State College is a very popular early evening destination for the surrounding community. Starting off on the paved track, this hike heads off into the trees for a woodsy, sometimes steep, jaunt. After the balloon, head uphill to the Education Building for a surprisingly clear echo.

DESCRIPTION

Jeff State, as it is commonly called, is a small but very fine community college. I took my first college classes there way back in 1981 and graduated a couple of years later.

Head toward the track, then begin walking in a counterclockwise direction. Approach the first of many "fitness stations" along the route on your left. I've seen only a few people use these;

DIRECTIONS

From I-59 heading north, take the Tallapoosa Street exit, bear around left, then back to the right, heading north on AL 79. Mark your mileage from the first traffic signal, located across from a Shell station to the right. Stay on AL 79 through Tarrant City to turn at the second Jefferson State entrance (at the Hilldale Baptist Church sign), about 10 miles, on the right. Pass a park on your right and head uphill to the walking track, which is on the right (past the tennis courts and ball fields). Park in the lot on your right.

Alternate directions: From 1st Avenue North, turn onto 39th Street North, cross Messer Airport Highway, and bear right then left onto 40th Street North. Cross Richard Arrington Jr. Boulevard. Pass Stockham Valve on your right (now closed), then pass W. C. Patton Park on the right. Pass under I-59 and the road becomes the three-lane AL 79. Continue as noted above.

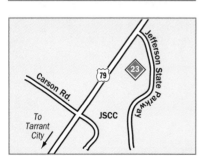

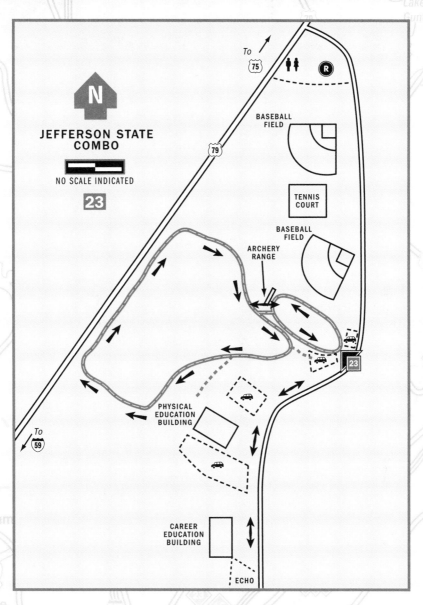

JEFFERSON STATE COMBO

NO SCALE INDICATED

23

To 75

BASEBALL FIELD

TENNIS COURT

BASEBALL FIELD

ARCHERY RANGE

23

PHYSICAL EDUCATION BUILDING

To 59

CAREER EDUCATION BUILDING

ECHO

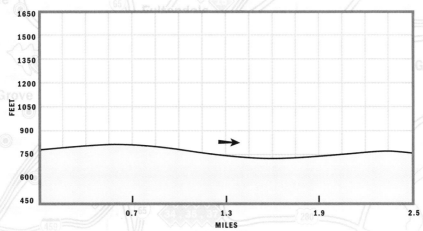

most people come here in the early evening to walk or run around the track, especially in warmer weather. While several nighttime lights help illuminate the track at night, it's wise to always walk with a friend after dark.

As you walk, pass a stand of tall pines and then a ball field to the right. (The college's successful baseball team was the 2002 state champion in its division.) Approach the track's first turn to the left, and follow it around past an archery range to the right. As with the fitness stations, I've rarely seen anyone actually shooting arrows here.

As you round the curve, look for a water fountain where you'll turn back to the right. Walk up the dirt path into the trees and bear to the left. With a field to your right and pines to your left, continue along the packed-dirt trail sprinkled with gravel and roots. If you bring a stroller on this hike, it should have the larger bicycle-type tires (at least 12 inches in diameter) to handle the ruts and downed trees you may encounter.

At a fitness station on the right, turn right (don't go straight) and walk across the edge of a putting green to the right. Ignore a road that ascends uphill to the left; take the pebbled path in front of you. Soon, the trail becomes steep and lined with brambles as you approach and pass another fitness station on the right. The path begins to drop around to the right, with a brushy area to the left, and enters the first woodland part of the trail. Where the trail diverges, noted by a directional arrow pointing to the left, go straight and then bear left at the next intersection, passing two large oak trees on the right.

You'll glimpse the traffic on AL 79 through the trees as you descend the widening trail and then curve around to the left. Approach fitness station no. 7 on the right as the trail takes on a thin blanket of pine needles. Passing through an area of large pines and walking directly toward AL 79, reach a T-intersection and turn right toward fitness station no. 8. With traffic whizzing by about 20 feet to the left on the other side of the trees, pass the fitness station and continue straight.

As you walk through some tall hardwoods, possibly the area of an old home site, look for a mammoth oak on the right that has lost all but 20 feet of its trunk. Wild, scary tree-sized limbs shoot out of the trunk's top.

Small clearings appear on either side of the trail, which descends slightly into a bottomland that can get mucky after heavy rains. As the "golf course" area begins to appear through the trees to the right, the trail curves right. Continue straight and begin climbing as you glimpse a house off to the left.

Pass through and over several downed trees that cross the trail, the result of a strong thunderstorm that swept through the area. Pass fitness station no. 10 and continue up the steep, rocky trail, which levels out and bears to the right.

Approach a trail junction. To the left a path heads behind the archery range, then leads into someone's backyard. I do not recommend strolling that way, even if arrows are not flying. To the right, the path leads back to the start of the woodland loop.

Turn left and walk back down to the walking track, heading around toward the parking lot. Walk through the parking lot and turn right onto Jefferson State Parkway, staying inside the marked walking path (painted white line). This is the out-and-back trip that leads to the echo.

Walk up the steep road, passing the Leroy Brown Health and Physical Education Building on the right. Begin descending and soon pass a stand of ivy-covered pines on the right as you approach the Harold C. Martin Career Education Building. Head right into the parking lot and bear around left to head straight uphill. Look for a steep slope straight ahead with an old set of now-defunct wooden steps, which once led to the parking lot above. Walk to the base of the steps, turn, and face the Brown building.

Wait until there are no cars passing by and loudly say, "Hello!" You'll get a perfect echo. But don't get carried away here, especially if there are classes inside. Head back downhill to the left and return to the parking area.

NEARBY ACTIVITIES

The drive through Tarrant City and up AL 79 is worth the trip alone. Tarrant City is probably the hardest-working holdout of the old iron-and-steel-attitude that built Birmingham. What catches your eye immediately are the huge stacks of the ABC Coke plant located to the left of 79. A division of Drummond Company, Inc., ABC processes coke, which is sold by the boxcar load. Coke is bituminous coal that has been baked at high temperatures in the absence of oxygen. The resulting carbon product is used in the manufacture of steel. All of that coal baking makes for some mighty streams of white smoke (steam gases from the cooling process in the quench tower), which gives the ABC plant an eerie, hellish appearance even in daylight. Drive by at night and add the drama of flames from the burn off of coke-processing gases.

Heading out of hardscrabble Tarrant City, you can't miss the Dolcito Quarry operation on the left, a division of Vulcan Materials. This facility makes everything you need to pave an interstate, including asphalt aggregate, base material, chemical stone, ground calcium carbonate, concrete aggregate, manufactured sand, and recrushed concrete. To add to this industrial drama, the next mile of highway is lined with giant earth-moving equipment. It's as if Tarrant City was founded to facilitate the ripping open of the earth.

From Tarrant City to Jefferson State, view a classic zoning quilt of churches, bowling alleys, pawnshops, vinyl siding manufacturers, liquor stores, used car lots, and trailer parks.

For a quick bite to eat on the way back home, you can stop at signless Ken's Hickory Pit Barbecue, which is on the right side of AL 79 just after you access it from Jefferson State Parkway, (205) 853-6488. It's a gritty, workingman's table, but the food is tasty. Or head back into Tarrant City and have a meat-and-three at the Cedar House Cafeteria near the ABC Coke plant, on the right, (205) 841-1001.

JEMISON PARK NATURE TRAIL

IN BRIEF

This satisfying suburban hike follows Shades Creek along Mountain Brook Parkway, then crosses the Parkway to follow Watkins Creek for about half a mile. Expect to meet walkers, joggers, and lots of area residents exercising their huskies and labs.

DESCRIPTION

This suburban park, dedicated in 1952, honors the memory of businessman Robert Jemison Jr., a descendant of pioneer business entrepreneurs. Jemison founded the Jemison Real Estate and Insurance Company in 1903 and developed the Tutwiler Hotel in 1910. Jemison's real estate accomplishments include development of the Mountain Brook area, home to his namesake park.

DIRECTIONS

From US 31, exit south onto AL 149, Lakeshore Drive. Pass Brookwood Village shopping mall on the right. Pass under US 280. (You can access Mountain Brook Parkway from US 280 as well; be sure to head away from the mall.) Begin looking for an open parallel parking space along the right side of Mountain Brook Parkway, which AL 149 has become. If spaces are scarce, parking is also available near the elementary school soccer field about half a mile north of Mountain Brook Parkway on Cahaba Road (left at the second traffic light after US 280). A sidewalk/gravel trail leads past the field, across a street, through some woods, and across the two-lane Parkway to Jemison Park proper.

Alternate directions: From US 78 East (Crestwood Boulevard), turn right onto Montevallo Road. Drive 3.5 miles and turn left onto Overbrook Road. Turn right onto Mountain Brook Parkway at the light and look for the park on the left.

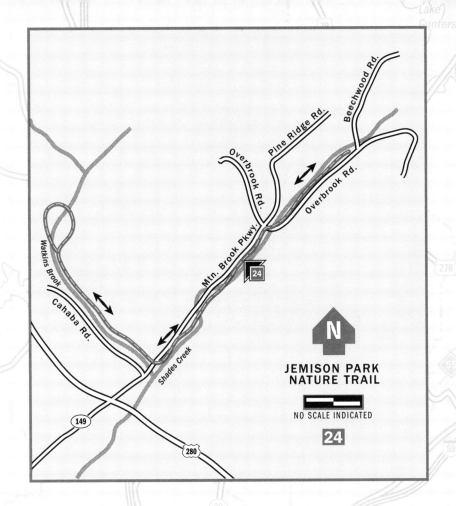

JEMISON PARK
NATURE TRAIL

NO SCALE INDICATED

24

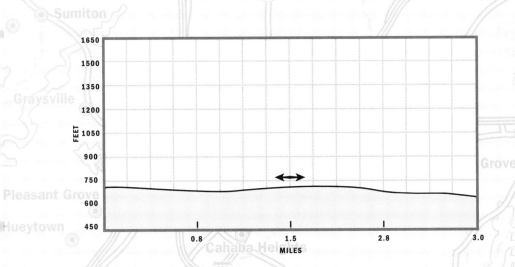

Sublime Shades Creek

Viewed from above, the trail through this 52-acre suburban woodland appears as a reverse L. Actually two out-and-backs placed together, this hike starts roughly in the middle of the L's longer back and heads southwest, following Shades Creek most of the way. This walk begins at the northern end of the park, which abuts Mountain Brook Parkway, near a creek crossing marked by a yellow sign. This spot is easily accessed from the available roadside parking, but any parking spot makes a suitable trailhead.

During times of heavy rain, this area can flood, as evidenced by the leaves and debris plastered on tree limbs along the bank. The land between the sidewalk and Shades Creek is Jemison Park. Follow the creek downstream; this stretch of Shades Creek is about 20 feet wide on average and deep enough to float a small boat.

As part of the Jemison Park Interpretive Program, signs along the way mark and identify various plants and trees and illuminate area wildlife. The first of these interpretive signs you'll pass details the activity of beaver that live in the area. As you walk, you'll also find benches on which to rest and perhaps do a bit of bird- or people-watching.

Soon, cross a small stream that flows beneath the sidewalk. In several places along this stretch, small streams and drainages flow into Shades Creek. An interpretive wildflower sign is next. In the spring, you'll see color-charged trillium—a small three-leafed, three-petaled flower—for several weeks. The rarer trout lily blooms here between March and April, but for just a few days. Jemison Park is also home to some magnificent, old pine, sycamore, and oak trees. Gray smooth-trunked beech trees, which like to grow near moving water, are common here, too.

Cross a bridge over Shades Creek, which now flows on your right. Walk past one end of a private, U-shaped cobblestone driveway leading to a large white home on the left; the road is to your right. In the spring, bright yellow forsythia line the edge of the sidewalk here. You might also spy a unique house across the creek on your right. This is Perryman's Mill, or rather a replica of the actual working mill that once stood there. After crossing over the other end of the private drive, walk over another bridge spanning the creek, which now returns to your left. Pass by a historic marker for Perryman's Mill. The mill is now a private residence, and is not open to the public, which may explain the marker's distance from the mill-*cum*-home.

Look for a "Beware of Snakes" sign as you pass a wooded area to the left that soon yields to a clearing with three picnic tables. After crossing a small drainage, you'll see the trail and creek come together, giving a close-up view of this surprisingly scenic waterway.

After passing an American beech interpretive sign, pass a bench facing the creek on the left and then admire the tall stately winged elms and giant tulip poplars, which are both labeled. Cross a small drainage and locate a sign on trail-left detailing the yellow-flowering ragwort (not to be confused with ragweed) that blooms from March through April. If you haven't seen anyone walking a dog yet, you must be out in some bad weather; this path is one of the primo dog-walking trails in Birmingham.

After you cross another drainage to the creek, approach a bridge, and see what looks like a bird feeder on the left. It actually holds copies of the "Bird List of Jemison Park." Prepared by the Friends of Jemison Park, the brochure is a checklist of birds that you may see in the park. Those named as abundant or common include mourning doves, red-bellied woodpeckers, and the common grackle. Birds that you may see occasionally include the belted kingfisher and turkey vulture (soaring above). Birds that can be found only rarely include the Canada warbler and the Acadian flycatcher. The brochure also contains lists of mammals and amphibians that live in and around the park.

With the list in hand, do not cross the bridge in front of you, but turn right and cross Mountain Brook Parkway to hike along Watkins Creek. Walk through a wood rail fence and onto the Jemison Park/Watkins Trace Trail, which is a wide gravel path about 0.4 miles long. With the creek flowing against you to your left, and the trail most likely busy with joggers, hike northwest through the mixed hardwood/pine forest. Interpretive signs continue through here as you pass a private home on the right and approach a trail fork. Go left and cross the creek on strategically placed stones. You'll have to make about a four-foot leap here. If that's too much, veer right and up the wooden stairs to Watkins Road, omitting the small loop option at the trail's end.

After crossing the creek, follow the trail as it loops to the right and passes a labeled white oak. Cross a small wooden footbridge and reach Watkins Road. Across the road, a stretch of sidewalk passes a soccer field adjacent to Mountain Brook Elementary. Turn right, go across the bridge then down the wooden steps. Look for a signed river birch tree on your left. Pass a private home on the left, cross another small wooden footbridge, and pass a labeled American beech to complete the loop. Now trace your steps back southeast to busy Mountain Brook Parkway.

At the Parkway, cross, turn left onto the sidewalk, and retrace your path to the creek crossing marked with a yellow sign. Step out into the middle of the wide creek on cement steps. If no one is waiting for you to cross (only one person at a time here) stop and gaze upstream. Cross over, head up and off to the left and then pass onto another sidewalk, with the creek to your left and woods on your right.

Heading north/northeast look for a sign that explains the floodplain nature of Jemison Park. The park comprises a mile of floodplain along Shades Creek, which drains 135 square miles of land between Red Mountain and Shades Mountain. The water flows through Jemison Park and eventually empties into the Cahaba River.

Follow the curvy sidewalk trail to a small, isolated picnic table on the left. This is the best spot along the trail for a picnic. The trail soon changes to gravel where an arched stone bridge comes up on the left, with Shades Creek flowing beneath it. Approach the road that crosses the bridge and look across to the right for the trail. Here the trail drops down, crosses a drainage, and heads northeast. Up to your right is Overbrook Road, which is lined with fashionable older homes.

This gravel stint is noticeably more rustic, and it undulates with the terrain, though never more than 10 to 20 feet. Except for the view of the nearby road, it's easy to forget you're walking through the heart of suburbia on this bucolic stretch.

With Shades Creek still running to your left, pass between two very tall beech trees and an oak. Across the creek, you'll see a picnic area, which you can access by turning left and crossing the road bridge at the trail's end. This is the turnaround.

NEARBY ACTIVITIES

The Birmingham Zoo and the Botanical Gardens are nearby. From Mountain Brook Parkway, take Cahaba Road north, towards Birmingham, through Mountain Brook Village. The road soon forks, just after an access road to US 280 turns left. To reach the zoo, follow the left fork to the entrance on your left. For the gardens, also good for a pleasant stroll, veer right then turn left at the entrance. Of course if you need to shop or eat lunch, Brookwood Village is just a stone's throw away.

LAKE CHINNABEE LOOP

An impoundment of Cheaha Creek, 17-acre Lake Chinnabee is a great place to bring the kids to spend the day—or weekend at one of eight campsites. This loop takes you around the scenic lake.

DESCRIPTION

Located to the west of Talladega Mountain and just south of the Cleburne County line, Lake Chinnabee lies quietly hidden in the depths of the Talladega National Forest. A small dam located on the lake's western arm creates the lake, impounding the waters of Cheaha Creek. The lake is sheltered by surrounding forest and is home to wildlife such as largemouth bass, bream, painted wood ducks, and sun-basking turtles.

To begin the hike, head southeast past the rest rooms on your left, with Cheaha Creek flowing off to your right. Walking against its flow, pass picnic tables and grills on the right and soon reach a dirt path. Cheaha Creek begins to slow as it approaches the lake, pooling its clear, amber-tinged water to a depth of two to three feet. You'll find creek-companion beech trees here, along with tulip poplar, hickory, loblolly pine, chestnut oak, white oak, and Alabama's state wildflower, the oak-leaf hydrangea.

DIRECTIONS

From the intersection of I-459 and I-20, head east toward Anniston. Drive 50 miles and take the first Anniston exit onto AL 21 South. At 13.8 miles, turn left onto CR 398 East. Drive 3.4 miles and turn right onto Cheaha Road. Pass through Camp Mac. Follow the Cheaha State Park signs along a narrow, twisting paved road. After 9 miles on Cheaha Road, turn right onto FS 646. Drive 1.3 miles and enter the Lake Chinnabee Recreation Area. Park in a lot on your left. Walk toward the rest rooms to begin the loop.

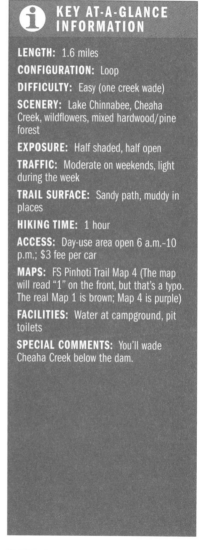

KEY AT-A-GLANCE INFORMATION

LENGTH: 1.6 miles

CONFIGURATION: Loop

DIFFICULTY: Easy (one creek wade)

SCENERY: Lake Chinnabee, Cheaha Creek, wildflowers, mixed hardwood/pine forest

EXPOSURE: Half shaded, half open

TRAFFIC: Moderate on weekends, light during the week

TRAIL SURFACE: Sandy path, muddy in places

HIKING TIME: 1 hour

ACCESS: Day-use area open 6 a.m.–10 p.m.; $3 fee per car

MAPS: FS Pinhoti Trail Map 4 (The map will read "1" on the front, but that's a typo. The real Map 1 is brown; Map 4 is purple)

FACILITIES: Water at campground, pit toilets

SPECIAL COMMENTS: You'll wade Cheaha Creek below the dam.

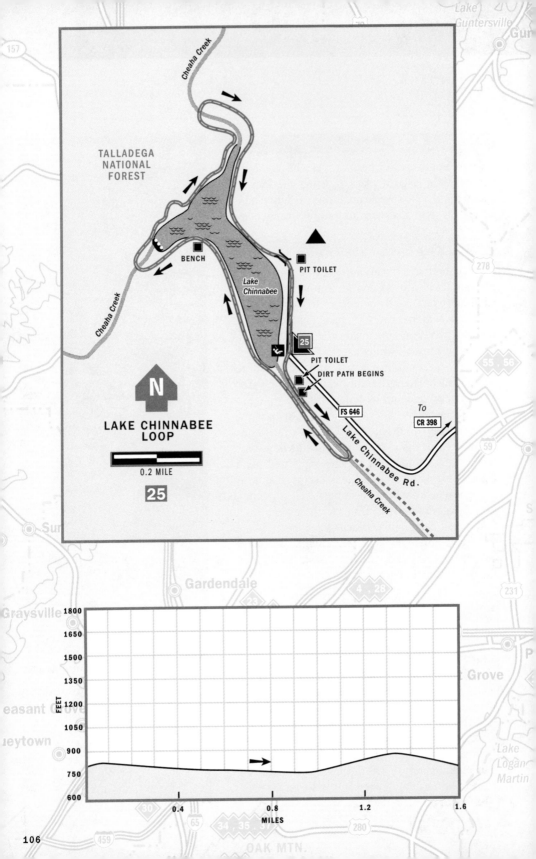

TALLADEGA
NATIONAL
FOREST

BENCH

PIT TOILET

Lake
Chinnabee

25

PIT TOILET

DIRT PATH BEGINS

FS 646

To
CR 398

Lake Chinnabee Rd.

Cheaha Creek

Cheaha Creek

Cheaha Creek

N

LAKE CHINNABEE
LOOP

0.2 MILE

25

FEET

1800
1650
1500
1350
1200
1050
900
750
600

0.4   0.8   1.2   1.6
MILES

Soon find a "Cheaha Lake Trail" sign that points right. This is the first of three creek crossings you'll make along the way. Rock hop across on stones and bear right onto a narrow dirt trail lined with wildflowers such as hepatica, black-eyed Susan, and galax. More silvery, smooth-barked beeches and mountain laurel also grace the trail as it traverses a steep, wooded hillside.

With the creek flowing down to your right, heading northwest in a clockwise direction, the trail climbs above the creek about 50 feet. Begin to head down, and at 0.18 miles, the creek begins to deaden into the lake. Cross a feeder brook at 0.24 miles, dipping up and down along the steep ridge. Just ahead of your arrival, turtles sunning on fallen trees skitter from their perches, plopping into the lake. With dragonflies performing precision flight maneuvers around you, the trail bends left, following the lake to a simple wooden bench at half a mile.

Heading southwest down to lake level, watch out for poison ivy that may encroach on the trail. You'll be able to hear the splashing overflow as you approach a small dam on your right, constructed in the 1930s. Water spills over the top, crashing down a stairstepped face about 30 feet to a pool below. The path is cushioned through here with pine needles.

When you see a wider dirt road heading straight ahead, turn right to follow the footpath down to the creek through a very scrubby patch of land littered with downed trees. Pick a spot to cross the creek and then resume the trail, bearing right, on the other side. You'll have to wade here, but it's easy, especially if you leave your boots on. Pass the dam again as the trail traces the shore beside a slope covered with ferns.

At 0.7 miles, bear away from the lake and head up a ravine, north, and then bear sharply right back toward the lake. You may spot the red crest of a pileated woodpecker along the way, or at least hear its impressive tree-pounding hammer. According to one ranger, the Forest Service is making efforts to revive the habitat of the pileated woodpecker, accommodating the loss of habitat due to the Southern pine beetle.

Dropping downhill at 0.8 miles, begin to trace a slough that leads to another feeder creek. The lake here is shallow and choked with vegetation, providing largemouth bass with prime hunting grounds. The slough narrows and winds back into the woods to the creek's mouth. This often-wet area is home to more beeches, ferns, and wildflowers.

Head into an increasingly boggy area to reach the creek at 1 mile. Cross on stones, bear right, and begin to climb back above the lake. Look down into the water and you might be able to see the rounded, pebbly spawning beds of bream. An interpretive sign notes that painted wood ducks frequent the area. They often nest as high as 50 feet above ground, but will also nest in wooden boxes placed on posts that are sunk into the lake.

At 1.25 miles, the main body of the lake widens as you head south. The trail's best open views of the lake are found here, with hillside meadows to your left. Much of the slope's open, meadow-like quality is the result of tree damage caused by Hurricane Opal in October 1995.

Approach the recreational area's small campground at 1.3 miles, cross a feeder stream on a small footbridge, bear right, and cross another footbridge. You'll see the campground pit toilets on your left. From here you can follow a narrow paved road back to the parking area, passing the play area on your right. It's a bit scruffy, but has a slide and swings.

NEARBY ACTIVITIES

After the hike, eat an apple and then head up the Chinnabee Silent Trail to Devil's Den, a popular swimming hole about half a mile from Lake Chinnabee. See p. 35 for more information.

From June through August, a lifeguard is on duty at Cheaha Lake in nearby Cheaha State Park. Paddleboats are rented at the lake for $5 per hour. The lake is open 9:30 a.m.–5 p.m. You can fish here, but you'll need a fishing license (available at the park store).

There are several short trails inside the park, including Cheaha Lake (p. 31), Bald Rock Boardwalk (p. 17), and the Pulpit Rock Trail (p. 187).

LAKESHORE TRAIL
(HOMEWOOD SHADES CREEK GREENWAY)

IN BRIEF

Wander beneath sycamore and oak trees beside lazy Shades Creek as you follow Birmingham's newest greenway.

DESCRIPTION

Many cities throughout the US are improving neighborhoods by creating greenways. These multi-use paths are often built on abandoned rail lines or follow beneath city right-of-ways in areas that can't otherwise be developed. While lacking the more remote quality of state parks and forests, they still offer a refreshing escape from the hustle of the city.

Lakeshore Trail is Birmingham's newest greenway. A project of the city of Homewood, it will eventually connect the Jemison Park Nature Trail with West Homewood Park. For now, you can walk this pleasant three-mile section between Brookwood Village and Columbiana Road. This is a multiuse trail, so expect to see runners, walkers, inline skaters, and bikers. The paved-path is wide enough to accommodate all these uses, but do keep an ear out for approaching cyclists.

From the parking lot, cross back over Brookwood Boulevard and head toward the rust-colored pedestrian bridge. Cross Shades Creek, and take a sharp left onto a wide paved path. If you like

DIRECTIONS

From I-65, take Exit 255 onto AL 149 (Lakeshore Drive), heading west toward Brookwood Village. After passing under US 31, turn right at first light onto Brookwood Boulevard, then head up the hill and take the first entrance on the left into the trailhead parking lot. To make this a shorter, one-way hike (using two cars, of course, turn right onto Columbiana Road after exiting the interstate, then take a quick left to reach the west end trailhead parking.

KEY AT-A-GLANCE INFORMATION

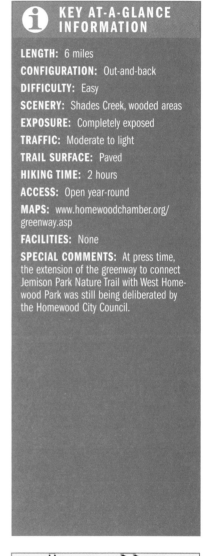

LENGTH: 6 miles

CONFIGURATION: Out-and-back

DIFFICULTY: Easy

SCENERY: Shades Creek, wooded areas

EXPOSURE: Completely exposed

TRAFFIC: Moderate to light

TRAIL SURFACE: Paved

HIKING TIME: 2 hours

ACCESS: Open year-round

MAPS: www.homewoodchamber.org/greenway.asp

FACILITIES: None

SPECIAL COMMENTS: At press time, the extension of the greenway to connect Jemison Park Nature Trail with West Homewood Park was still being deliberated by the Homewood City Council.

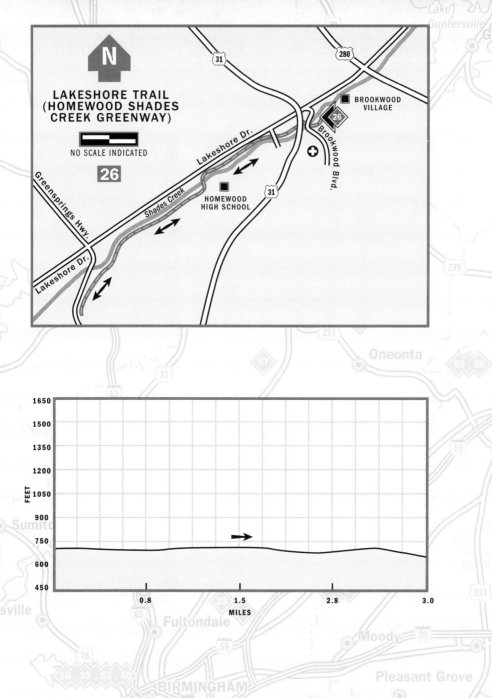

kudzu, then you'll be tickled pink at the vast areas of this Japanese import on both sides of the trail. Introduced to the United States in 1876, kudzu has been promoted as a garden ornamental, as cattle forage, and for hillside erosion control. But now that it covers millions of acres in the Southeast, kudzu has become a pest to many.

Walk with the flow of the creek, passing beneath Highway 31 and the steady clickety clack of rushing vehicles. Brookwood Medical Plaza looms up to your left. You'll notice the flatness and openness of this trail right away. If the sun's out, you may want to bring along the shades and a hat. The trail curves widely at first, generally heading west as it follows Lakeshore Drive. Pass behind a mirrored building and notice a small scattering of hardwoods, pine, and more kudzu to the left. The creek is sluggish through here, but the songbirds are energetic. To my surprise, I spotted a blue heron stalking dinner in the creek on my hike.

After passing the 2200 Lakeshore Building on your right, cross a paved road. With the Fort William C. Mulkey National Guard Armory up to your left, descend slightly as the trail dips below the level of Lakeshore into a brushy area. Cross a small stream that feeds into Shades Creek and regain the level of Lakeshore. Here you'll experience the closest proximity to the busy four-lane highway on the hike; a guardrail stands between the trail and the road.

With Shades Creek still on your left, look for a wide spot in the creek, one of the better fishing spots in this suburban area (Alabama fishing license required).

Cross a brief rise in the trail, with a stone wall on trail left. As the path dips down below the level of Lakeshore once more, look for the main entrance to Samford University across the road to your right. Chartered as Howard College in Marion, Alabama, in 1841, the school moved to Birmingham in 1887. The private university moved to its current location in 1957. If you left your watch at home, you can look to the campus bell tower to check the time.

Samford University plans to revitalize this portion of the greenway from Homewood High School back to US 31. In conjunction with Vulcan Materials, the Friends of Shades Creek, the Alabama Rivers Alliance, and the Birmingham Audubon Society, the university's biology department is working to eliminate invasive plants such as kudzu and privet, encouraging the growth of native species such as azalea and mountain laurel. There is also a long-term plan to develop the area as a bird sanctuary.

Pass Homewood High and its playing fields on your left, and then get ready to go down. Bear left onto a pedestrian bridge and cross the creek. The road in front of you, University Park East, goes up to the high school. Curve back around left and descend to pass beneath the road, continuing west as you emerge back into the open from beneath the road.

Shades Creek is on your right, providing a nice barrier between you and Lakeshore Parkway along the best stretch of the trail. Pass beneath a low-clearance bridge and enter an area of towering pines. A minor network of small paths leave the main trail here, but you should stay on the main trail. Pass a wooden footbridge and assisted living complex to your left, cross a small bridge over another Shades Creek feeder, and pass a block of garden homes buffered by sycamores.

A raised empty field will appear to your left, above a swampy area scattered with tall hardwoods, including large sweetgums. As the trail bends around to the left, the turnaround is not far away. Off to your right, beyond a swath of trees, is Green Springs Highway.

The trail begins to parallel Green Springs Highway and passes a marshy tree-filled area to the left. When the trail bears west again, approach a gravel road and parking lot. Turn around here and enjoy the walk back to the parking area.

NEARBY ACTIVITIES

The Jemison Park Nature Trail is just a mile away from where you parked. You can walk there by paralleling Lakeshore Drive (heading east) through the Brookwood Mall parking lot. (See p. 100 for more details.) If your stroll worked up an appetite, a few food favorites in nearby Homewood include O'Carr's Deli (2909 18th Street South), Savage's Bakery (2916 18th Street South), and Nabeel's (1706 Oxmoor Road). Applebee's and the other offerings at Brookwood Village are just a short walk from the parking area. Visit www.birminghammenus.com for menus and more information.

LAKESIDE PARK LOOP

IN BRIEF

This hike's first half beckons those wishing for a cool summer's walk beneath maples, pines, and oaks, while the second half offers good views and access to 15,000-acre Logan Martin Lake.

DESCRIPTION

Pell City is a small town where residents and visitors enjoy nearby Logan Martin Lake's 275 miles of shoreline. Located on the lake, Lakeside Park, home to the Pell City Civic Center, is the local hub for outdoor recreation, including walking, tennis, baseball, softball, soccer, football, and fishing.

To begin, walk beneath the Rosa Lorene Morton Nature Trail sign and enter the wooded portion of this hike (the sign may be down). A few years ago, this small patch of woods completely enclosed this gravelly and leaf-strewn trail, but now there are wide clearings to the left. The trail is not blazed, but it is easy to follow. Cross a small wooden footbridge and continue walking through an area of tall maples, pines, oaks, and other trees.

A path appears from the left, but continue up steeply. The trail then levels into easy walking, before bearing right, and diverging from the paved

DIRECTIONS

From Birmingham, access I-20 East. From the intersection of I-459 with I-20, it is 21.5 miles to the Pell City/US 231 exit (Exit 158). Bear to the right onto US 231 South and drive through Pell City. At 3.2 miles from I-20, turn left onto AL 34 East, which goes to Talladega. Drive past Cropwell Commons on the right and soon turn left (still on AL 34) at a video rental store. Pell City Civic Center will be on your right. Continue a short distance and turn right into Pell City Lakeside Park. Pass through the gate onto Veterans Drive and continue until the first parking area on the left. Pull in and park.

KEY AT-A-GLANCE INFORMATION

LENGTH: 2 miles

CONFIGURATION: Loop

DIFFICULTY: Easy

SCENERY: Logan Martin Lake, ducks, hardwood/pine forest

EXPOSURE: Mostly exposed

TRAFFIC: Moderate on paved path, light on the Rosa Lorene Morton Nature Trail

TRAIL SURFACE: Dirt, gravel, pavement

HIKING TIME: 1 hour

ACCESS: Open March 1–November 30, 8 a.m.–6 p.m.; closed December 1–February 28 (although people still walk in the park)

MAPS: None

FACILITIES: Rest rooms, pay phone, water at Pell City Civic Center; rest rooms at pavilion and ball field

SPECIAL COMMENTS: Crowds of people abound in this area during Saturday ballgames. Most other times, you'll have the place to yourself. To reserve a pavilion for a family picnic, call (205) 338-9713. No alcohol is allowed in the park.

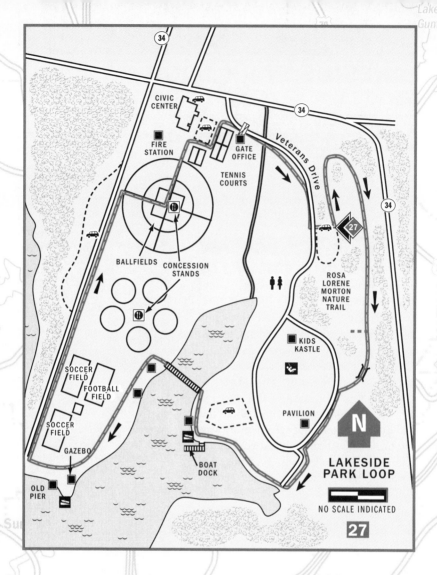

LAKESIDE PARK LOOP

NO SCALE INDICATED

27

CIVIC CENTER

FIRE STATION

GATE OFFICE

TENNIS COURTS

BALLFIELDS

CONCESSION STANDS

Veterans Drive

ROSA LORENE MORTON NATURE TRAIL

KIDS KASTLE

PAVILION

SOCCER FIELD

FOOTBALL FIELD

SOCCER FIELD

GAZEBO

OLD PIER

BOAT DOCK

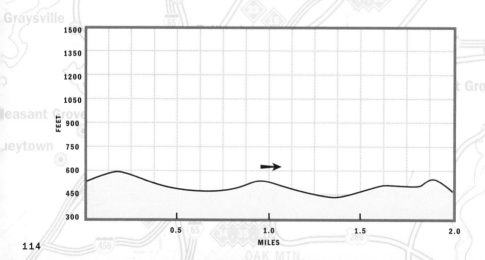

trail. Small mulberry and mimosa trees appear alongside the trail, and a tall yellow maple looms on the right. Next, watch for a large, strangled tree on the right, in the grips of several hairy vines running up its trunk.

During one of my walks here, I encountered dozens of trees that had fallen due to a recent storm. Pell City does a great job of maintaining this park; when I returned not long after, the path had been cleared.

As the trail bears around to the right, walk into an open area and drop down into a thorny, scrubby area where the trail flattens. Ignore a side trail that leaves right and continue straight. Cross a second small footbridge, reach the trail's end, and exit the woods onto Veteran's Drive. To shorten the hike considerably, turn right and follow the road, which will lead you 0.15 miles back to your vehicle. Otherwise, continue the hike by turning left.

Pass a pavilion with a rest room across the road, on your right. Walk either on the road or on the grassy shoulder as you head toward Logan Martin Lake. Pass a volleyball court to your right and glimpse the lake through the trees ahead. The road bends right, but continue straight onto a wide, pine-needled dirt road to intersect the paved walking path. Bear right onto the eight-foot-wide paved path and pass a contemplation bench. Off to your left, view Logan Martin Lake and/or a mud flat depending on the lake's water level, which is regulated not only by rainfall, but also by dams located at either end of the lake.

When the Coosa River was dammed in 1964, the nearby town of Easonville disappeared beneath the waters. A remnant of the old town, the Coosa Valley Missionary Baptist Church, is visible on the north side of US 231 south. The church and its cemetery were moved across the highway to their present location, just a couple of miles south of Pell City.

Approach a large parking area and turn left toward the lake. A floating boat pier lies to the left. Swimming is allowed, though you do so at your own risk. Beside the boat pier is a boat launch area. If you want to launch your bass boat here, you must pay a $3 fee at the entrance station. Next, a T-shaped pier stretches out over the water on your left where you'll usually be greeted by a passel of ducks looking for a handout. Fishing is allowed only if you have an Alabama fishing license on your person.

Next, look ahead for a large, arched wooden walkway that spans a slough. Cross it to the other side, a good place to cast a plastic worm or maybe pull a Jitterbug in the late evening. The land you cross over to is a ballfield-covered peninsula that juts out narrowly into the lake. Turn left onto the paved trail, which passes playing fields for soccer, baseball, and football, located to your right.

Pass a red bench, a small gazebo, another red bench, and walk toward a larger covered gazebo out on the point. Most evenings, the lake calms and mirrors the sinking sun's red and orange goodbyes.

At the gazebo, the paved trail dead-ends. Turn right and walk near the lake's edge toward a pier. (If the water's down, you can walk out onto dry spits of land and explore the lake bottom.) Reach an old boat launch and an old wooden pier on the left. Here, bear right and head back toward the civic center, with the playing fields to your right, a vast parking area to your left, and the lake beyond that.

On this long, straight, level segment of the hike, you can walk on the paved parking access road or walk to the side in the grass. Pass a maintenance outbuilding on your left, a walkway that goes right, and then a gazebo. The main gated entrance to the parking area looms ahead. At the next paved walk, turn right and meander between two baseball fields. Pass a water fountain to your left and approach a concession stand that is open during games. Turn left at the concession stand to pass tennis courts on your right. Exit into the civic center parking lot; inside are rest rooms and water if you need them.

Bear around to the right through the parking lot and toward the gated entrance to the park, passing a second set of tennis courts. Bear right onto Veteran's Drive for the walk back to the parking lot where you left your vehicle. Walking alongside the road in the grass, passing over a drainage pipe, you might see a blue heron poking around in the culvert's shallow water, as I did during my visit.

Before turning into the parking lot, pass a rest area with benches on your right, which is also the finish/start line for the Pell City Sports Complex Walking Track.

NEARBY ACTIVITIES

Just around to the left of the parking area is the playground complex called Kids Kastle and is designed for kids ages 2 to 5. A Tot Lot inside is designed for the younger kids. Features include a small climbing wall, endless stairs and turrets, a swinging bridge, sand galore, slides, swings, and benches for old folks like me to sit on.

Heading back into town on US 231 North, there are several places to eat, including the Pell City Steak House. Pass through town and cross I-20 for the Western Sizzlin' buffet or a sackfull of Krystals. For barbecue, you've got a lot of choices. Continue down 231 North for a couple of miles into Coal City and look for Paul's Barbecue on the right. Or, from the park, turn right onto Highway 34 and drive 1.2 miles to Old Time Barbecue, which is on the right next to a Citgo station.

MAPLEBRIDGE–HORSESHOE RAMBLE

IN BRIEF

This trail makes the most of a quarter-mile-long slope, using multiple switchbacks to carry you back and forth, as you slowly wend your way uphill.

DESCRIPTION

Considering that most of Trussville Sport Complex's 125 acres is occupied by a wealth of ball fields, trail builders have made the most of the surrounding forest by constructing maze-like trails. Hikers should be aware that trails here accommodate hikers as well as mountain bikers. Don't fret, though. If it weren't for members of the Birmingham Urban Mountain Pedalers (BUMP), much of this trail system would not exist. Not only are they actively constructing new trails at the Complex, but the bike traffic also keeps much of the trail system from being engulfed by scrub.

From your vehicle, walk toward the marked Maplebridge Trail and turn right. Initially the trail is a wide paved pedestrian walkway that heads east. Pass a field to your left and then a bank of longleaf pines to your right, heading south toward the ball fields on the right. Pass through a clearing and, as

DIRECTIONS

From I-59 North, take Exit 141. Go right onto Chalkville Road toward Trussville. Drive 1 mile and turn left onto Oak Street, which promptly becomes Cherokee Drive. Cross an old stone bridge to see the park entrance on your left. Turn left and drive through the park until you see the Maplebridge Trail sign on your right. Park in the large lot adjacent to the sign.

Alternate directions: From I-459 North, take Exit 32 (Trussville/US 11). Turn right onto US 11. Drive 2.8 miles and turn left onto Chalkville Road North. Drive 0.5 miles and turn right onto Oak Street, then follow the directions above.

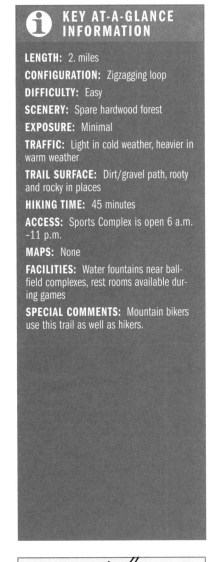

KEY AT-A-GLANCE INFORMATION

LENGTH: 2. miles

CONFIGURATION: Zigzagging loop

DIFFICULTY: Easy

SCENERY: Spare hardwood forest

EXPOSURE: Minimal

TRAFFIC: Light in cold weather, heavier in warm weather

TRAIL SURFACE: Dirt/gravel path, rooty and rocky in places

HIKING TIME: 45 minutes

ACCESS: Sports Complex is open 6 a.m. –11 p.m.

MAPS: None

FACILITIES: Water fountains near ball-field complexes, rest rooms available during games

SPECIAL COMMENTS: Mountain bikers use this trail as well as hikers.

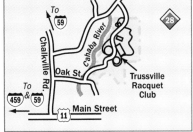

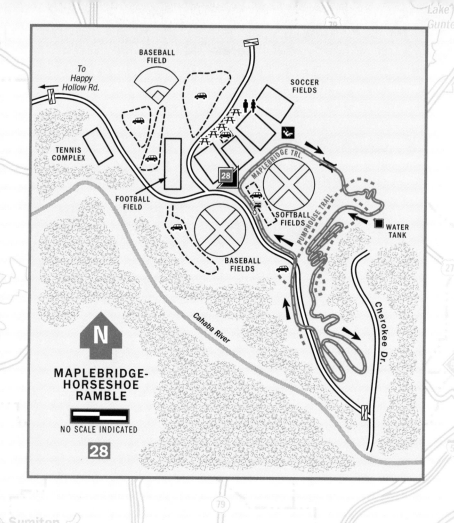

BASEBALL FIELD

To Happy Hollow Rd.

SOCCER FIELDS

TENNIS COMPLEX

MAPLEBRIDGE TRL.

FOOTBALL FIELD

28

SOFTBALL FIELDS

PUMPHOUSE TRAIL

WATER TANK

BASEBALL FIELDS

Cahaba River

Cherokee Dr.

N

MAPLEBRIDGE-
HORSESHOE
RAMBLE

NO SCALE INDICATED

28

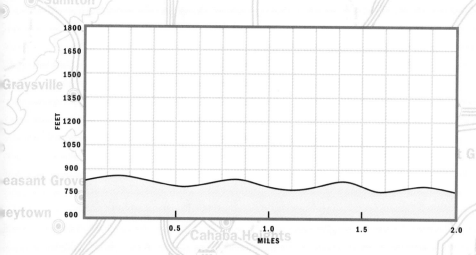

you approach a play area, bear right on a route that alternates between a rocky path and a smoother, needle-covered trail.

Walk by homes on your left with a scrub mix of privet and other invasive ornamentals to your right. Cross a wooden footbridge that passes over a wet-weather drainage and enter a mixed hardwood/pine forest. Now walking on gravel, camber right and pass a small brick utility building on your right. This marks a quarter-mile.

Turn right onto a wider path, then immediately turn back left, heading up and onto the Horseshoe Trail. The path shoots straight up the steep hillside to a small water tower. To heat your thighs on this extra bit of trail, just go up. The last third of this quarter-mile out-and-back is very steep before it dead-ends at the water tower. Otherwise, take the first left at a hiker sign onto a flat, winding path, where the switchbacks are so tight that you can often step from one to another.

Double back and pass through a hardwood forest choked with vines, Russian olive, privet, and occasional downed trees. Double back again, now heading south, to pass a small magnolia and a few beeches. Step over the occasional piece of sandstone on the forest floor, then take a hairpin turn right, heading north/northeast. At a trail marker, bear back right and hike downhill briefly to reach a trail intersection. If you turn left, you'll head back up to the water tower. Instead, turn right, then immediately bear back to the left. The total distance traveled so far is about half a mile (0.7 miles if you took the earlier out-and-back option up to the water tower).

Look for ball fields visible through the trees on your right and a portion of the trail you will soon reach on your left. Continue walking, eventually reaching a series of switchbacks leading uphill. Trail segments between switchbacks parallel the ridge above, and shorten in length as you gain elevation. Except for the short climbs between parallel segments, the trail is fairly level. The scenery is pleasant but mediocre, with the occasional rock pile and stand of pesky mimosa.

After the final switchback, the trail sets off on a wild curvy trek through the woods. If there are bikes on the trail, you'll be able to hear them long before you see them. Soon you'll hit a level section of trail, with the Complex road visible through trees on your right. You'll see a post-lined trail to your left, but it is not part of this hike.

Twisting down, encounter a bass-boat-sized chunk of sedimentary rock on your left and then a trailer-sized boulder. Bear right and, with the road visible straight ahead, take a sharp left to the southwest. Encounter lots of downed pines to the sides of the trail and enter a wild area rife with beetle-ridden pines. Where the path meets a big pile of broken pavement, bear right and down, winding through more scrub.

Again the road appears straight ahead; bear left and briefly parallel the road. Bear away from the road, then the road reappears on your left as you pass over a path lined with smooth rock. Heading northeast, exit the woods and briefly walk along the road for about 0.1 mile. Then duck back into the forest on the left side of the road.

Head down into a boggy area of ferns, downed trees, pines, and mixed hardwoods. Look for a 25-foot magnolia on trail-right. When you intersect a wide unmarked trail, turn right and walk briefly through an even boggier area and then out into a gravel parking lot. Veer right and you'll see the parking lot across the road where you parked your vehicle.

MARTIN WILDLIFE PARK TRAIL

KEY AT-A-GLANCE INFORMATION

LENGTH: 2.9 miles

CONFIGURATION: Combo

DIFFICULTY: Easy

SCENERY: H. Neely Henry Lake, boggy island, waterfowl

EXPOSURE: Exposed except for island loop

TRAFFIC: Moderate/heavy, except on island

TRAIL SURFACE: Wide gravel path, boardwalks, muddy dirt path (on island)

HIKING TIME: 1–1.5 hours

ACCESS: Trailhead never closed

MAPS: None

FACILITIES: Gadsden Mall has rest rooms, phone, food court, shopping

SPECIAL COMMENTS: 27.5 miles north on I-59 is a rest area; all pets must be on a leash in the park. There are two connected trails within the wildlife park, the Green Trail and the Brown Trail.

IN BRIEF

Have you ever wanted to explore a small, wooded island in the middle of a big lake? It might be a muddy affair, but here's your chance.

DESCRIPTION

Not too many malls have a nature trail nearby, but Gadsden Mall does. The land bordering H. Neely Henry Lake is too swampy for commercial development, and—as is often the case—since there was not much else to do with it, the land was set aside as an urban green space. But such efforts to transform flood plains and other undesirable acreage into useful recreational space are much appreciated by hikers, bikers, and others who enjoy the outdoors. The park was opened on October 15, 1991, and dedicated to James D. Martin, a Commissioner of the Alabama Department of Conservation and a former Representative to the U.S. Congress.

To begin, walk past the park's sign, pass a row of ornamental shrubs on your left, and cross an arched footbridge over a slough of the lake onto the Green Trail. Right away views of the lake open up to your left. There are some power lines visible down the backbone of the trail system, but otherwise the area is wild and scrubby.

In summer, dragonflies hover and zip along the banks. Wildflowers abound on both sides of the trail, including trumpeter vine, Queen Anne's

DIRECTIONS

From the intersection of I-459 and I-59 near Trussville, drive 44.3 miles to Exit 182/I-759; follow I-759 East for 5 miles to Exit 4B. Bear around onto US 431 North and drive 0.5 miles. Turn left at the first traffic light and drive to the back of the mall with the mall on your left. Park near the James D. Martin Wildlife Park sign.

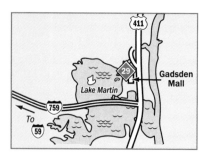

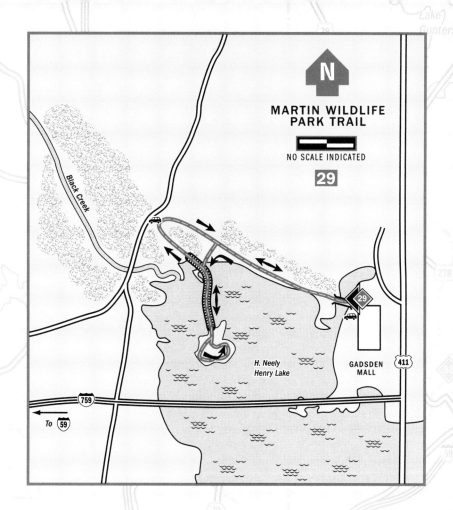

MARTIN WILDLIFE
PARK TRAIL

NO SCALE INDICATED

29

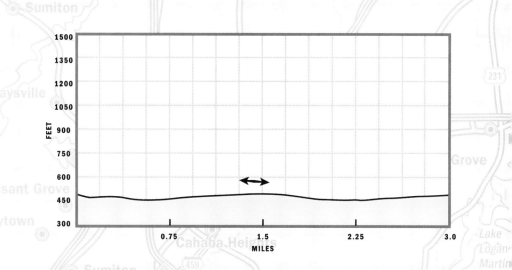

lace, black-eyed Susan, and others. Walking on the wide gravel path, you'll see a variety of trees, including the southern catalpa, which has large, heart-shaped leaves.

Pass a dirt access road and a water-treatment facility on your right, then pass a peninsula of land to your left that juts into the lake. The lake soon opens up again with sweeping views across the water. Back on your right, the scrub picks up again, harboring swampy bogs and pools.

In addition to the bright orange blooms of trumpeter vine, also known as orange honeysuckle, you'll see splashes of colorful morning glories from amid the grasses, reeds, and weeds. At 0.4 miles, pass a wetland pond to your right and look out toward tiny islands in the lake on your left. If it's early summer, you'll see Queen Anne's lace and red clover through here.

Pass a half-mile marker sign, and then turn left toward the lake to continue the Green Trail at 0.6 miles. Enter a short patch of woods—a shady spot to rest—and soon step onto the beginning of a long boardwalk that will take you out to a small lake island. The boardwalk is in good shape and is a popular place to jog as well as fish. Out over the water, reach any intersection with the Brown Trail, another arm of the boardwalk that you'll take on your way back.

The best wildlife viewing on this route is from the boardwalk. With clear views out over the lake to your left and good views of a reedy swamp to your left, you'll see lots of waterfowl, including white egrets, sandhill cranes, an occasional blue heron, and even kingfishers. Continue straight on the boardwalk, passing a small walkout on the left, headed south toward the island.

At the end of the boardwalk, walk down into the moist scruffy woods of the island. When the Coosa River was dammed, creating Neely Henry Lake, the rising water created numerous small islands such as this. Pass two benches and proceed on a gravely woodland path that can get muddy after a heavy rain, flanked by tall pines, water oak, red oak, and sweetgum. Step up onto a short, elevated boardwalk, passing over a wet, marshy area.

Head around toward a bench that overlooks the lake and then bear left to continue your counterclockwise tour of the flat island. Pass another bench as the trail traces the water's edge. A section of trail is often underwater here, so you might have to edge around it. Lots of orange-flowering trumpeter vines grow on the island, adding some unexpected color to the dank, dim environment.

I was happily surprised to see very few buzzing bugs along this trail. Nothing sought me out, other than a few sweat-loving gnats. At 1.25 miles, you may have to skirt a couple of successive watery areas before returning to the elevated boardwalk that will put you on track to re-access the long boardwalk across the lake.

Back at the Y split, the Green Trail goes right, and the Brown Trail goes straight. Follow the Brown Trail boardwalk as it penetrates a slough while heading toward shore. Reach the end of Brown Trail's boardwalk section and pick up the gravel path at 1.8 miles. Soon, reach a trail parking area on your left and begin to head southeast back toward the Green Trail. Pass the entrance to the boardwalk on your right at 2.2 miles, then retrace the long straight Green Trail back to the mall parking area.

MOSS ROCK PRESERVE TRAIL

IN BRIEF

Hoover's newest city park is known primarily as a rock-climbing venue, but the path to the boulders, and beyond to the falls of Hurricane Branch, makes a great hiking venue as well.

DESCRIPTION

Known for years as the Shades Crest Boulder Fields, this wooded suburban enclave was long at risk for development. Although hemmed in on all sides by housing communities, the 250-acre plot was finally set aside as a nature park. That's good news not only for climbers, but for hikers (and mountain bikers) as well.

From Shades Crest Park, you'll cross the road to enter the pine/hardwood forest and encounter a narrow stream traversed by a rickety wooden bridge. The stream, though, is small and easy enough to step across. The path you'll follow is a rocky dirt affair scattered with small bits of forest debris.

The pines in Moss Rock Preserve have endured a tough bout with the Southern pine beetle. Dead, decaying pines and snapped pine trunks litter the forest floor. The hardwoods you'll find here include black maple, red maple, red oak, and tulip poplar. The woods are peaceful, but if you stop and listen, you can distinguish a vague roar of traffic off to the east.

Heading north, ignore a trail that leads left at 0.1 mile. Continue straight and meander slowly

KEY AT-A-GLANCE INFORMATION

LENGTH: 1.2 miles

CONFIGURATION: Out-and-back

DIFFICULTY: Easy/moderate

SCENERY: House-sized boulders, Hurricane Branch

EXPOSURE: Mostly shaded

TRAFFIC: Moderate/heavy on weekends, light on weekdays

TRAIL SURFACE: Rocky, rooty woodland path, steep in places

HIKING TIME: 1 hour

ACCESS: Trailhead never closed

MAPS: None

FACILITIES: None

SPECIAL COMMENTS: Our area's premier bouldering destination, this park is maintained by community volunteers. To find out more or to volunteer, visit www.hooveral.org.

DIRECTIONS

From I-459, exit onto US 31 North and turn left onto Patton Chapel Road heading south. Drive 1.5 miles and turn left onto Chapel Lane. Drive 0.5 miles and turn right onto Al Seier Road. Drive 1.3 miles and turn left into the parking area for Shades Mountain Park. From the parking area, the trailhead is just across Al Seier Road.

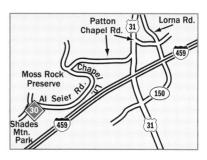

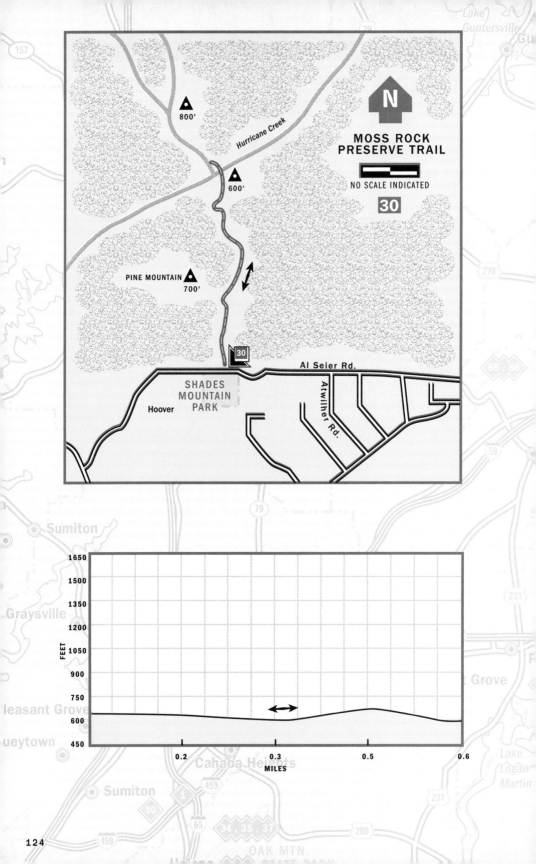

MOSS ROCK
PRESERVE TRAIL

NO SCALE INDICATED

30

800'

600'

PINE MOUNTAIN
700'

Hurricane Creek

30

Al Seier Rd.

SHADES
MOUNTAIN
PARK

Hoover

Atwilher Rd.

downhill. At 0.12 miles, cross a wet-weather drainage that has attracted numerous large beech trees. The path is level through here, passing among sweetgum, tulip poplar, and unlucky horizontal pine trees. There are a couple of spots where you'll have to jag around a downed tree, but most of the fallen pines had been cut and pushed aside at the time of my visit.

Emerge from the tree cover and reach a paved road that penetrates into a housing development known as The Preserve, then bear left to pick up the trail on the other side. Head up a set of 4x4 posts laid into the ground as stairs, then walk back into the forest.

As you encounter a rutted path that crosses the trail, the bouldering area spreads out just below you. Go straight and walk down into an amazing landscape of house-sized rocks. The sloping boulder-covered hillside that leads down to a ravine, carved by Hurricane Branch, is divided into three areas: Ozzy (straight ahead), Lost Roof (off to the left), and Grass Man (to your right). To download a schematic of the boulder fields, complete with a listing of named and unnamed climbing routes, visit www.drtopo.com/alabama/shades.pdf.

Follow the trail down into the Ozzy Area, which is comprised of a long boulder wall and a nearly circular collection of giant sandstone blocks. Bear around right and downhill, following the trail with the 30-foot-high boulder wall on your right. Roughly 50 feet long, the wall ends with two large tulip poplars guarding the perimeter. Here, now heading into the Grass Man area, bear left and continue downhill, twisting to a T in the trail. At the T, bear left and continue down and northwest, passing small boulders on your left.

At the bottom of the ravine, cross small, clear Hurricane Branch, which flows from left to right. The water is cool, about a foot deep in places, and is home to a few darting minnows. Rock-hop across and climb up the slope. The trail will shortly lead you to a long, sloping waterfall that a mountain biker I met along the trail called "magical." It's definitely a pleasant surprise to discover such a scenic spot in the middle of the 'burbs.

To return to the parking area, retrace your path through the boulder fields. There are several trails that lead through the rocks, so you may wind up taking a slightly different route back to the top of the slope.

NEARBY ACTIVITIES

For a less-wild urban walk, visit the manicured grounds of Aldridge Gardens (p. 9).

NOCCALULA FALLS HISTORIC GORGE TRAIL

KEY AT-A-GLANCE INFORMATION

LENGTH: 1.4 miles

CONFIGURATION: Loop

DIFFICULTY: Difficult (due to rough trail surface and creek crossing)

SCENERY: Noccalula Falls, sandstone bluffs, Black Creek, historic sites

EXPOSURE: Mostly shaded

TRAFFIC: Moderate around falls, light beyond falls

TRAIL SURFACE: Very rocky dirt path

HIKING TIME: 2 hours

ACCESS: 8 a.m–10 p.m., daily; $2 park entrance fee for adults, $2 for children, includes admission to Pioneer Village

MAPS: Map, historic guide brochure available at entrance to Pioneer Village

FACILITIES: Rest rooms, water, vending, snacks, phone, picnic tables, covered pavilions (rented by the hour)

SPECIAL COMMENTS: This trail is rough (overgrown and hard to follow at times); you will have to wade across Black Creek to complete the loop.

IN BRIEF

Enjoy a cool, misty view of 90-foot Noccalula Falls from behind its falling curtain of water and then loop through a rugged, wooded gorge passing numerous historic sites.

DESCRIPTION

Once across the bridge, bear right and follow the metal fence as it traces the bluff edge. Below and to your right is Black Creek gorge and the spectacular sight of Noccalula Falls as it plunges into a large, dark pool. A bronze statue of the falls' namesake stands here at bluff's edge.

According to legend, a young American Indian princess could not abide her father's desire for her to marry a man of his choosing. Instead, as the wedding ceremony was being prepared, she leapt to her death from the spot marked by the statue. No one knows if the legend is true, but there is historical evidence to support the story, including Native American rock art found near the spot where the princess is thought to have fallen.

There are two distinct experiences you can have at this City of Gadsden park. You can admire the beauty of the falls from a distance, wander the nicely landscaped grounds, tour the Pioneer Village, or even attend a wedding—they are popular here. Or you can come here gritting your teeth for a rough-and-tumble hike down in the gorge. If you want to do both, I suggest that you take care of

DIRECTIONS

From the intersection of I-59 North and I-459, drive 45 miles up I-59 toward Gadsden and take Exit 183. Go to the second traffic light and turn right onto US 431 South/US 278 East. Drive 3.8 miles and turn left on AL 211 North. Drive 1.7 miles and turn left into the Noccalula Falls parking area (past Jack's). Park and walk toward the arched bridge that spans Black Creek.

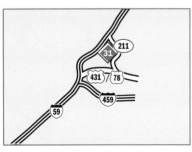

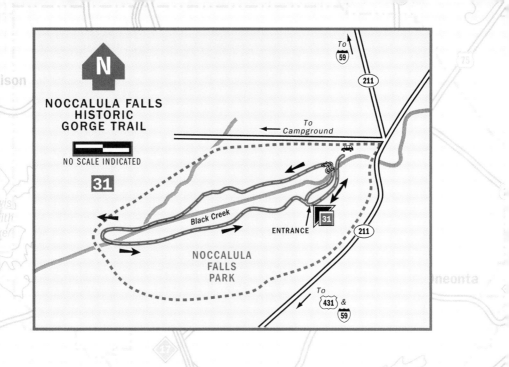

NOCCALULA FALLS HISTORIC GORGE TRAIL

NO SCALE INDICATED

31

Black Creek

ENTRANCE

31

NOCCALULA FALLS PARK

To Campground

To 59

211

211

To 431 & 59

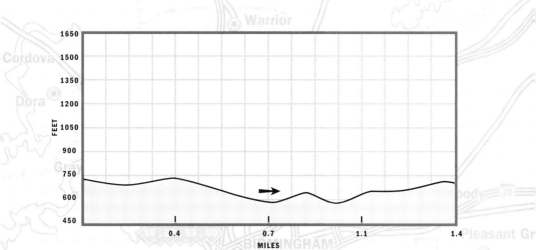

the civilized activities before you descend into the gorge. Because when you come out, you'll be sweaty, wet, maybe dirty, and very tired.

Continuing beyond the statue, pass beneath the crown of a hollow tulip poplar that rises more than 100 feet from the gorge floor. Follow the fence to the entrance booth, where you'll pay a fee and pick up an interpretive brochure that describes various points of interest you'll encounter on the trail. Many of the numbered posts, though, are missing or obscured, so you won't be able to find all of the sights.

Immediately bear right; reach the gorge bottom via two long flights of steep, metal stairs. The falls have long been an attraction, and some form of stairs has led down to them since the 1870s. Once in the humid still valley, walk toward the roaring falls (unless it's a hot, dry summer when the falls may slack to a trickle), following along an ancient rock face leaning out over the trail on your right. The higher rock layers are sandstone; the lower layers are a softer shale.

You'll find an abundance of oak-leaf hydrangea, moss-covered rocks, a number of side trails that scatter toward the creek, and lots of stones and boulders. At the trail split, bear right, heading uphill on a surface that can be wet and slick. Along the way, watch carefully for faded blue blazes on trees and rocks that mark the trail.

As you approach the falls, the roar multiplies. Walk carefully into the vast, open, sloping room that has formed behind the falls. The entire area is wet and supports a variety of mosses. There is no distinct path behind the falls, so you'll have to pick your way across a jumble of slick shale blocks that have peeled from the roof above. When you are directly behind the falls, you'll be an unnerving 100 feet away from the plunge pool inside a tremendous cavelike overhang. Viewed from here, the water thunders down from above and creates a mild pummeling breeze.

Emerge from the falls overhang, and at a trail fork, go up and to the right. Look for American holly, chinkapin oak, sweetgum, chestnut oak, large pines, and pignut hickory, many draped in the hairy vines of old-growth poison ivy. You may see a stray duck or two resting on the trail as well. Passing among apartment-complex-size boulders on a path choked with oak-leaf hydrangea, you'll have any number of opportunities to leave the main trail and explore. Just be careful, especially near the creek. There have been tragic drownings.

Push by a stand of mountain laurel and look for a cave-like hollow up in the rock face to your right, where in the extremely humid, wet environment, pockets of fern thrive. Go left at a T in the trail. According to the trail brochure, pot shards, flint chips, and other artifacts were found near trail marker 14 marking this as a temporary shelter for Native Americans passing through the gorge.

Just after the overhang you'll encounter a variety of "invasive" (non-native) plants, including Russian olive, privet, mimosa, and wild blackberry. Half a mile into the trail, the path reaches down to the Black Creek and then bears right. Here, the creek is about 30 feet across and 3- to 4-feet deep, with a sandy bank along the shore. With cicadas buzzing in the trees, reach a manmade channel. The channel was dug in the late nineteenth century to reach the coal that lies below the surface here.

Go around the channel to the right and, where the trail splits, go left. Follow along the creek as it deepens and takes on a dirty, chocolate brown color. Look just ahead for the remnants of an old dam, which still manages to hold back the water.

Cross Cascade Creek on stones before the feeder stream enters Black Creek from the right. Then, Black Creek begins to choke down and forms chutes as it flows among large boulders. Just before you reach Poor Man's Squeeze, a narrow ledge that you must circumvent to continue forward, look across the creek and see an old concrete structure. This bunker-like building was a pump house that supplied water to a nearby cotton mill.

Just before you would otherwise be forced to mount Poor Man's Squeeze, you cross the creek and resume the trail on the other side. There is no bridge or easy way to rock-hop across. But at the point in front of Poor Man's Squeeze, you'll be able to step down into the water and wade to the far bank. The water's not too cold and is generally about knee-deep for an adult. The rocky bottom is a bit slippery. Be cautious here. If the creek is swollen, don't cross. Just go back the way you came in and then hike back to the pump house from the other side. In case you're curious, there are trails beyond Poor Man's Squeeze (I followed them for about a mile), but I would suggest sticking with the official trail to avoid potential trespassing.

Look across the creek and you'll see a mid-stream boulder with a large rusty bolt sticking out. A bridge used to cross here, part of the Old Woodliffe Road. Known as Chalybeate Springs, the area was a large park in the 1930s that drew tourists seeking the healing spring waters. Unless you brought a spare pair of wading sneakers for the occasion, I would suggest that you leave your hiking boots on to ford the creek.

Once across, bear left and pass the pump house, heading east. Between here and the exit to the top, the trail is often hard to follow. Be sure and look carefully for blue blazes to stay on track. This side of the gorge is both rocky and brushy and contains tangles of mountain laurel and devil wood. Numerous trees across the trail will slow you down as well. You'll encounter short, steep sections and walk beneath impressive rock overhangs that lean out over the trail.

When you reach 4x4s placed into the trail, step up to a wider path (Old Woodliffe Road) and go left. Going right will take you on an alternate path back to the creek crossing. After some welcome level walking, begin to see the falls through the trees. Soon the trail comes full circle, and you'll reach the stairs on your right. Take them up and retrace your path back to the parking lot, a tired and sweaty hiker with wet feet—it's worth the trouble, though.

▶ NEARBY ACTIVITIES

Visit the park's various attractions, which include a petting zoo ($1 admission), a train ride around the park ($1–1.50), a large playground, a miniature-golf course, and the botanical gardens with over 25,000 azaleas. Call (256) 549-4663 for park information or (256) 543-7412 for campground information ($15–20 per night). The $2 fee you pay to access the trail also gains you admission to Pioneer Village. The collection of hand-hewn log buildings reflects the simple but hard life of the early settlers to this area. The easiest way to satisfy your hunger while at the park is to bring a picnic lunch. There is also a Jack's near the park entrance.

NUBBIN CREEK LOOP

KEY AT-A-GLANCE INFORMATION

LENGTH: 7 miles

CONFIGURATION: Balloon

DIFFICULTY: Difficult

SCENERY: Small waterfalls, ridge-line views, boulder gardens

EXPOSURE: Mostly shaded

TRAFFIC: Very light in cold weather; Boy Scouts in warmer weather

TRAIL SURFACE: Dirt, rocks, roots

HIKING TIME: 4 hours

ACCESS: Open year-round

MAPS: FS Pinhoti Trail Map 4 (The map will read "1" on the front but that's a typo. The real Map 1 is brown; Map 4 is purple) both available in country store

FACILITIES: None at trailhead; rest rooms, country store, and restaurant at nearby Cheaha State Park

SPECIAL COMMENTS: The Pinhoti portion of the trail is very rocky.

IN BRIEF

This rugged hike features portions of three Cheaha Wilderness trails: Nubbin Creek Trail, the Pinhoti Trail, and the Odum Trail. The path often travels across and through quartzite boulder fields, making it hard on the feet, but the views, especially from the Pinhoti portion, are sweeping.

DESCRIPTION

Walk about 50 feet along the Nubbin Creek Trail to find the trailhead map board and registration box on your left. Take a moment and fill out the information card and drop it in the box. If you come up missing, this is the first place rescuers will look (assuming you told someone where you were going).

Initially, the trail is easy as it passes through a mixed hardwood forest. Blue blazes infrequently painted on trees mark the way. Hike through a

DIRECTIONS

Take I-20 East from Birmingham for 55 miles to Exit 191. Bear right onto US 431 South. Follow the signs to Cheaha State Park. Drive 2 miles and turn right onto CR 131. In half a mile, turn left onto AL 281 South, the Talladega Scenic Drive. Drive 8.8 miles to CR 49 and turn left. (There are two scenic overlooks on the way up, both on the right: at 1.5 miles and 6.5 miles from the intersection of CR 131 and US 281.) Drive 3.4 miles and head right at a Y-intersection. Union D. Baptist Church will be on your right, a cemetery to your left. The road gradually goes from blacktop to rough pavement to dirt. Stay on the main road (do not turn left or right where the road curves). Watch for the Nubbin Creek Trailhead sign on the right. Turn in and park. Facing the road, the trail will be visible on your left.

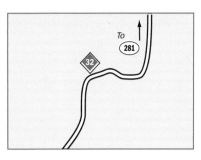

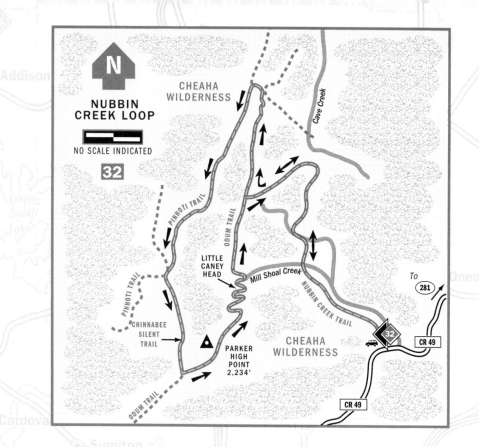

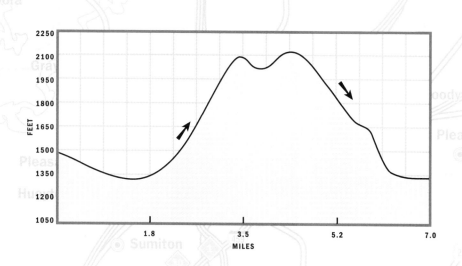

patch of small pines on the right and look for ferns growing along the trail's edge. Pass through a brushy area with many downed pines that have been snapped off near the base of their trunks. Pine beetles are epidemic in this area, weakening trees before finally killing them. The ground here slopes down from left to right, as Mill Shoal Creek rushes unseen below on its way to meet up with Nubbin Creek. A steep, narrow trail off to the right leads down to the water. Continue along the main trail, heading roughly northwest.

Approach the first creek crossing (Mill Shoal) and admire some small waterfalls as you step across the eight-foot-wide stream on stones. The trail then hooks left, gently ascending with the creek to your left. Next, cross a tiny stream running left to right that feeds into Mill Shoal Creek. Here look for the oddly lobed leaves of the mulberry tree (and in May or June, the tree's sweet fruit, which resembles an elongated blackberry).

Ascend through a lightly forested area and pass a triple-trunked oak on your left. Cross one dry streambed, then another. The trail continues and crosses another dry drainage, passing over stones in the trail. Cross a small ridge and begin to descend into a shallow valley. A very noisy creek runs down to your right. Shortly, reach this unnamed creek, which flows to Mill Shoal Creek. On your left will be some very scenic, small cascades above the cold, clear water that pools to a depth of two feet. Step across on stones and ascend on the other side.

The trail heads roughly northeast, with the ground dropping away to the right. Cross the faint remains of an old logging road. You may have to cross several downed trees at this point, where your first views of nearby hills and ridges appear to the east. From here the creek below is audible, competing with the sound of wind in the trees.

Come alongside another small creek, walking against its flow. The trail abruptly turns right and crosses the stream. After crossing, turn back to your right, heading north. The creek veers away to the right, out you will come alongside yet another stream. Walk against the flow of this six-foot-wide stream, swing toward it, cross it, and turn right.

While the trail meanders, heading north/northeast, pass through an area strewn with rocks and small boulders. Walk along a stretch of trail with very small pines (five to six feet) growing at the trail's edge, and pass through to a level stretch of trail. At a large pine, the trail bears sharply left, heading southwest as it gently ascends between two small ridges about 1,000 feet apart. Even in cool weather, you should be in a nice lathery sweat by now.

The breeze will pick up slightly as you ascend through this mixed forest thinly populated with hardwoods. The slope begins to shift through here, heading up to the right and down to the left. Up above, a ridge line is visible as the trail heads due west. Listen for a creek down to the left as you walk along relatively flat terrain.

As you near the end of Nubbin Creek Trail, approach a signboard that indicates directions to the Odum Trail, Cave Creek Trail, Pinhoti Trail, and Cheaha State Park. Turn right to follow the connector trail due north to the Pinhoti Trail. The trail may be hidden beneath leaves here, so look carefully. You'll also notice that this portion of the trail is not blazed.

Pass two large boulders and walk through a small rock garden. Cross a couple of large downed trees and then a foot-wide stream flowing left to right. Continue north up a steady slope, then jog downhill where you'll straddle a very large tree that blocks the trail.

It's curious that if you hike this trail in October, you'll most likely run through spider web after spider web. Every 50 feet, another juicy brown spider about as big as the end of your thumb has stretched its web across the trail. But by November, the webs are gone until warmer weather returns.

Slowly ascend as the trail crosses the pined slope at a shallow angle. At the next signed intersection (showing the direction to Nubbin Creek Road and Cheaha State Park), turn left, following the red blazes to the Pinhoti Trail. Walk beneath a tree that lies across the trail, then arrive on top of the main ridge amid large limestone boulders covered with rock paper and moss. Pass a fire ring and camping spot amid the rocks. I'm not sure why anyone would want to camp here. There's no water, the wind is cold at night, and the ground is rocky.

Now at an altitude of 2,200 feet, look west into the wide valley as you continue north down the descending trail. Come to an area with three signposts, two of which are standing. Looking over the valley below, turn left onto the Pinhoti Trail. On this trail section, watch for metal, diamond-shaped markers of the Pinhoti as well as blue blazes, though these markers are visible fairly infrequently. The trail here runs roughly south along the ridge, with the picturesque valley down and away to your right. Be prepared for a lot of boulder hopping.

The trail tames briefly, but then resumes its rocky nature. Drop down a bit, with a 20-foot-high rock face to your left, and look for this hike's best scenic viewing spot atop large rocks that jut out beyond the ridge edge. Be very, very careful if you decide to take in the unobstructed view. The green (in summer) valley below spreads out north and south and extends west for miles.

Back on the trail, continue hiking south on a stony path, blocks of layered and fractured sedimentary rock. Pass a few scrub pines clinging to the rock edge and notice your first blue blaze in quite awhile. Encounter several house-sized boulders on the left. More rock hopping follows, followed by even more rock hopping, which may jar your boots loose and necessitate a re-lacing.

The down-slope to the right eases up as the land below begins to rise to meet you. As the trail flattens out, be careful not to lose the trail, especially in winter after the leaves have fallen. Pass a double-trunked oak to your right; the trunk forks about seven feet up.

After a fire ring appears on your left, walk through an area of small- to medium-sized pines. Emerge into an open, flat camping area, with fire rings both to the right and left, then approach a signpost. The Pinhoti continues straight ahead, but turn left onto the Odum Trail, which may be difficult to find at first. As you continue roughly south, the trail will become more obvious. Start climbing on the rooty dirt path; you'll notice a very faint yellow blaze on a pine tree to your right. Follow the Odum Trail's yellow blazes, which will take you to the next junction.

Reach an area of pleasant, level woodland walking. You may be lucky enough to see a wild turkey or a white-tailed deer through here. Where the trail slowly bends its way around to the left, an area of many downed trees will appear.

An easy, level area of walking ensues. After an area of young pines off to the left, reach a tangle of downed trees and large boulders that you will have to snake through.

Eventually, the trail begins to ascend as you approach a limestone outcropping where two signs are located. The Odum Trail continues right, and the Nubbin Creek Trail goes left (north) and back to this hike's trailhead. From this point, it is 4 miles to the parking area.

Look for a blue blaze, on a tree to trail-left, which will lead you back to the balloon string. Hike among large boulders with a view over the ridge to the southeast. Pass a large pile of rocks to the left and watch for a double blue-blaze, which indicates a tricky turn. Turn back sharply left. On the map, this portion of the trail appears wavy, like a couple of Ss stacked one atop the other. Weave back and forth, reaching a memorial consisting of a small wooden cross.

The trail then wanders, descending gently as the slope now drops down to the left. Enjoy some pleasant woodsy walking on a clearly-defined path, passing among pines and hardwoods. A fire ring and campsite will appear on the right.

Cross Mill Shoal Creek on stones, then ascend the ridge at a slant as the land now slopes down to the right. Hiking on level ground, watch on trail-left for a small, capped pipe in the ground. This is a USGS Land Survey marker. Beyond the marker, blazes are sparse and many downed trees cross the trail. A ridge soon looms in front of you as the trail drops down into a thicket. Pass a double-trunked oak and then some small hickory trees.

The loop portion of the hike ends just beyond here, and the Nubbin Creek Trail turns right and leads back to the parking lot. It's still 2 miles away, but the walk is all downhill and very scenic. Near the end of the return you'll reach a Y-intersection that you may not have noticed on the way in. Go right.

▶ NEARBY ACTIVITIES

From CR 49, turn left onto AL 281 and drive a couple of miles to the Cheaha State Park. The country store is stocked with snacks, energy drinks, basic camping supplies, Pinhoti Trail maps, and other sundries. It is open 8 a.m.–5 p.m. Up the hill from the store is the Cheaha State Park Lodge and Restaurant. The breakfast and lunch buffets here are tasty, and great views can be had from the window-side tables. For more information call (800) ALA-PARK or visit www.alapark.com.

The Talladega Superspeedway is visible from I-20. It seats 143,000 race fans and thousands more in the 215-acre infield. Attractions include the Talladega/Texaco Walk of Fame inside Davey Allison Memorial Park and the International Motorsports Hall of Fame; call (256) 362-RACE or visit www.talladegasuperspeedway.com for more information.

Get a bite to eat on the way back at one of many restaurants in Oxford or Anniston. If you want some catfish, hold on until Exit 162. Head off of I-20 onto US 78. The Ark is about half mile on the right. Call (205) 338-7420 for more information.

OAK HILL CEMETERY WALK

▶ IN BRIEF

Enjoy a fascinating walk through Birmingham's history, strolling around the city's first cemetery. Early Birmingham movers and shakers are buried here, including iron and steel magnates Henry F. DeBardeleben and Colonel James Withers Sloss, black community pioneer William R. Pettiford, and the first mayor of Birmingham, Robert E. Henley.

▶ DESCRIPTION

This walk begins at the Pioneer Memorial Building, an attractive, gray Indiana limestone, Tudorstyle structure. In addition to administrative space, the building houses a museum downstairs (in development) and contains the original chapel used for burial ceremonies at the cemetery. Founded in 1871 as City Cemetery, Oak Hill was deeded to the city of Birmingham in 1873. The National Register of Historical Places added Oak Hill to its roster in 1977.

The cemetery's interment records, dating back to 1873, are kept in the chapel. These handwritten records list the interred's name, age, cause of death, and physician. Some 1800s causes of death include teething, croup, pistol shot, poisoning, and railroad accidents. Other primary documents on file include personal records of those buried at Oak Hill and records of plot sales. To enhance your walk, you'll want to step inside and obtain a free interpretive cemetery map.

Although Oak Hill is still an active cemetery with an occasional burial, the few remaining plots

ⓘ KEY AT-A-GLANCE INFORMATION

LENGTH: 0.8 miles

CONFIGURATION: Loop

DIFFICULTY: Easy

SCENERY: Tombs and memorials of Birmingham pioneers; stately hardwoods and magnolias

EXPOSURE: Moderate shade

TRAFFIC: Light, busiest in spring

TRAIL SURFACE: Wide, paved path and grassy carriage lanes

HIKING TIME: 30 minutes to 1 hour, depending on linger factor

ACCESS: Gates open 8 a.m.–4:30 p.m., Monday–Friday

MAPS: Cemetery map available at the Pioneer Memorial Building (visible as you pass through the gates)

FACILITIES: None

SPECIAL COMMENTS: Contact Executive Director Stuart Oates at (205) 251-6532 for information on researching the cemetery interment records.

▶ DIRECTIONS

Oak Hill is located in the downtown area near the Civic Center, on the corner of 11th Avenue North and 19th Street North. Entrance to the cemetery is from 19th Street North. Pull in and park on the cemetery's paved roads near the office, pulling slightly to the side.

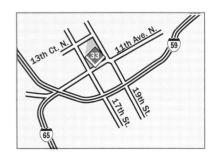

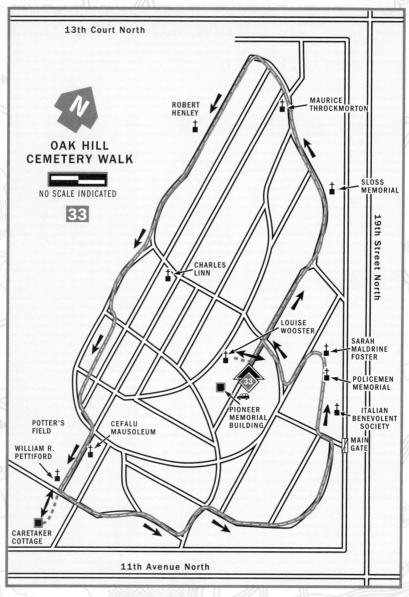

OAK HILL CEMETERY WALK

NO SCALE INDICATED

33

13th Court North

ROBERT HENLEY

MAURICE THROCKMORTON

SLOSS MEMORIAL

19th Street North

CHARLES LINN

LOUISE WOOSTER

SARAH MALDRINE FOSTER

PIONEER MEMORIAL BUILDING

POLICEMEN MEMORIAL

ITALIAN BENEVOLENT SOCIETY

POTTER'S FIELD

CEFALU MAUSOLEUM

WILLIAM R. PETTIFORD

MAIN GATE

CARETAKER COTTAGE

11th Avenue North

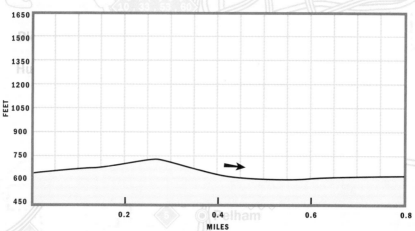

have been owned by local families for generations. A rather egalitarian final resting place from the cemetery's inception, all races and colors have been buried here. The interment records list numerous white physicians as having attended to black patients, long before the doors of legal segregation were closed.

A scenic, urban escape, Oak Hill attracts people from local businesses for a brown-bag lunch beneath the shade of towering red oaks. Others who frequent the cemetery are power walkers, joggers, people interested in genealogy, students, and artists.

There are a few rules of common-sense etiquette you should observe. While walking through the grounds, you should not step on the tombs, sit or climb on the walls, or litter.

To orient yourself, standing in front of the chapel, look to your south/southeast. On your left stands the Civic Center, and further left is the Social Security Administration building. Look to your right for a glimpse of Red Mountain in the distance.

This walk is taken along a counter-

Foster monument

clockwise circuit of the cemetery, so begin by bearing left and heading north. At once the eyes are drawn away from the ornate tombs and graves and up into the crowns of stately old trees such as magnolia, red oak, and live oak. In summer, crape myrtle adds a bright pink flair to the landscape. Closer to the ground you'll find lots of ornamental shrubbery.

At Block 10, bear to your left, following the smooth paved path. Across from the cemetery on your right is Author Shopes Park. Also off to your right is the historic Fountain Heights neighborhood.

To your right, inside the cemetery wall, is the Sloss memorial. A railroad man and iron maker, Colonel James Withers Sloss organized the Sloss Steel and Iron Company, an enterprise that defines Birmingham's industrial heritage to the present day. Directly across from Sloss is the grave of John Burford Sr. Burford has the distinction of being the only Revolutionary War veteran buried at Oak Hill. Also buried here are many Civil War veterans, including Union soldiers who settled in Birmingham after the war.

Continue and soon reach the plot of Birmingham Postmaster Maurice B. Throckmorton, located on the left. Throckmorton was accidentally shot and killed during one of Birmingham's more infamous nineteenth-century moments, the Hawes Riot of 1888. The riot began as an angry crowd descended on the Jefferson County Jail, where Richard Hawes was being held on charges that he murdered his wife and two daughters.

Walking uphill to the northwest, look for a 60-foot magnolia tree on your right, along with Block 33. Due to their damaging roots and large amount of leaf litter, planting of magnolias at Oak Hill was banned in 1906. The grounds are bird friendly, and you will see and hear robins, cardinals, and even hawks on the lookout for a meal of squab. At the top of the slope reach Block 27 on your right and bear left, heading south. The large cedar of Lebanon on the right marks the interment of Robert Henley, who was appointed as the first mayor of Birmingham in 1871.

After passing Block 9 on your left, reach Block 15 on your right. Here, turn left and walk downhill about 30 feet. Turn right, leave the paved walk, and walk onto a wide, grassy carriage way. Heading south, soon approach a knoll overlooking Potter's Field, where hundreds of bodies lie buried. Reserved for the poor and used for victims of the cholera outbreak of 1873, the graves of Potter's Field are unmarked. Mary Hawes and her two daughters, whose murders sparked the Hawes Riots of 1888, are buried here. They are thought to be near a small ornamental tree that lies near, but is not associated with, a headstone that reads "Mom Rest in Peace."

When you see the Cefalu Mausoleum built by Rosario Cefalu, turn right onto the paved path and head south toward the cemetery's maintenance shed, which sits near a five-room caretaker's cottage (1880s) that is no longer in use. There are plans to refurbish the cottage into a visitor center or museum.

Facing the cottage, turn back and walk toward the African-American section of the cemetery. At a Y in the path, the section to your left contains the graves of African-American pioneers, including William R. Pettiford and Arthur H. Parker. Pettiford founded the Alabama Penny Savings Bank. Parker High School is named after Arthur H. Parker.

Walking east/northeast, with the Civic Center straight ahead in the distance, bear back to the left. The path twists and turns, but stick to the outer perimeter, soon coming to Block 3 on your left. Bending left, follow the contour of 11th Avenue, which runs to your right. Two mausoleums will appear. To your left is the George Westbrook family mausoleum. Made of hewn stone, it is the largest mausoleum at Oak Hill. A smaller mausoleum, built by Dr. Malvern Due is on the right.

When you reach the main entrance road, with the main gate to your right, bear left. To your right will be the Italian section of Oak Hill. Begun by an association of Italian grocers, the Italian Benevolent Society established this part of Oak Hill for Italian immigrants, many who died in Birmingham without family.

Walking northwest, approach a monument to the first two Birmingham police officers to die in the line of duty. Beyond that is the most photographed monument at Oak Hill, an angel holding a cross, which marks the grave of Sarah Maldrine Foster. At the Foster memorial bear left, walking carefully in the grass toward the chapel.

To end your Oak Hill expedition, visit the burial site of Birmingham's Grand Madam Louise Wooster. A larger-than-life character who supposedly was a lover to John Wilkes Booth, she is thought to have served as the model for the madam depicted in Margaret Mitchell's *Gone with the Wind*. Although she may have indulged in the sinful arts, Wooster did not flee the 1873 cholera epidemic as many wealthy residents did. Instead she converted her house of ill repute into a hospital where she helped the sick and the dying.

OAK MOUNTAIN HIKE AND BIKE

▶ IN BRIEF

This counterclockwise loop takes you on a tough, hilly walk through the heart of Oak Mountain State Park. But, don't expect to relax on the bike-ride portion, which takes you back to the North Trailhead along the northernmost ridge of Double Oak Mountain.

▶ DESCRIPTION

This hike/bike combo will test your mettle. Hiking and biking both rely on leg strength, but if you are primarily a hiker or primarily a biker, you'll find that the two activities sap different muscle groups. Together, you should have a thoroughly tired set of legs after this workout.

You'll be more comfortable and have more fun if you prepare for this hike/bike. Make sure you layer with a pair of padded bike shorts as the base. Since your legs will be pumping the entire distance, go for a pair of loose hiking shorts to

▶ DIRECTIONS

Take I-65 South to Exit 246 (US 119/Cahaba Valley Road). Turn right at the light onto US 119, then make a quick left at the first light onto State Park Road. Travel 2 miles to a 4-way stop. Turn left onto John Findlay Drive and soon enter the park. The Information Center will be on the right (with rest rooms and maps). Stop your car and pay the day-use fee at the entrance-gate kiosk, then continue along Findlay Drive for 2 miles. Turn right onto Terrace Drive, drive up the hill past the BMX track, and park in the large lot on the right (at the corner of Terrace Drive and Day Use Road). Locate the bike chaining bars, secure your bike, then return to the intersection of Terrace Drive and Findlay Drive. Turn right and drive 3.5 miles to the North Trailhead, which will be on your left. Park and cross Findlay to the trailhead cluster and access the Yellow Trail.

KEY AT-A-GLANCE INFORMATION

LENGTH: Hike, 5.5 miles; bike, 8.5 miles

CONFIGURATION: Loop

DIFFICULTY: Difficult

SCENERY: Lake Tranquility, hardwood forest mixed with pines, streams on hike portion; ridge views, sandstone boulder formations, and streams on bike portion

EXPOSURE: Minimal for both, although more exposed on bike portion

TRAFFIC: Light on the Yellow Trail, except near trailheads; Red Trail busy near North Trailhead

TRAIL SURFACE: Dirt forest path with rooty, rocky sections

HIKING TIME: Hike, 3 hours; bike, 1.5 hours

ACCESS: Park is open year-round; gate opens at 7 a.m. and closes at 6 p.m.; $2 per person to enter the park

MAPS: Oak Mountain State Park Trail System

FACILITIES: Portable toilet at North Trailhead parking lot; rest rooms, water, phone, vending, picnic tables, reservable pavilions available in the day-use area—call (205) 620-2524.

SPECIAL COMMENTS: This hike combines the Yellow hiking trail with the Red biking trail to form a 14-mile loop. Make sure you have a helmet; secure it to your bike or carry it as you hike.

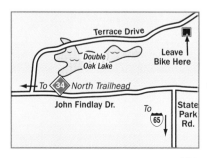

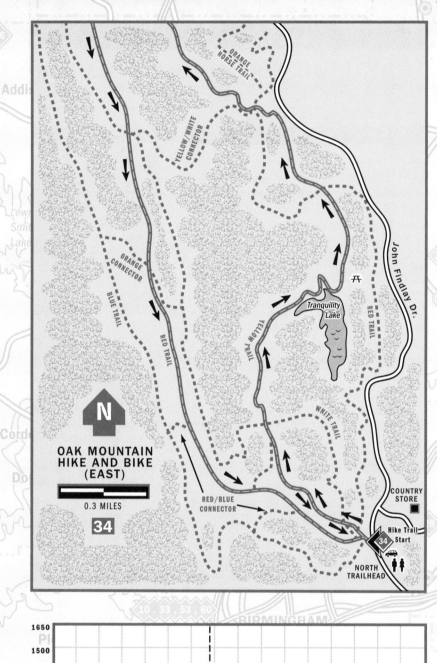

OAK MOUNTAIN HIKE AND BIKE (EAST)

0.3 MILES

34

ORANGE HORSE TRAIL

YELLOW/WHITE CONNECTOR

ORANGE CONNECTOR

BLUE TRAIL

RED TRAIL

YELLOW TRAIL

Tranquility Lake

RED TRAIL

John Findlay Dr.

WHITE TRAIL

RED/BLUE CONNECTOR

COUNTRY STORE

Hike Trail Start

NORTH TRAILHEAD

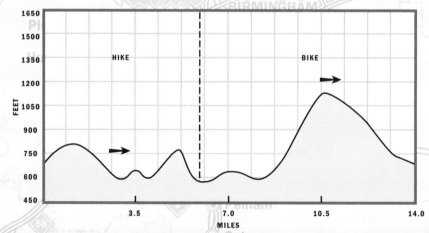

FEET		
1650		
1500		
1350	HIKE	BIKE
1200		
1050		
900		
750		
600		
450		

3.5 7.0 10.5 14.0
MILES

round out your lower body (unless it's really cold). Gauge the weather and layer your upper body accordingly; it's better to get hot and strip down than to get cold and stay cold. If it's below 50 degrees, I take a hat or a toboggan along. Shoes are a quandary if you're used to pedaling with cleats or special biking shoes. I keep it simple, though, and wear a pair of lightweight hiking boots for the hike and bike.

HIKE

I often hike alone, which has its merits. But nothing will make a walk in the woods more pleasant than the company of family or friends. For this little adventure my friend Kai, an exchange student from Germany, tagged along. As good-natured as they come, Kai was so quiet I often had to look back to make sure he was still there.

From the North Trailhead, walk in 100 feet and turn right onto the Yellow Trail at a sign that reads "Maggie's Glen 1.3 Miles." While this hike intersects and follows portions of other trails, you should remain on the Yellow Trail until you reach your bike. Cross over a creek onto a dirt trail laced with pebbles, roots, and rocks, and pause to admire this forest's initial offerings of maple, oak, and pine. After a short climb, meander easily, heading generally south.

Pass a patch of pine seedlings on trail-right and then climb higher into an area of young pines. The abundance of new pines is soon explained by a ridge segment of trail littered with dead ones, victims of the Southern pine beetle. Descend and, as the trail levels, the forest resumes a hardwood/pine mix. The next ascent emerges onto another level area with scattered decaying pines and only a few six- to eight-foot pine stumps. Amid this woody rubble, the trail appears to go both left and right; go right, stepping over and stooping under numerous downed trees.

Continue straight, winding downhill past living trees showing evidence of an old fire. Once down in the V-shaped ravine, small beech trees six to ten feet tall appear. In winter, look for the beech's distinct coppery leaves.

The path descends steeply into Maggie's Glen, about 1.3 miles into the hike. A peaceful area, the glen consists of four wooden benches and a covered information board. Use the bridge to cross over the six-foot-wide stream and bear right. Cross a feeder stream and begin to climb steadily uphill. The White Trail briefly joins this trail section, then heads left; continue straight on the Yellow Trail. As you continue southwest, crossing a couple of streams, the trail winds gently through hushed woods. You'll soon begin to curve right, gradually heading northwest on a course that will bring you to Lake Tranquility. Pass a brown sign with a "2" on it and a tent camping area on trail-right. Stay straight at a double-trunked oak and continue downhill.

Approach a small creek, then enter a wet area that is home to numerous, tall, beech trees. Some people carve initials into the smooth gray-white bark, but this ultimately harms the tree. Pass a fallen beech that is miraculously still growing, sideways. At a junction, follow the red arrows left and cross a footbridge.

Following the creek northwest toward Lake Tranquility, the trail rises above, then descends back to lake level before hanging a sharp left to acutely camber around a small slough. At the end of the slough, bear around right and look up over your left shoulder to see a few old unused cabins. The lake spreads out to your right, with a clear view across to a pavilion and Oak Mountain's newer cabin rental area.

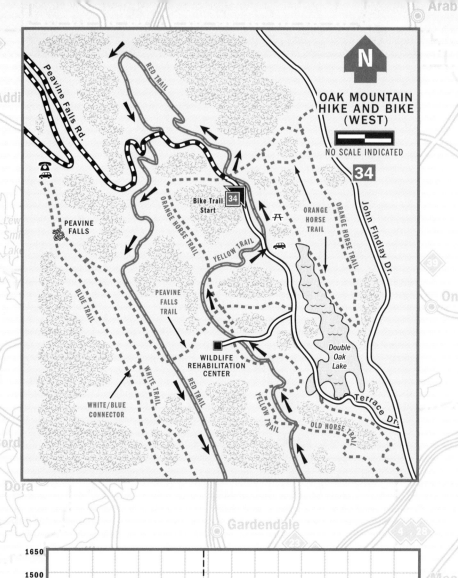

OAK MOUNTAIN
HIKE AND BIKE
(WEST)

NO SCALE INDICATED

34

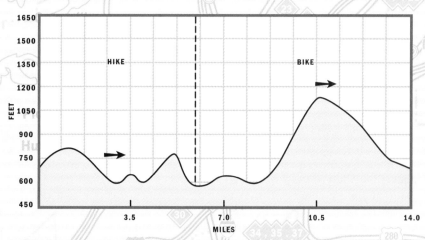

Continue along the lakeshore while getting closer to the dam, which was built by CCC volunteers between 1935 and 1941, along with a group camp and many other structures and trails. Use a short boardwalk to cross over the dam, while the rush of foaming water cascades beside you.

At the bottom of the dam, the trail travels left, following the dam's outflow. Pass a dilapidated picnic table off to your right, cut off a bend in the stream, and soon return to the stream. Looking across the water, you'll see a day-use area complete with pavilions and picnic tables. Where the trail forks, stay right, passing a couple of yucca plants. Bear right across the stream on a footbridge; enter an open area and turn left. Heading due west, look for a yellow carsonite marker in the ground, pass a creek to your left, and enter a brushy area filled with scrub, grasses, yucca, and beech.

As you meander, now working your way south/southwest, cross a small creek and pass a scrubby area, accompanied by the sounds of frogs trilling and croaking in warmer months. Soon, cross another footbridge just prior to crossing the Red Trail. Stay straight on the Yellow Trail, cross a small stream, and take a steep uphill climb. At a double yellow blaze, bear around right, heading southwest. With a clear view up to your left of Double Oak Mountain's northern ridge looming in the distance, roll easily into an area of downed pines soon reaching a wide cleared area.

After a long pleasant walk, descend to meet the Red Trail again. Turn left and briefly join the Red Trail, cross a footbridge, and then turn right back onto the Yellow Trail in a flat area that heads south into the woods. After a long uphill climb, top a small knob with an old fire ring on your right.

By now, your legs have thoroughly warmed and your mind should be shifting into a nice forest-numb gear. From brief finger ridges to narrow V-shaped ravines, continue working south until you reach a tiny gap in an area of large chestnut oaks. Look for a double yellow blaze, turn left, then bear back around right and begin to climb at an angle to the hillside slope. Up on top of the next ridge, which is lined with pine, you can go left or right, but go right and take a long downhill walk into a flat valley floor that is home to numerous beeches.

At a large oak with a yellow blaze and a horseshoe marker, you can go either right or left. First, go left about 40 feet to see a pile of old rusted barrel hoops, evidence of an old moonshine operation. Backtrack and then go down to the right to stay on the Yellow Trail, heading roughly west. After crossing a small stream and then passing through a narrow valley, look for a creek on your left.

Be careful here; watch for a small white sign that reads "hand lead horses across stream." This is where the Yellow Trail crosses as well. If you miss this turn, you'll wind up at Double Oak Lake. Cross the creek, jog up, and follow the yellow blazes downhill toward another creek. Cross it and then pop up on the other side.

After a steep up and down, close in on a green water tank and a small brick outbuilding to your right. Exit the woods, feeling like Grizzly Adams, and cross a paved road (the Wildlife Rescue Center is up the steep road to your left). Back in the woods, begin a nice series of roller coaster hills and valleys. After a steep descent to a creek, bear around left, take a footbridge across the creek to stay on the Yellow Trail, soon reaching an intersection with the Peavine Trail.

Continue straight until the trail forks, then go right and follow yellow blazes up into a longleaf pine thicket. Bear left at a double yellow blaze and begin to pay closer attention to the trail. You may see riders on horseback through here, as the Yellow Trail occasionally shares a section with the orange- or horseshoe-symbol-blazed Horse Trail.

At the next horse trail sign, turn right and head downhill, roughly north. Look ahead for the yellow blazes, which are very faint through here. Soon, veer right and, where the two trails diverge, go right onto the Yellow Trail for a couple of seriously steep ascents and descents. At a double yellow blaze, walk down to a two-foot-wide creek, cross it, then go left and up a final steep uphill. After the last steep downhill, intersect Peavine Falls Road and go right to see the parking area where you left your bike.

BIKE

Before you retrieve your bike, you may want to powder your nose at the rest room or down a beverage from a drink machine here. You can fill your water bottle at the rest room, but be prepared to see flecks of unknown debris floating in it. Better yet, leave filled bottles on your bike or ride down and fill up at the visitor center.

After unlocking your bike, head the wrong way down the one-way road that circles the picnic area. The entrance to the Red Trail will be immediately on your left. The narrow, dirt, mountain-bike single-track roughly follows Peavine Falls Road for a short distance, then crosses it and dips back into the southern hardwood forest. If you're not experienced with trail riding, you'll want to keep a heads-up throughout this challenging ride. The trail is very rooty, snakes between handlebar-grabbing trailside trees, and seems to climb forever.

After crossing Peavine Falls Road, take a hard right across a wooden bridge. You'll have to pop onto this short, narrow span while keeping your balance. After you negotiate a curvy, climbing path replete with tricky switchbacks, enjoy a nice, long, winding downhill. Bear right onto the gravelly Peavine Falls Road, grind it out for about 0.2 miles, and then roll back into the woods on your left. Cross the road once more and engage your legs for a long, steep climb. Along the way up, you'll bunny-hop a log, cross two short wooden bridges, and traverse a stone slab in the ground. The trail then bends around right and takes on a very rocky section, complete with a stream flowing down a portion of the trail. Continue uphill, heading roughly east, and wind to the top of the northernmost Double Oak ridge to bear left onto a wide dirt road, which is the Red Trail.

The ensuing ridge ride is a small relief to your aching thighs, but the long, slight incline never lets you rest completely. When you approach a covered shelter on your left, you may want to take a break and enjoy the view of Double Oak Lake below.

The trail continues ascending as it passes a "3.5 miles to North Trailhead" sign. Soon, though, the trail levels and surprises you with a much-deserved descent, followed by an inevitable, but short, climb. Reach a trail split, with orange blazes to the left and red to the right, and follow the red blazes down a much wider dirt path. This fast downhill section is the icing on the cake, but moderate your speed when approaching folks walking the trail. The drop-off is fast as you curve down, passing a creek on your right and then left. Where the creek crosses the trail, it flows through U-shaped concrete culverts. Hitting one of these culverts at full throttle is a real thrill (a wet one usually). After plowing into and out of four successive culverts, the trail bears sharply left over a wooden bridge and then swings back around to right.

Zigzagging along the creek downhill, enjoy more culverts before you make one last short climb. See the North Trailhead area straight ahead, where you left your vehicle.

OAK MOUNTAIN LOOP

▶ IN BRIEF

Sandwiched between a huff-and-puff approach and an easy and flat walk through the woods, bag both ridges of Double Oak Mountain in this hypnotic, meandering hike.

▶ DESCRIPTION

On a cold, cloudy day in December, this hike that runs along both of Double Oak Mountain's ridges wore me out. The initial rolling ascent up the South Rim Trail (Blue Trail) to reach the southern ridge had me gasping for air. But the reward was a long meandering stroll along and just below Double Oak Mountain's two ridges. Running roughly southwest to northeast, the parallel ridges are separated by a narrow, rolling valley. Whereas the walk out along the ridge seemingly floats on a smooth track, the walk back traces the narrow, rocky backbone of Double Oak's northern ridge. When I finished this hike, I crawled stiffly into my little truck somewhat dazed and cold.

To begin, pass a metal gate and the North Trailhead signboard. Walk straight and take the Blue Trail on the left. Immediately start climbing through a steep hardwood forest, primarily of maple and oak but mixed with pine. Dotted with

▶ DIRECTIONS

Take I-65 South to Exit 246 (US 119/Cahaba Valley Road). Turn right at the light onto 119, then make a quick left at the first light onto State Park Road. Travel 2 miles to a four-way stop. Turn left onto John Findlay Drive and soon enter the park. The Information Center will be on the right (with rest rooms and maps). Stop your car, pay the day-use fee at the entrance-gate kiosk, then continue along Findlay Drive for 5.5 miles to the North Trailhead parking area, which will be on your left. Park and cross Findlay to the trailhead cluster.

KEY AT-A-GLANCE INFORMATION

LENGTH: 10 miles

CONFIGURATION: Loop

DIFFICULTY: Difficult (due to length)

SCENERY: Mixed hardwood/pine forest, ridge-line views, airplane wreckage, bubbling streams

EXPOSURE: Minimal

TRAFFIC: Light on outer reaches of trail, heavier closer to the trailhead

TRAIL SURFACE: Dirt woodland path with roots, rocks

HIKING TIME: 5 hours

ACCESS: Park is open year-round; gate opens at 7 a.m. and closes at 6 p.m.; $2 per person to enter the park

MAPS: Oak Mountain State Park Trail System

FACILITIES: Port-o-potty at North Trailhead parking lot, rest rooms, water, phone, vending, picnic tables, reservable pavilions available in the day-use area—call (205) 620-2524.

SPECIAL COMMENTS: This hike combines major portions of the Blue South Rim Trail and the White Shackleford Point Trail to make a 10-mile loop.

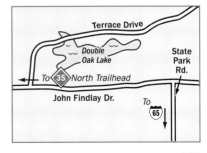

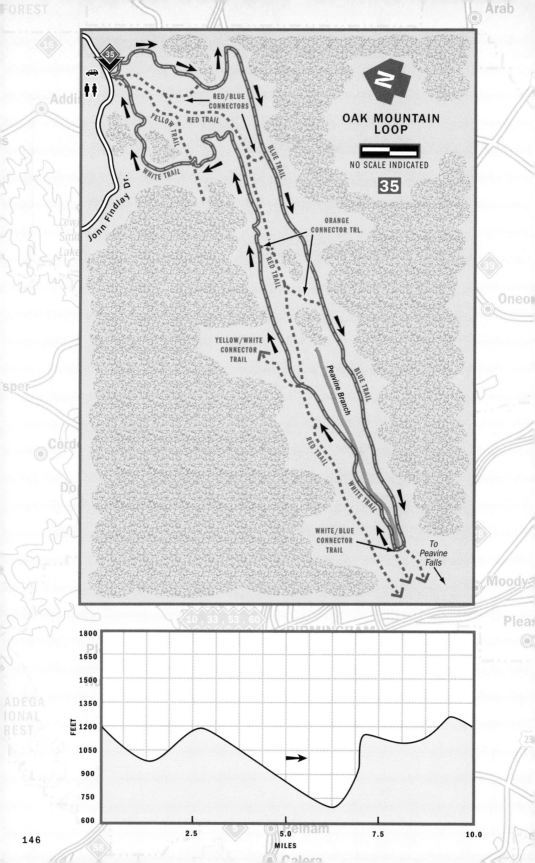

OAK MOUNTAIN
LOOP

NO SCALE INDICATED

35

RED/BLUE
CONNECTORS

YELLOW TRAIL

RED TRAIL

WHITE TRAIL

Jonn Findlay Dr.

BLUE TRAIL

ORANGE
CONNECTOR TRL.

RED TRAIL

YELLOW/WHITE
CONNECTOR
TRAIL

Peavine Branch

BLUE TRAIL

RED TRAIL

WHITE TRAIL

WHITE/BLUE
CONNECTOR
TRAIL

To
Peavine
Falls

FEET

1800
1650
1500
1350
1200
1050
900
750
600

2.5   5.0   7.5   10.0

MILES

ice-cream-scoop hills separated by V-shaped valleys, the trail will level briefly as it ascends in a southward direction, meandering up and over rises topped with pine. Pass by a double-trunked oak on your right and over stone and log work placed into the trail to control erosion. Traveling southwest, you'll repeatedly bob up and down (although more up than down as you gain elevation). Soon, cross a small stream that flows from left to right, pop up on the other side, and bear left onto a rocky section of trail. These woods are permeated by an intense quiet, broken in the fall only by the scuttling of robins through the leaves.

As you continue to gain altitude, the scattered rocks and boulders on the forest floor gain weight and the climb steepens. Pass some refrigerator-sized boulders, and continue up with a steep drop to your right. The trail will level here with more big boulders squeezing the trail. Look over your shoulder to the southwest to view a distinct but unnamed peak. You'll soon encounter a small trail that leaves left, but continue straight, enjoying a level walk in an area of pines that has a nice woodland feel.

The trail turns back to the northeast by a stream flowing in a ravine to your right. Take an easy uphill segment that leads to a final push to the ridge top. With the boulder-strewn ridge above you, plod up the very steep, rooty trail and follow (or grab onto) a cable encased in white PVC pipe. Ignore a path that goes to the left and bear right at a blue-blazed sign to begin a long ridge walk.

Heading southwest, pass through an area of pines, green lichen-stained boulders, and downed trees, into a clearing with an old campsite. With small pines popping up in light gaps left by the numerous downed trees, meander easily as the ridge narrows. Reach a Red/Blue Connector Trail sign and continue straight. If you think you need to bail, go ahead and turn right onto the connector, which will take you to the Red Trail. Bear right onto the Red Trail and follow it back to the trailhead.

Continue parallel to the ridge on your left, descend slightly, and look to your right for an aging airplane frame, which came to an untimely halt here many years ago. Look uphill to your left to the ridge 100 feet away where the plane must have first hit the ground. If you climb up to the ridge here, you may find smaller bits of wreckage as well as long views to the south, overlooking small lakes and farms. Back on the Blue Trail, continue a pleasant, meandering walk. If it's late fall or early winter, the shuffle and scrape of leaves against your hiking boots is hypnotizing.

Reach a sign that reads "3.2 miles Peavine Falls." A small trail that goes up to your left leads to a bouldering area. It was right about here that I saw a tangle of Mylar balloons trapped in the upper reaches of a tall oak. I've always wondered where those things float off to.

Soon the pace picks up as the trail begins to roll away from the ridge. Stride up onto a finger ridge as a small wooded valley develops between the trail and the ridge. Reach the first steep descent in a few miles, cross a small stream, and then pop up on other side. Where the trail forks, with blue blazes going right and left, head right and down to the northwest, with a stream to your right. At the bottom of this steep descent, approach Peavine Branch and cross it on a small footbridge made of 2x6-inch boards.

Look for a sign with white arrows and turn right onto the White Trail, which initially follows Peavine Branch. Peavine Branch is six feet across, clear, and about a foot deep. Head through a rocky, brushy area and then cut off a creek bend by following the trail to the left into a grassy forest meadow. After climbing to the top of a rocky ridge, look for a Yellow/White Connector Trail sign. Stay on the White Trail, which crosses the Red Trail. Head up through rocks, bear around right, and where the connector leaves sharply left, continue straight, heading north/northeast along the White Trail.

Walking along the narrow, rocky ridge, with broken views to the left, pass a trailer-sized boulder and five car-sized boulders. Accompanied by the dull thump of your shoes on the path and the hollow sound of rubber on stone, keep an eye out for the white blazes through this scrubby area.

Approach a cluster of trail signs, and continue on the White Trail past a "No Camping Reclamation Area" sign on trail-left. Known as Shackleford Point, you'll also find two Geodetic Survey markers here, but the Shackleford Point sign is missing. The most obvious marker is bronze and anchored in cement. You may have to poke around to find the other.

Having had a relatively easy time on the White Trail, get out your shoe brakes as you edge out onto the point of the ridge and descend steeply down a rocky section. After crossing a 2x4 step-down, the trail bears left. Keep an eye out for the white blazes. If you think you're off track, backtrack until you locate a white blaze and start over.

Where the ridge narrows to less than eight feet, you might want to supplement your shoe brakes with a pair of goat hooves. With a steep, rocky drop to your right, the trail jags left and down. Look for a vague white blaze on a tree, skirt around the tree left, and then continue north, zigzagging down the hillside. Switchbacking and rolling down, down, down, pass over 4x4s in the trail and by a sign cluster. Bear right with the white arrows, briefly joining the popular Yellow Trail, and descend into Maggie's Glen. Cross a small, energetic stream on a footbridge and enter the glen, which is home to four wooden benches, a sheltered map board, and a "No Camping This is a Reclamation Area" sign.

Be careful here. You'll see a sign, "White Trail," that points to the right. This sign, though, is for hikers coming from the opposite direction and is actually pointing them to cross the creek. You'll be tempted to turn right and follow the water upstream, but don't. Instead, after crossing the creek, turn left and follow the white blazes northwest, walking with the creek, which soon drops away on your left.

Pass a few small beeches and follow the white blazes through an area of pine-beetle-damaged trees. Cross over a tiny stream on a footbridge to spot a parallel trail off to your left. From here you can see Findlay Drive.

Approach an intersection, continue forward downhill, and cross another creek by footbridge. Turn left and arrive back at the parking area, a very tired yet satisfied human being. If you're lucky like I was, you may see deer feeding along the road as you drive out.

▶ NEARBY ACTIVITIES

Canoe and paddleboat rentals are available at Double Oak Lake Marina (on Terrace Drive) for $7–12 per hour. Someone 16 years old or older must be in each boat. Open seasonally in warm weather; call (205) 620-2524.

Take the kids to the park's Demonstration Farm on Findlay Drive. The farm features a wide variety of animals for petting and viewing, such as peacocks, goats, cows, horses, and chickens. Admission is free; call (205) 620-2526.

If you like to hit the little white ball, head over to the 18-hole golf course that abuts Findlay Drive. There are four sets of tees, a Pro Shop, and snack bar. Call (205) 620-2522 to reserve tee times.

The beach, located off of Terrace Drive behind Park Headquarters, is open year-round. It's crowded in the summer and deserted in the winter. Swimming is allowed during daylight hours and only in the roped areas. Dressing rooms, beach attendants, and a snack bar are seasonal.

The favorite off-trail activity at Oak Mountain seems to be the time-honored picnic. The primary area for picnicking is in the day-use area located along Terrace Drive. For large parties, a pavilion with tables, a roof, and grills can be reserved; call (205) 620-2524. Warm-weather weekends get crowded fast.

OAK MOUNTAIN:
LAKE TRANQUILITY LOOP

KEY AT-A-GLANCE INFORMATION

LENGTH: 7 miles

CONFIGURATION: Lopsided figure-8

DIFFICULTY: Moderate

SCENERY: Ridge views, mixed hardwood/pine forest, gurgling streams, stone dam, and Lake Tranquility

EXPOSURE: Minimal

TRAFFIC: Moderate in warm weather, light in cold weather

TRAIL SURFACE: Forested dirt path, rooty and rocky in places

HIKING TIME: 4 hours

ACCESS: Park is open year-round; gate opens at 7 a.m. and closes at 6 p.m.; $2 per person entry fee

MAPS: Oak Mountain State Park Trail System

FACILITIES: Portable toilet at North Trailhead parking lot; rest rooms, water, phone, vending, picnic tables, and reservable pavilions in the day-use area—call (205) 620-2524.

SPECIAL COMMENTS: This hike combines portions of the White Shackleford Point Trail, the Yellow Foothills Trail, and the Yellow/White Connector to form a 7-mile hike. The lake is called Old Lake on USGS topos.

IN BRIEF

Get over the tough part of this hike first with a steep climb up to the northern ridge of Double Oak Mountain. The reward will be a long walk along a narrow scenic ridge, topped with a shoreline tour of Oak Mountain State Park's lesser-known lake, Lake Tranquility.

DESCRIPTION

I hiked this trail in December on a cool, overcast day. Within the first 2 miles, I was sweating and had to stop and remove my jacket and my hat. Shortly, though, up on the windy ridge, I cooled quickly and re-donned my hat in a hurry. In summer, the sweating begins as soon as you step out of your vehicle. In either season, it's important to stay hydrated and not overheat or chill.

This is a beautiful hike that takes you through a variety of terrain. Steep ascents will have you huffing, but the long ridge walk and a long rolling downhill to Lake Tranquility will give you plenty of time to catch your breath. This hike is no cakewalk, but the strenuous elements are nicely spaced, making for an enjoyable outing.

Cross Findlay Drive and walk toward and past the trailhead gate and map board. A hundred

DIRECTIONS

Take I-65 South to Exit 246 (US 119/Cahaba Valley Road). Turn right at the light onto US 119, then make a quick left at the first light onto State Park Road. Travel 2 miles to a 4-way stop. Turn left onto John Findlay Drive and soon enter Oak Mountain State Park. The Information Center will be on the right (with rest rooms and maps). Stop your car and pay the day-use fee at the entrance-gate kiosk before continuing along Findlay Drive for 5.5 miles to the North Trailhead, which will be on your left. Park and cross Findlay to the trailhead cluster.

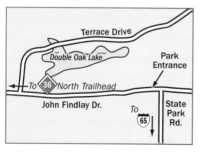

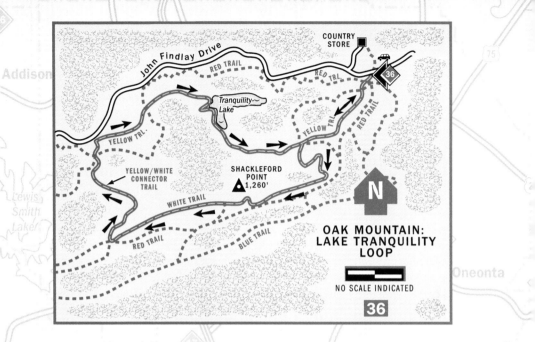

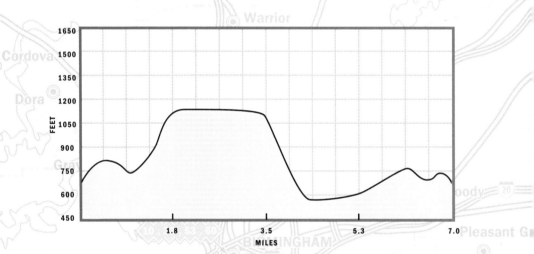

feet in, turn right onto the White Trail. A sign here with a yellow-and-white arrow reads, "Maggie's Glen 1.3 miles." After crossing a small creek the footpath is narrow, rooty, and rocky as it climbs south through a hardwood forest typified by chestnut oak, white oak, and black maple.

Reach a junction where the Yellow and White Trails split. Go left on the White Trail, which climbs and winds to the southwest. Approach a steep V-shaped valley on the right. On this hike, I was amazed to see a chipmunk run up a pine tree, although I could have mistaken the furry creature's identity. If it was a chipmunk, that's the first one I've ever seen climb a tree.

Take a deep breath and gear down for a short, steep ascent, as you head up and south into a chaotic, level area of pine. Many trees have been cut and removed, but many still remain where they fell. A glance at any of the downed trees reveals a litter of tiny bore holes, the calling card of the Southern pine beetle. However, in the light gaps created by the pine damage, many new and healthy looking pines are growing.

Pass through the damaged trees, descend south, then hike up and right when the trail forks. Drop down into hardwoods then back up into more pine-beetle-damaged pines. On a cleared ridge with many jagged six-foot pine stumps, at a small oak with a yellow blaze, skirt to the right around a large mass of tree debris to stay on the trail.

Keep forward as you occasionally duck under and hurdle over the downed trees. The trail bears back right, heading west. When I hiked this trail there were two signs reading "Area Closed Erosion Zone" and "Ground Under Repair," indicating hikers should not leave the trail.

After stepping over a few more downed trees, enter a mixed pine/hardwood forest where healthy pines are present. As you descend, coppery-leafed (winter), smooth-trunked beech trees dot the area. As you might expect given the water-loving beeches, you'll begin to hear a trickle off to the left. Begin a steep descent down a ridge to peaceful Maggie's Glen. A swift, little creek runs past the four benches and map board located here. The small creekside spot would be the perfect place for a picnic. A sign here notes, "No Camping, Reclamation Area."

Take the footbridge over the creek, cross a feeder stream, then head uphill as the feeder runs downhill to your left. At the next junction, bear left onto the marked White Trail and start an earnest steady climb southeast, cross a tiny stream on an increasingly rocky and steep trail.

The trail goes back left to the north/northeast and, passing through some car-sized boulders, turns back southeast. Look off to your left for a distinct tree-covered peak. This is where you will begin to circle around to the right and up onto a rocky ridge. While you're hiking straight up, heading southwest, be observant. You'll be tempted to pull left and stray onto the left side of the ridge. But don't do that or you'll get lost. Look for an old, gnarled pine on your right that has a very faint white blaze. Here, make a sharp right and walk up onto the ridgetop. Once on top, you'll be picking your way southwest with steep slopes on both your right and left. Pass an apartment complex of boulders on your left. You may want to scramble up to the left here and take in the nice view to the north.

After a few short, steep, rocky pitches, the trail levels out in an area with a few pines and lots of chestnut oak. As you descend, look for a glade of small stones on trail-left before the ridge makes a definite dip, then ascends to a higher ridge line, still running southwest.

Pass up through boulders, veer left, and step up a few 2x4s placed in the trail. Zigzag briefly as the slope peters out into a flat area atop the ridge. Arrive shortly at what's known as Shackleford Point, where you'll find two Geodetic Survey markers here. The most obvious is a bronze marker anchored in cement, but you may have to poke around to find the other. The walking through here is pleasant and fairly level, and you'll pass through a lot of tangled brush.

Pass a "No Camping, Reclamation Area" sign on your right to reach a trail fork with numerous signs. Bear right to stay on the White Trail as it meanders atop a narrow, flat ridge dotted with small, grassy meadows. The trail eases to the left side of the ridge and becomes a narrow rut at times. Walk through an area of large boulders on either side of the trail, then return to the ridge's center.

Soon the trail heads down to reach another signed junction. The White Trail continues straight, but bear right onto the Yellow/White Connector and drop down over the ridge edge. Descending north, the ridge you've been walking appears over your right shoulder. Meander steeply down, passing yellow-and-white blazes painted on trees and cross a tiny wet-weather stream that bubbles out of the slope on your right. The trail can get thin through here, especially under heavy leaf cover.

Reach, and pass through, a small cleft. A horse trail goes right, so stay straight on the connector as you walk north up and over a short rise. The trail veers sharply left, then begins an easy walk down a small finger ridge. The trail levels out, dips off the end of the ridge, then roller coasters back up. There will be water to the right and to the left, with lots of beeches growing here. Steeply descend and a stream to your left will flow with you, then cross in front of you, working its way to the other creek on your right. After a rain, this can be a mushy area.

Walking north/northwest, see ferns, beeches, pines, and oaks. You'll also see a footbridge off to the left, which leads to the Yellow Trail. You can also just keep straight, then very shortly emerge onto the Red Trail. Turn left onto the Red Trail (watch out for mountain bikes), cross a wide wooden bridge, and then turn right onto the Yellow Trail (there will be a yellow carsonite marker here). Head northeast, with a stream down to your right, and begin a brief climb.

The trail meanders west, and walking here is easy. Look for a small holly tree on trail-left and a double-trunk chestnut oak on trail-right. It was here, on my cold winter hike, that the sun managed to peek through the clouds for a few minutes. Immediately birds in the trees around me responded with bursts of song and the air seemed to warm instantly.

Still meandering, you'll soon head up and north through an area dominated by pines. Glide down a steep, smooth slope and reach a stream to your right with a feeder coming in from the left. Cross the feeder, then the Red Trail, then the six-foot-wide creek on a footbridge, and hike uphill. Climb at an angle to the slope, heading east as it levels, and the path begins to wind once again.

Soon turn back to the left, heading north, and walk through an area dominated by six- to ten-foot pines. Look for a stream to your left, flowing in a southwesterly direction. Come alongside the vigorous stream, which is about ten feet wide and two to three feet deep in places. Cross it on a footbridge and look upstream to see a dam of downed trees and debris that raises the water level behind it a good two feet.

Exit the bridge into a marshy area, heading north/northeast, and pass a very large, triple-trunk white oak. Here, the creek is on your right and the bank on the far side is very steep. The trail winds, heading east, and passes a large open field to your left. This is a day-use area that is accessed off of Findlay Drive. You'll see a pavilion, picnic tables, grills, and lots of open play area to toss a Frisbee.

Yellow blazes will head left, but go right toward the creek and a yellow carson-ite marker in the ground. With the pavilion on the left, follow the trail around the creek bank until you see a footbridge that spans the creek. After crossing, turn left and walk to the northeast, turn right onto a log-lined path, and soon see an old picnic table with a fire ring on your left. It was here, on my hike, that the warm sun retreated, causing the temperature to drop about 10 degrees in a short period.

A fenced-in area appears up on your right across the creek, a water treatment facility for the park. Ahead is a sign that reads "No Fishing," and just beyond that a small dam with water rushing down its outflow face. Walk toward the lake dam, which holds back the source of the creek you've been following.

You can walk out onto the dam, although a sign makes it clear that you should not. From the dam, Lake Tranquility spreads out in front of you. I haven't walked around the lake but I estimate that it's a couple of miles. Cross a boardwalk up and over the dam and snake along the lake's edge. You'll a see pavilion across the lake to your left and abandoned cabins ahead. Cross a stream that feeds into the lake and then bear back left and wind along with continuous views of the blue-green water.

Ascend up and south as the lake drops away on your left. Another lake feeder drains into the lake as you leave the lake and re-enter the woods. You'll pass a cabin that sits high atop a steep hill to your right, then cross a footbridge toward a giant beech on the other side.

The woodsy trail ascends to a fork, so stay right to remain on the Yellow Trail. Lots of beeches grow in this low, wet area. One stubborn beech that has fallen across the creek, continues to grow, sideways. Walk against this stream, five feet wide here, to meet the two streams that converge to form it. Head east through a gap and around left, following the stream. Look for a pile of old, rusted barrel hoops on the right. This is the site of an old moonshine still, one of many that operated in these hills not so long ago.

Gain the slope ahead, hiking away from the creek, before descending to rejoin it. Continuing down, cross the stream, cross another stream, and walk easily down and east through a solid hardwood forest.

When you reach the next junction of the Yellow and White trails, you'll know your journey is coming to a close. Go straight, cross another stream, then cross the footbridge into Maggies Glen. To reach the trailhead, go straight up the hill in front of you and follow the Yellow Trail out.

OAK MOUNTAIN:
PEAVINE FALLS COMBO

This strenuous loop packs plenty of steep punches on both ends, with lots of pleasant ridge-and-valley walking in between.

Heading straight up and into the forest, the Peavine Trail gets down to business right from the start, heading southeast into an area of pines and hardwoods, primarily hickory, oak, and maple. Look off to your left for the Tree Top Trail boardwalk and its outdoor raptor exhibits. The Peavine Trail continues to rise, then slopes down; the terrain resembles so many giant ice-cream scoops stacked together. Although there are brief respites of leveling, this trail continues to ascend steeply while heading roughly south.

Pass an orienteering post on trail-left labeled "No. 7" and continue a pattern of steep pitches broken by short, flat areas. When the climbing becomes easier and the trail begins to meander, look for a trail intersection. Bear right to the southwest, briefly following a horse trail, then

Take I-65 South to Exit 246 (US 119/Cahaba Valley Road). Turn right at the light onto US 119, then make a quick left at the first light onto State Park Road. Travel 2 miles to a four-way stop. Turn left onto John Findlay Drive and soon enter the park. The Information Center will be on the right (with rest rooms and maps). Stop your car, pay the day-use fee at the entrance-gate kiosk, and continue along Findlay Drive for 2 miles. Turn right onto Terrace Drive, drive up the hill 1 mile, and park on the right in one of the large paved lots. The Tree Top Trail will be visible across Terrace Drive. The string to this balloon hike is the Peavine Trail, which begins about 50 feet beyond the right of the Tree Top Trail.

KEY AT-A-GLANCE INFORMATION

LENGTH: 7 miles

CONFIGURATION: Balloon

DIFFICULTY: Moderate to difficult

SCENERY: Hardwood forest, Peavine Branch, Peavine Falls

EXPOSURE: Minimal

TRAFFIC: Light, except around Peavine Falls

TRAIL SURFACE: Woodland path, rooty and rocky in places

HIKING TIME: 4 hours

ACCESS: Park is open year-round; gate opens at 7 a.m. and closes at 6 p.m.; $2 per person to enter the park

MAPS: Oak Mountain State Park Trail System

FACILITIES: Port-o-potty at Peavine Falls parking lot, rest rooms, water, phone, vending, picnic tables, reservable pavilions available in the day-use area—call (205) 620-2524.

SPECIAL COMMENTS: This trail combines the Peavine Falls Trail (blazed green), with portions of the Shackleford Point Trail (white), the Yellow/White Connector, and the Yellow Trail.

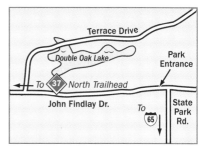

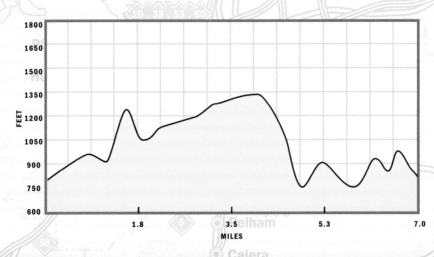

RED TRAIL

RED TRAIL

ORANGE TRAIL

RED TRAIL

PEAVINE
FALLS

YELLOW TRL.

To
Park
Entrance

PARK
OFFICE

37

Double
Oak
Lake

Terrace Dr.

John Findlay Dr.

WHITE/BLUE
CONNECTOR
TRAIL

GREEN TRL.
(PEAVINE TRL.)

WHITE TRAIL

BLUE TRAIL

RED TRAIL

YELLOW TRAIL

Peavine Branch

N

OAK MOUNTAIN:
PEAVINE FALLS COMBO

NO SCALE INDICATED

37

WHITE TRAIL

RED TRAIL

YELLOW/WHITE
CONNECTOR

MILES

FEET

1800
1650
1500
1350
1200
1050
900
750
600

1.8   3.5   5.3   7.0

turn back left and descend a steep hill to stay on the Peavine Trail, now heading east. On a weekday, the quiet through these woods is palpable.

When you reach a junction with the Yellow Trail, continue straight on the Peavine Trail as you roll through a pine thicket. Look up to see a long ridge ahead; you'll eventually reach the ridge, but for now stay in the small valley, where a breeze may pick up as you make your way through an area of sandstone and quartzite. Leave the pines to re-enter hardwood forest. The trail through here may be faint, especially under a blanket of winter leaves.

The trail becomes rockier, turns back sharply to the left, and begins to climb to the southeast. Step over six 4x4s and a couple of fenceposts placed in the trail. As the trail again thins a bit, watch for a sharp right turn. Switching back to the west, angle up to the ridge above, then switchback again.

Ascend through a very rocky area, then switchback left at a slingshot-trunk tree on your right, now heading south/southwest. After one more switchback, which will swing you back to the northeast, see a 20-foot rock wall ahead that runs north-south along the ridge. Emerge and turn right onto a wide dirt road (the Red Trail) on Double Oak Mountain. Walking southwest down the Red Trail, the rock wall fades into the slope on your right. When you see the Peavine Falls sign, turn left to regain the trail.

Ascend roughly south, hiking parallel to the Red Trail down below. The path flattens and transforms into a pleasant, meandering ridge top walk through groves of small, wiry trees that recall a Hobbit forest. At a car-sized boulder, the trail dips down to the right, then crosses over to the left side of the ridge. The trail forks briefly, then rejoins itself. Pass a small boulder garden on trail-left, continue straight, and pass through another boulder garden, this one tinted pale green with lichens.

Ignore the first side trail that leads down to the left. But after the trail forks and rejoins itself again in a ridge top meadow, another side trail goes down left to a minor overlook. Back on the Peavine Trail, continue your easy ridge top walk. The trail surroundings morph and blend gradually from scrub and cedar to a wide grassy area. Follow the trail as it bears right and descends steeply through a grove of young pines. The path soon widens, becoming gravelly, and traverses a small footbridge into the Peavine Falls parking lot.

Bear around left to the wide, dirt Peavine Falls Trail. There is a newer gravel path to the falls, the Peavine Falls Trail Project, located at the far end of the parking lot. This newer trail was created to ease the impact on the older Peavine Falls Trail, which has become worn and slick with use. You can take either route, but this description follows the blue blazes of the old trail.

The walk is an easy downhill stroll through a hardwood-pine forest. If you're lucky, you may glimpse a wild turkey through here on an uncrowded day. Pass large boulders to your left and step over numerous exposed roots in the trail. As opposing slopes squeeze the trail, reach a small stream on your right. Here, the newer access trail comes in on your right. With the sound of rushing water nearing, cross Peavine Branch on a wooden footbridge into a very rocky area.

Peavine Branch cuts through the rock here, drops into a chute, and then plunges over a 15-foot ledge to a pool below. From there, the creek continues flowing southeast. To see the falls, follow a path along the left side of the small canyon until the waterfall comes into view. The bottom is 100 feet straight down, so be very careful.

Retrace your steps, recross the footbridge, and turn right. Bypass a "trail closed" sign on a side trail to the left and continue straight ahead on a level path that roughly follows the creek. The trail you're now on is the white-blazed Shackleford Point Trail, or simply the White Trail.

Ascend gently, passing a carved beech and sun-stippled pools in the creek. The terrain is rocky here, nothing spectacular but with a peaceful air of great age—broken branches, downed trees, kind of like walking across the top of an old man's head.

Pass a footbridge on your right, which leads to the Blue Trail, but stay straight. After passing a tiny island in the stream, the trail veers left off to the north/northeast, away from the stream into a grassy area. The creek will reappear downhill to your right, about 100 feet away. The trail begins to roll varying its bearing from east to northeast. Where the path bears left back to the north, cross three 4x4s built into the trailbed and descend into a bucolic meadow. I was lucky to see three brilliantly colored bluebirds here.

Hike up through boulders, step onto the Red Trail, spot a Yellow/White Connector Trail sign, and turn onto the connector. Stay on the connector as it rises up and over the ridge to engage a downward slope, heading north/northwest. Following the yellow/white blazes on this very steep descent, you may have to hold yourself back occasionally by grabbing onto trailside trees.

Travel through another area of ice-cream scoops and gouges into a small valley. Stay with the yellow/white blazes and, at a double yellow/white blaze, make a sharp left. The trail will soon plunge down, passing, to your left, a stream, an old campsite, and a post labeled "4." The trail through here can get mushy in wet weather, and you may have to hop across a few downed trees.

When you see a footbridge off to the left, take it, and find yourself on the Yellow Trail heading southwest. The Yellow Trail is the park's roller-coaster trail, and its short, steep climbs and drops make thighs in need of a good burn sing with joy. To add to the mix, traverse narrow ridges, move through V-shaped valleys, and cross over a tiny gravel bald. Whether it was low blood sugar or the rustic setting, a very distinct feeling of isolation hit me along this segment. Continue through a bowl-like depression, where the trail thins a bit, and then skirt a tangle of trees. Come to a double yellow blaze and turn sharply to the left.

Where you reach a thick area of pines and a horse trail to your left, bear right to stay on the Yellow Trail. Take a steep downhill on pine needles to run into a set of three yellow markers. Be alert here and go right to stay on the trail. But to see a pile of old rusted barrel hoop bands and part of an old barrel, evidence of an old moonshine still, go straight a short distance then return to the Yellow Trail.

The trail soon encounters another tricky spot. You'll be able to see part of Double Oak Lake through the trees to your right. Step steeply down to your left, though, and cross a small creek. Then trudge up a steep slope to a tree painted with several yellow blazes and an orange horseshoe blaze. Take a sharp right, plunge down then up, and parallel a ridge on your right until you see a green water tank and a small utility building.

Cross a steep paved road (that leads up to the Wildlife Rescue Center) and quickly re-enter the woods. Although you're near a mostly downhill run on the Peavine Trail, the jagged landscape ahead looks like a piece of crumpled paper.

Heading south, you'll intersect the woodland portion of the Tree Top Trail. You can turn right here and follow the trail to the elevated boardwalk and its outdoor raptor enclosures, which will lead you out to the parking area. But if you want the full workout, don't stop yet. Bear left, cross a footbridge, and plunge up into yet another steep ascent. You'll almost have to lean into the hill as you climb.

Soon, though, the trail levels out, then drops down steeply into a small valley. After one more battle with gravity, emerge through a notch and find the Peavine Trail. Turn right and take the Peavine back to the parking area to conclude this excellent loop. (Just as a reminder, after you access the Peavine Trail, go right at the top of the first hill to return to your vehicle.)

▶ **NEARBY ACTIVITIES**

Canoe and paddleboat rentals are available at Double Oak Lake Marina (on Terrace Drive) for $7–12 per hour. Someone 16 years old or older must be in each boat. Open seasonally in warm weather; call (205) 620-2524.

Take the kids to the park's Demonstration Farm on Findlay Drive. The farm features a wide variety of animals for petting and viewing such as peacocks, goats, cows, horses, and chickens. Admission is free; call (205) 620-2526.

If you like to hit the little white ball, head over to the 18-hole golf course that abuts Findlay Drive. There are four sets of tees, a Pro Shop, and snack bar. Call (205) 620-2522 to reserve tee times.

The beach, located off of Terrace Drive behind Park Headquarters, is open year-round. It's crowded in the summer and deserted in the winter. Swimming is allowed during daylight hours and only in the roped areas. Dressing rooms, beach attendants, and a snack bar are seasonal.

OAK MOUNTAIN: TREE TOP (C. EARL STEPHENS) NATURE TRAIL

KEY AT-A-GLANCE INFORMATION

LENGTH: 1 mile

CONFIGURATION: Out-and-back

DIFFICULTY: Easy/moderate

SCENERY: Wild animal rehab exhibits, hardwood forest

EXPOSURE: Minimal

TRAFFIC: Boardwalk crowded on warm-weather weekends; trail to Wildlife Center less traveled; all parts of trail quiet during the week

TRAIL SURFACE: 750 feet of boardwalk, rocky, rooty forest trail

HIKING TIME: 1–2 hours to take in all the sights, including a tour of the Wildlife Center

ACCESS: Park is open year-round; gate opens at 7 a.m. and closes at 6 p.m.; $2 per person to enter the park.

MAPS: Alabama Wildlife Rehabilitation Center map (available at Wildlife Center); no trail detail for the Tree Top appears on the Oak Mountain Trail System map

FACILITIES: Rest rooms, water, phone, vending, picnic tables, reservable pavilions available in the day-use area—call (205) 620-2524.

SPECIAL COMMENTS: The initial boardwalk portion of the trail is easy and wheelchair traversable, but the trail up to the Wildlife Center is steep and rough.

IN BRIEF

Take a short hike and learn a long lesson about injured wildlife rehabilitation. The first part of the walk offers close-up views of birds of prey. Visit the Wildlife Center, where injured raccoons, opossums, and other animals are on the mend.

DESCRIPTION

The Alabama Wildlife Rehabilitation Center maintains a unique and mutually beneficial relationship with Oak Mountain State Park. The park provides the land and the main building free to the center. In exchange the center rescues, rehabilitates, and returns hundreds of wild animals back to their natural environments.

To begin the hike, cross Terrace Drive and step across a small footbridge. After walking up a series of steps, cross a small bubbling stream and continue climbing to reach the main boardwalk.

The first exhibit is one of six large, fenced enclosures that are home to the Wildlife Center's injured birds. Many of the birds, such as the barred owl in this exhibit, are permanently disabled. The

DIRECTIONS

Take I-65 South to Exit 246 (US 119/Cahaba Valley Road). Turn right at the light onto US 119, then make a quick left at the first light onto State Park Road. Travel 2 miles to a four-way stop. Turn left onto John Findlay Drive and soon enter the park. The Information Center will be on the right (with rest rooms and maps). Stop your car and pay the day-use fee at the entrance-gate kiosk, then continue along Findlay Drive for 2 miles. Turn right onto Terrace Drive, drive up the hill 1 mile, and park on the right in one of the large paved lots. The Tree Top Trail will be visible across Terrace Drive. For those in need of handicapped parking, a special parking area is located next to the trailhead.

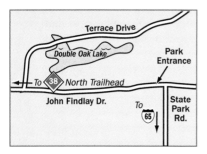

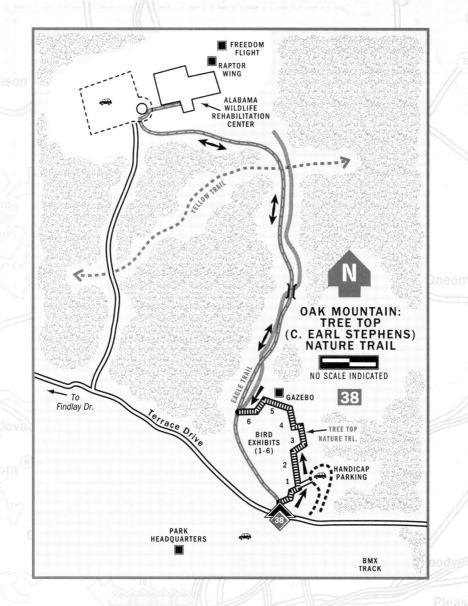

FREEDOM FLIGHT

RAPTOR WING

ALABAMA WILDLIFE REHABILITATION CENTER

YELLOW TRAIL

EAGLE TRAIL

To Findlay Dr.

Terrace Drive

N

OAK MOUNTAIN: TREE TOP (C. EARL STEPHENS) NATURE TRAIL

NO SCALE INDICATED

38

GAZEBO

6 5 4 3 2 1

BIRD EXHIBITS (1-6)

TREE TOP NATURE TRL.

HANDICAP PARKING

38

PARK HEADQUARTERS

BMX TRACK

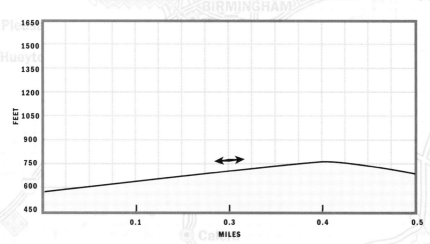

enclosures, which are attached to the boardwalk, are built high above the ground into the lower tree canopy, which includes white oak, pine, persimmon, and maple. If you come here during the spring, the red flower blossoms of blooming buckeye litter the forest floor.

Each enclosure, along with interpretive information about the injured birds, features a blind with small windows that visitors can peer through to view the birds. However, your best views are from the side, looking straight into the towering cages. Although the birds become somewhat accustomed to seeing a parade of onlookers, they still shy from loud noise and sudden movement.

An exhibit, like the second one (black vultures) on my visit, may be empty. Although some disabled birds will live out their lives here, many are rehabilitated and released. Even those who are permanent residents help other guests, such as immature birds, to complete their rehab by keeping them company and teaching them basic skills like how to eat a mouse.

The third exhibit may or may not contain a screech owl. It was vacant when I visited. One of my most spine-chilling memories involves one of these nighttime-hunting birds. While camping overnight in North Georgia, I dozed in my sleeping bag, soaking in the utter silence outside my small tent. Without warning, a piercing cry that I would associate with someone being murdered nearly paralyzed me. It was a screech owl on the prowl.

At the fourth exhibit, gaze on a rare albino turkey vulture. Found in Piedmont, Alabama, the bird sustained serious injuries during a tornado there. Pass resting benches to your left and continue toward exhibit five, which houses two great horned owls. These guys are not the least bit friendly and pack a menacing, aggressive hiss.

Follow the boardwalk as it bears left and crosses a creek. With a covered gazebo to your right, approach the sixth exhibit, which shelters two red-tailed hawks, the largest of all Alabama hawks. Named Drummond and Perry, one was hit by a car and the other injured after becoming tangled in fishing line.

The boardwalk then bears right and ends. Here, step down onto the forest floor, turn right, and pick up the Eagle Trail, which leads up to the Wildlife Center. The trail is pebbly and rooty but initially level as it heads south/southeast against the flow of a small creek to your right. The trail bends eastward, passes a heavily carved beech tree, then ascends. Soon, step across the creek on stones and pass two more carved beeches. These water-loving trees are wrapped in a smooth gray bark that must be irresistible to passersby with pocketknives, but keep your knife sheathed please; carving the bark ultimately harms beech trees. In fall and winter, beeches keep their distinct coppery leaves.

With the creek on your left, ascend the narrow ravine between two steep hills. Cross a footbridge back over the creek again and continue uphill, heading east. At an intersection with the Yellow Trail, camber to the right and onto the Yellow Trail. Look for another footbridge across the creek to your right, cross it, reach a fork, and go left. This is the really steep portion of the hike.

Heading northeast and ascending, the Wildlife Center will come into view up the slope to your right. Top out at a paved drive and turn right back to the center, passing a large parking lot on your left. Turn right into the center's entrance walkway.

Enter the cozy stone and timber building and you're likely to see a handful of volunteers going about the daily business of wildlife rescue and rehabilitation. Just inside, you'll find photo exhibits, a stuffed black bear, and a large sitting room with woodland views. Kids and adults alike will enjoy the animal exhibits. Depending on the animals that are being cared for, you'll probably see snakes, turtles, squirrels, and other injured or orphaned animals. Be aware that the animal nursery, where baby birds and mammals are nursed back to health, is a quiet zone. My young daughter was thrilled to watch a volunteer (through a one-way mirror) carefully syringe-feed a nest full of tufted titmice.

Celebrating its 25th year, the Wildlife Center is a hopping place with dedicated volunteers and staff. In 2001 alone, the center took in 500 animal orphans and treated 155 birds with broken wings, 190 animals injured by cats, 72 animals injured by dogs, 9 animals injured by illegal gunshot, 14 animals injured from trapping (which included glue traps and melted candy), and 3 hummingbirds that had become entangled in spider webs—and that's just a partial list. The release of rehabilitated wildlife is a highlight of the Wildlife Center's activity. In 2001, wildlife releases included 31 robins, 15 blue jays, 21 cardinals, 26 mockingbirds, 14 barn owls, 33 cottontail bunnies, and 2 snapping turtles.

Cindy Lowry, the center's development assistant, notes that volunteer orientation occurs once a month. Staffed seven days a week, three shifts per day, the Wildlife Center treats an average of 3,000 distressed wild animals each year. Training levels, she says, progress as a volunteer becomes more experienced. To inquire about volunteering, call (205) 320-6189 or visit www.alawildliferehab.org. If you find an injured wild animal, call the center's hotline at (205) 621-3333.

After cooling down (or warming up) inside, exit the Wildlife Center through the mammal room onto a gravel path. Immediately to your right, don't miss the new raptor exhibit, which contains more birds of prey such as vultures and owls (and even a raccoon on my visit). Past the raptor exhibit look for the Freedom Flight building, where injured birds are taught to fly again. I was able to watch as two red-tailed hawks stretched their healing wings in preparation for release.

To return to your vehicle, retrace your steps to the front of the center and turn left back down the Eagle Trail, which leads to the boardwalk. At the intersection with the Tree Top Trail, you may walk back along the boardwalk or loop back through the woods on a narrow nature trail.

▶ NEARBY ACTIVITIES

Canoe and paddleboat rentals are available at Double Oak Lake Marina (on Terrace Drive) for $7–12 per hour. Someone 16 years old or older must be in each boat. Open seasonally in warm weather; call (205) 620-2524.

Take the kids to the park's Demonstration Farm on Findlay Drive. The farm features a wide variety of animals for petting and viewing, such as peacocks, goats, cows, horses, and chickens. Admission is free; call (205) 620-2526.

If you like to hit the little white ball, head over to the 18-hole golf course that abuts Findlay Drive. There are four sets of tees, a Pro Shop, and snack bar. Call (205) 620-2522 to reserve tee times.

The beach, located off of Terrace Drive behind Park Headquarters, is open year-round. It's crowded in the summer and deserted in the winter. Swimming is allowed during daylight hours and only in the roped areas. Dressing rooms, beach attendants, and a snack bar are seasonal.

The favorite off-trail activity at Oak Mountain seems to be the time-honored picnic. The primary area for picnicking is in the day-use area located along Terrace Drive. For large parties, a pavilion with tables, a roof, and grills can be reserved; call (205) 620-2524. Warm-weather weekends get crowded fast.

PALISADES PARK NATURE TRAIL

▶ IN BRIEF

What began as an Eagle Scout project is now a pleasant walk through the woods of Blount County. Take along the Self Guiding Nature Trail brochure to help identify pignut hickory, Tupelo gum, and many other trees native to this area.

▶ DESCRIPTION

Located on Ebell Mountain, at the tail end of the Southern Appalachians, the thinly soiled lime-stone and sandstone substrate of Palisades Park was once part of a vast seabed. Thrust upward over 200 million years ago, the former seabed is now a rolling hardwood forest perched 1,000 feet above sea level.

Only 83 acres, Palisades Park is small but packed with history, nature, and adventure. Among area rock climbers, Palisades Park's quarter-mile of stony bluffline is a popular destination. Numerous vertical routes, ranging in difficulty from beginner to expert, grace the 60-foot cliff face. On the other end of the adrenaline spectrum, Palisade's nicely landscaped grounds, historic pioneer

▶ DIRECTIONS

From the intersection of Interstates 459 and 59, drive north on I-59 for 30 miles. Take Exit 166 and turn left onto US 231. Drive 14 miles to Oneonta and follow signs for US 231 North. In downtown Oneonta, the highway will bear left at a red light, then immediately bear back to the right. Drive 2.2 miles and turn right at a small "Palisades Park" sign onto an unmarked road. Bear right onto the next paved road and follow the park signs. About 1.5 miles from US 231, reach a stone Palisades Park sign and turn right. The park will appear shortly. Follow the road around to visitor parking and turn left into a large, sloped parking lot.

ℹ KEY AT-A-GLANCE INFORMATION

LENGTH: 1 mile

CONFIGURATION: Asymmetrical loop

DIFFICULTY: Easy

SCENERY: Labeled trees and plants, mixed hardwood/pine forest

EXPOSURE: Mostly shaded with a couple of exposed sections

TRAFFIC: Light, even if the park is crowded

TRAIL SURFACE: Rocky dirt path

HIKING TIME: 30–45 minutes, depending on how long you dawdle

ACCESS: 9 a.m.–9 p.m.; closed Christmas and New Year's days

MAPS: Self Guiding Nature Trail brochure and the Palisades Park Trails map available at the park office

FACILITIES: Rest rooms, soft-drink vending machines, pay phone, picnic pavilions, playground

SPECIAL COMMENTS: To reserve pavilions or for more information, call (205) 274-0017; no alcohol allowed in park; pets on leash only; climbing/rappelling permits are $2.

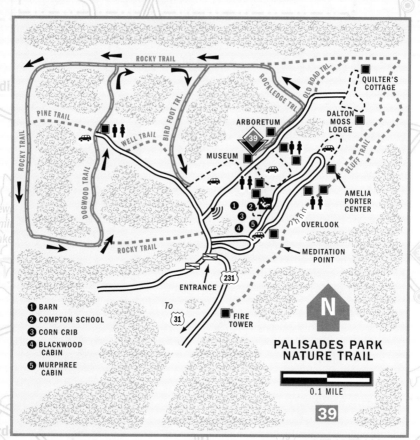

QUILTER'S COTTAGE

OLD ROAD TRL.

ROCKY TRAIL

ROCKLEDGE TRL.

PINE TRAIL

WELL TRAIL

BIRD FOOT TRL.

ROCKY TRAIL

DOGWOOD TRAIL

ARBORETUM

39

MUSEUM

DALTON MOSS LODGE

BLUFF TRAIL

AMELIA PORTER CENTER

OVERLOOK

ROCKY TRAIL

ENTRANCE

231

MEDITATION POINT

To
31

FIRE TOWER

1 BARN
2 COMPTON SCHOOL
3 CORN CRIB
4 BLACKWOOD CABIN
5 MURPHREE CABIN

N

PALISADES PARK
NATURE TRAIL

0.1 MILE

39

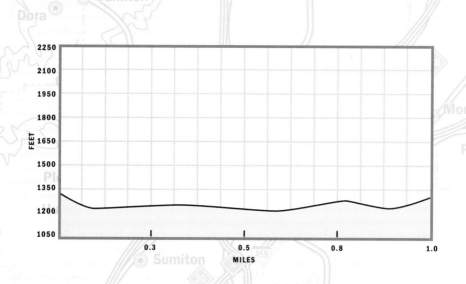

buildings, and large picnic pavilions attract families and groups in search of a relaxing afternoon barbecue. Whether picnicking or rappelling, though, all visitors enjoy the scenic vistas along this hike.

To begin, walk back down through the parking lot and head toward the clearly marked arboretum. Composed of eight short segments, the hike route described here will take you past all 14 numbered markers, which correspond to entries in the Self Guiding Nature Trail brochure. Before you head into the woods, give a nod of approval to Eagle Scout Matthew Gonsoulin. He, along with park staff, family, and fellow members of BSA Troop 97, created this trail.

At the bottom of the parking lot, bear right and pass over a small bridge toward an attractive wooden gazebo. Continue past the gazebo, walking on boulder-strewn ground through a small landscaped area. When you reach a post labeled "Rockledge Trail," turn left and enter the mixed hardwood/pine forest.

Traveling north and downhill on a forest path four- to five-feet wide, the woods are pleasant, quiet, and cool in the shade. Where the Rockledge Trail T-bones the Rocky Trail (well signed), turn left. Heading west, enjoy a gentle downhill stroll, keeping an eye out for poison ivy that grows along the trail.

If you're here in late spring or early summer, you'll see an abundance of wild blackberries growing among spiny brambles along the trail. Park rules disallow bringing a bucket and making a pie, but don't be afraid to sample one or two of the juicy berries. The berries are an important food source for the park's wild animals and birds. In fact, you'll see various purple scats fat with blackberry seeds along the way.

Reach an intersection with the Bird Foot Trail. Here you'll find stone benches and Marker 4. Look around to identify basket oak, blackjack oak, and pignut hickory. The bark of the basket oak peels easily into strips ideal for basket making. The nutshells of the pignut hickory were used by native Indians and settlers to dye cloth.

Continue straight on the Rocky Trail, still breezing downhill. While listening for black crows cawing as they soar on air currents above the forest canopy, you'll soon reach Marker 5 on the left, which highlights rock outcrops that are part of a wet-weather seep. Trees here include the highbush blueberry and red maple.

In rapid succession come to Markers 6 and then 7. At Marker 6, you should be able to easily spot the fringetrees. Also called "old man's beard," this member of the olive family is often used as an ornamental plant. At Marker 7, look for shortleaf pines and a red hawthorn (look for the sharp spines).

In addition to areas where trees have been removed to create light gaps (important for forest growth and diversity), you'll notice occasional beetle-damaged pines rotting on the ground. The perpetrator is the Southern pine beetle, a tiny, black, burrowing bug that weakens and kills pines. Across Alabama, the beetles remain epidemic in some areas, laying waste to thousands of pine acres.

As the trail meanders slightly downhill, you may run into a monarch butterfly flitting over the path or a shiny green junebug careening through the trees. Pass the Dogwood Trail on your left, but continue straight on the Rocky Trail to Marker 9, where you'll find another pignut hickory, this one leaning over the trail.

Duck under the hickory, pass another spot of pine-beetle damage, and approach Marker 10; be sure to take time to gaze up at a specimen of the mighty tulip poplar.

Good for building canoes and cabins, the tree can attain heights of 200 feet. After Marker 10, the trail begins to ascend for the first time.

At Marker 11, where you'll see a large basket oak and sassafras trees, a partial view opens to your right, revealing a distant ridge. Pass more sassafras along the trail, blackberry brambles, and an overgrown path that leads right. Bear southwest on the level Rocky Trail, passing through a healthy mix of shortleaf pine and red maple.

Markers 12 and 13 identify and illuminate tupelo gum, northern red oak, and the sourwood. Look on the back of a sourwood leaf to find tiny hairs running along the leaf's spine. Now traveling south, watch for two stone benches on trail-left. Rest for a spell here beneath the shade of a basket oak, red maple, and nearby dogwood.

Where the trail diverges and the Pine Trail leaves left, stay with the Rocky Trail going south. As you meander downhill, then uphill, scrubby areas filled with briars and grasses open to your right. On the trail's first steady ascent, pass remnants of an old barbed-wire fence on your left.

At the intersection with the Dogwood Trail, turn left and north. Named for the flowering dogwood, look for specimens of the petite, small-leafed tree along this trail. Around Easter, the trees put out attractive white blossoms. Continuing north, now plying a flat, curvy path, walk downhill and cross a wet-weather drainage. Pass through a gravel parking lot and reach Picnic Pavilion 7. This is the park's most isolated and private covered pavilion. With lots of parking and play area, rest rooms (locked when not in use), a swing, and grills, this would make a great spot for a family gathering. Be sure and plan ahead, though; reservations for the park's pavilions are taken up to a year in advance.

Pass through the pavilion and continue on the Dogwood Trail, stopping at Marker 8 on your left. On the sides of the trail, you'll see a curious, pleasing mix of bright green bryophytes and whitish lichens called reindeer moss. The bryophytes look like tiny pine trees. With the complementary reindeer moss, the scene resembles a tiny snow-covered forest.

The Dogwood Trail will soon T-bone the Rocky Trail. Turn right onto the Rocky Trail and walk along the only section of trail that you'll cover twice. Shortly reach the three stone benches that mark your right turn onto the final leg of the hike, the Bird Foot Trail. Heading south/southwest and uphill, pass Marker 3, which highlights groundwater seeps in the trail, and soon come to Marker 2, where you'll learn more about the abundance of wildlife foods contained in this forest.

After you pass the Well Trail on your right, reach Marker 1. The labeled Virginia pine here displays a gall about eight feet up on its trunk. This gall probably resulted from the tree's efforts to fight off an insect or fungal invader.

Exit the woods through a big patch of blackberry brambles and emerge through the Nature Trail's official entrance into a gravel parking lot. Ahead are the historic buildings and the playground. Over to your left is the parking lot where you left your vehicle.

After the hike, tour the park's collection of pioneer buildings. If you have kids, let them romp in the playground, which features a tall and very fast slide. You will, of course, be drawn to the bluff that looks out over a valley toward Sand Mountain. You can add a half-mile to your day, by walking the length of the bluff on the well-marked Bluff Trail. At the northern end of the Bluff Trail (past the Dalton Moss Lodge), the trail will turn sharply right and switchback down to reach the base of the bluff. In spring, the trail is crowded with the fragrant white blossoms of oak-leaf hydrangea. Shortly, though, the trail, which used to continue, disappears. Turn around and retrace your steps to the top of the bluff.

If you're not prepared to picnic, nearby Oneonta, in addition to plentiful fast-food establishments, is home to 'Round the Clock (homestyle veggies and meats), the Landmark (a bit more uptown), and Charlie's Barbecue.

PINHOTI TRAIL:
ADAMS GAP TO DISASTER

KEY AT-A-GLANCE INFORMATION

LENGTH: 5.2 miles

CONFIGURATION: Out-and-back

DIFFICULTY: Moderate (difficult if you walk down through the rubble)

SCENERY: Mixed hardwood/pine forest, both healthy and damaged

EXPOSURE: Minimal

TRAFFIC: Light on weekdays, moderate on weekends

TRAIL SURFACE: Dirt forest path

HIKING TIME: 3 hours

ACCESS: Trailhead never closed

MAPS: FS Pinhoti Trail Map 4 (The map will read "1" on the front but that's a typo. The real Map 1 is brown; Map 4 is purple) both available in country store

FACILITIES: None

SPECIAL COMMENTS: The extensive forest damage you'll encounter was caused by a combination of the Southern pine beetle and a very hot fire set by an arsonist in 1998.

IN BRIEF

Along this route, you'll witness the destructive power of beetles and fire on a remote section of Talladega Mountain as well as Nature's resilience.

DESCRIPTION

I began this trek in the Cheaha Wilderness as a hike/bike outing, but it evolved (or devolved), for reasons beyond my control, into a more straightforward out-and-back. The low that clear morning was a nippy 11 degrees, but the temp had climbed to 30 degrees by the time Kai, an unflappable exchange student from Germany, and I pulled into the Adams Gap trailhead of the 104-mile-long Pinhoti Trail. We set off into the cold, clear morning, intending to rendezvous with the Odum Scout Trail, which would take us to High Falls. There, we had already dropped the mountain bikes that we planned to ride back to our truck at Adams Gap.

Immediately upon accessing the rooty, dirt trail northward into the woods, I began to notice

DIRECTIONS

Take I-20 East from Birmingham for 55 miles to Exit 191. Bear right onto US 431 South and follow the signs to Cheaha State Park. Drive 2 miles and turn right onto CR 131. In half a mile, turn left onto AL 281 South, the Talladega Scenic Drive. There are two scenic overlooks on the way up: at 1.5 miles and 6.5 miles from the intersection of CR 131 and US 281, both on the right. , pass the lot signed "Cheaha Trailhead" on the left, 11.5 miles from the CR 131/US 281 intersection. Continue on 281 to the top of the mountain, passing the entrance to Cheaha State Park. Drive another 8 miles on AL 281 South, and the trailhead parking area will be on your right. From the parking area, cross the road to the brown hiker sign.

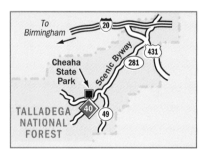

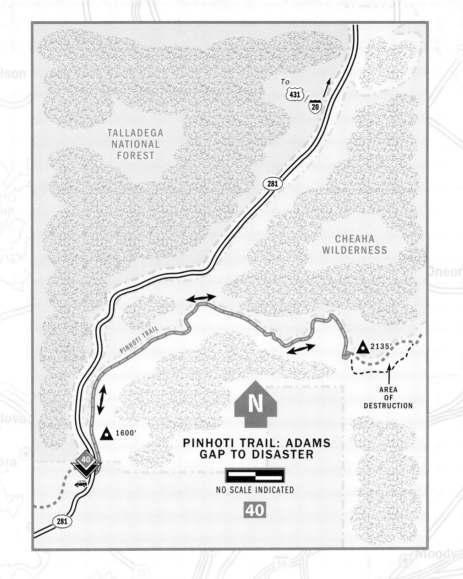

TALLADEGA
NATIONAL
FOREST

CHEAHA
WILDERNESS

To (431)
(20)

281

PINHOTI TRAIL

▲ 2135'

AREA
OF
DESTRUCTION

N

▲ 1600'

(40)

281

PINHOTI TRAIL: ADAMS
GAP TO DISASTER

NO SCALE INDICATED

40

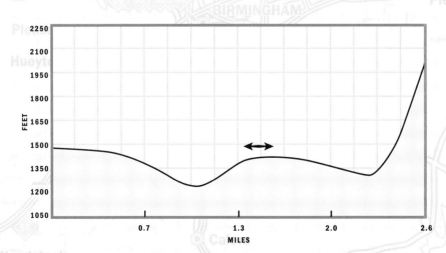

pine trees on the ground, as well as a few dead pines still standing, waiting for a gust of wind to snap their rotting trunks. Bark had sloughed from the dead trees, revealing hundreds of bore holes. Southern pine beetles strike again. The brown/black beetle, which is only about an eighth of inch long, infects pines of all species and sizes and is considered to be the most destructive forest agent in the state. The beetle lays its eggs on trees that have been weakened by drought, wind, and other forces. Pine-beetle attacks can decimate just a few trees in a single area, or a few thousand, in less than two months. Occasionally, the beetle even lays low healthy trees.

According to the Alabama Forestry Commission website, www.forestry.state.al.us, "The first indication of attack is usually the yellowing or browning of the needles. Examination of the trunk of the tree will usually reveal white, yellow, or sometimes red-brown pitch tubes, about as large as a wad of gum…Examination of infested trees by removal of the bark will show a distinctive winding S-shaped gallery pattern…Active spots or patches of infestation are distinctive also in that the center trees have dark reddish-brown foliage gradually changing until those on the edge have light greenish or yellowish green foliage…." From data obtained on aerial flights in 2001, the commission reported 2,540 pine-beetle-infestation spots, which contained an estimated 462,124 infected trees. During periods of a down pulpwood market, as in 2001, the method of control was to cut and leave the infected trees to rot.

We quickly passed through the first area of pine-beetle damage and settled into a route that crossed numerous rolling ravines. The forest through here is a nice mix of pines and hardwoods. The pines are mainly longleaf, white, and loblolly—I most often see the latter downed or dying upright. Repeatedly the path zigzags up a slope, over the crest, and down the opposite side. I ticked off 10, 12, 14 ravine crossings before the path assumed a winding course as it approached a looming ridge to the northeast. Chestnut oaks, black maple, and other hardwoods dominate the rock-strewn landscape.

At 3 miles, the path, which is part of the 104-mile-long Pinhoti Trail, turns sharply right at a signpost indicating that the trail heads straight up the slope. A wide, cleared path lies neatly among an amazing jumble of quartzite and sandstone. It was as if the royal hiking road through the rocks hinted at some glorious prize at the top. Kai and I began our slow plod up the steep incline. We had arrived later than expected and had only a limited amount of daylight. Already it was noon, and we had at least 8 miles of hiking left followed by 10 miles of mountain biking. Unless there's a clear sky with a full moon, nighttime in the Talladega National Forest is dark. And when it gets down to 10 degrees, that adds up to cold and dark.

We crested the ridge, dead pines sprinkled on the forest floor. We climbed over a few, now able to glimpse through the trees other hills and ridge lines in the distance. And then a funny thing happened—the trail stopped, disappeared.

Spread out before this east-facing slope, extending down into the valley below and beyond, hundreds, thousands, tens of thousands of pine trees lay dead. Trunks and limbs overlay more trunks and limbs. The only way through the mess was to walk on top of the mess. (*Note:* This is a good place to turn around. It's easy to get lost beyond this point.)

It appeared that our hike as planned had been foiled. But, where there's a will, there's a way, so we made a joint decision to attempt to locate the trail on the other side of this tangle of logs, which extended more than half a mile down a very steep slope. After climbing back to the west and up higher to get a better view of the situation, I gave us 30 minutes to get to the bottom and find the other side.

Picking my way down that pine-scented, pick-up-sticks clutter of dead, sere, brittle pines, I occasionally heard a slightly surprised, "Oh my!" or a matter-of-fact, "This seems quite difficult," from Kai following close behind.

After struggling down into a small, rocky basin, it became evident that the damage continued even farther north. I did manage to find a ragged blue blaze on a dead tree that still stood, but that was it. The half-hour I allotted to find the trail had more than passed. To get back safely (we were now well out of sight of where the trail ended) we needed to call it a day and walk out the way we came in.

Coming down was hard, but climbing back up this pine-trashed slope was twice the work. To try and minimize the length of the debris field, we skirted right. This route, however, put us on a nearly vertical hand-over-hand struggle up the slope. Finally topping out onto a cluster of jagged boulders, we sat down with a thud and partook of a little trail nutrition—raisins and water.

Rested, we picked our way back to where we expected to find the trail. But this is a vast area, and now that we had returned to partial tree cover, it was hard to navigate. In a minor sense, we were lost. It's never a good idea to panic or keep plunging ahead if you think you're lost. I didn't have my GPS to backtrack with, so out came the trusty map. We poured over various details, comparing where we thought we were with where we wanted to go. Checking the map, we were able to position ourselves in relation to the landmarks, a valley and two hills visible in the distance. Fortunately, we backed our way out of the unknown and to the trail using the map, compass, and visible landmarks. It's very easy to get off a trail, even a short one, and find yourself hopelessly disoriented. But with a little patience, and a map and a compass, (or even better a GPS unit) it's just as easy to get unlost. Keep that in mind when you venture into Alabama's wild lands, and be prepared.

Back on the trail, I settled in to enjoy the hike out, and Kai's spirits picked up noticeably. We each ate a Power Bar as the daylight began to fade slightly and the temperature once again dipped below freezing.

▶ NEARBY ACTIVITIES

Visit Cheaha State Park Campground on top of Cheaha Mountain. The country store is stocked with snacks, energy drinks, basic camping supplies, Pinhoti Trail maps, and other sundries. It is open 8 a.m.–5 p.m. Up the hill from the store is the Cheaha State Park Lodge and Restaurant, with tasty breakfast and lunch buffets and great views from the window-side tables. For more information, call (800) ALA-PARK or visit www.alapark.com.

PINHOTI TRAIL:
BLUE MOUNTAIN JAUNT

KEY AT-A-GLANCE INFORMATION

LENGTH: 5 miles

CONFIGURATION: Out-and-back

DIFFICULTY: Moderate/difficult

SCENERY: Hardwood forest, small streams, trail shelter

EXPOSURE: Minimal

TRAFFIC: Light year-round, heavier on weekends and during warm weather

TRAIL SURFACE: Rocky, dirt path

HIKING TIME: 2 hours

ACCESS: Cheaha Trailhead open year-round

MAPS: FS Pinhoti Trail Map 4 (The map will read "1" on the front but that's a typo. The real Map 1 is brown; Map 4 is purple) both available in country store.

FACILITIES: Garbage cans at trailhead; rest rooms, country store, restaurant at Cheaha State Park (2 miles farther on AL 281 South)

SPECIAL COMMENTS: Sturdy boots recommended. The drive up I-20 is fast; just be extra careful between Moody and Pell City, where an inordinate number of traffic fatalities have occurred in the past.

IN BRIEF

This Pinhoti Trail segment contains several steep sections of lean walking—you lean forward or you lean backward to keep your balance. The goal of this bun burner is to reach Blue Mountain Shelter, a wooden three-sided trail shelter with a loft.

DESCRIPTION

This trail will definitely give your heart a workout. I've followed this portion of the Pinhoti a half-dozen times, and the 2-mile hike to the shelter always seems longer than it really is. The day I visited, I had only two hours to complete it before I had to get back to Birmingham and pick up my daughter from child care. Needless to say, my pace was more spirited than usual. Yours certainly doesn't have to be.

Approach and pass through a rock-wall entrance, which displays leaf imprints along the way. Follow the trail into the woods and stay to the right. A sheltered map board appears shortly. Here you can check your bearings and fill out an information card (in the wooden box), which lets park rangers know who is on the trail.

With the map board to your left, begin your first uphill tread. The trail is steep, rooty, and rocky,

DIRECTIONS

Take I-20 East from Birmingham for 55 miles to Exit 191. Bear right onto US 431 South. Follow signs to Cheaha State Park. Drive 2 miles and turn right onto CR 131. In half a mile, turn left onto AL 281 South, the Talladega Scenic Drive. (You'll see two scenic overlooks on the way up: at 1.5 miles and 6.5 miles from the intersection of CR 131 and AL 281, both on right.) At 11.5 miles from the same intersection, turn left into "Cheaha Trailhead" parking lot. The trailhead is at the far end of the paved lot, marked by the stone entrance.

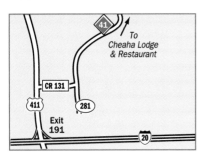

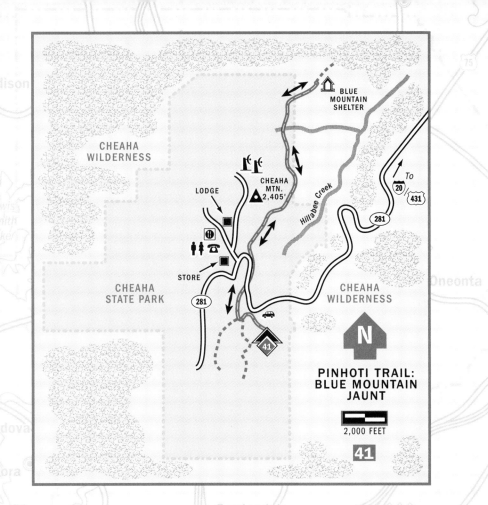

CHEAHA
WILDERNESS

BLUE
MOUNTAIN
SHELTER

LODGE

CHEAHA MTN.
2,405'

Hillabee Creek

To
20 / 431

281

STORE

CHEAHA
STATE PARK

281

CHEAHA
WILDERNESS

N

PINHOTI TRAIL:
BLUE MOUNTAIN
JAUNT

2,000 FEET

41

41

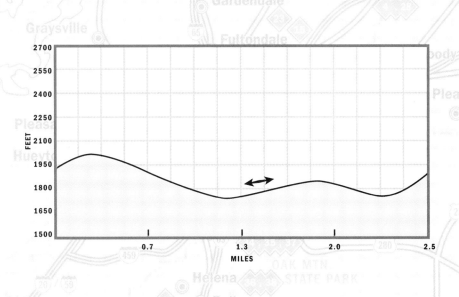

and there's more of that to come. The forest through here is a blend of Southern hardwoods with a variety of pines. Heading roughly north, reach a T-intersection and a signpost. The Pinhoti Trail goes both left and right; go right to reach the Blue Mountain Shelter, which is 2 miles from this point.

This initial section of trail gently hooks back to the right toward AL 281, which soon becomes visible through the trees. The trail makes a steep descent down some railroad-tie steps to cross two-lane AL 281. Head for the hiker sign across the road and descend down eight steps. Bear left at the stair bottom and take off to the north. Here, as with most of the inbound trail, the ground slopes steeply down from left to right.

Unlike other areas of the Pinhoti, this section is well marked with the diamond-shaped metal tags emblazoned with a three-toed turkey foot or the occasional white, turkey-foot blazes painted on trees. You'll also see an occasional blue blaze and near the middle of the hike, some big, sloppy, red paint splotches on a few trees; just ignore these blazes.

Not long after the steps, the trail levels a bit and the descent moderates. Continue heading north, with partially clear views of rolling hills to the east. Soon after sounds of water reach your ear, walk into a mucky area that leads to a small stream. Cross the stream, walk about 30 feet, and cross two more streambeds. In the summer, these streams dry up quickly. Below, and to the right, the streams merge into a larger flow.

The trail turns to the east as you pass between two large trees. Continue through another area of downed pines and then begin to head north again. While the trail continually maneuvers left and right, frequently changing your bearing, it generally leads in a north/northeast direction.

Walk through an area of very young pines, four- to five-feet high, and then pass a fine specimen of red maple. Descend the easterly trail with a steep slope and a scenic view off to the right. Continue down a steep descent toward a small creek. If there's been rain recently, the creek splashes noisily. To your left, the water flows smoothly down a slide of rock. Cross over, climb straight up on the other side, and bear around to the right, heading east.

The rocks in and around the trail begin to occur with greater frequency. Look for a large boulder to your left, and to your right (south) look for an antenna high atop a ridge. The trail bears left onto a fairly level path. About here I heard the crashing sounds of a white-tailed deer hoofing it through the brushy understory far below me.

Descend for awhile and watch for hawks that may be soaring the climes off to your right. The trail ascends again and becomes very rooty. Pass a fractured boulder on your right, which looks as if it could teeter over the edge any day. As the ascent steepens, and the trail heads northwest, look for a distinct peak in the distance off to the right. After the trail begins to descend again, pass a tree that appears to be growing straight out of a large rock.

The path snakes steeply down and may be hard to follow through here, especially in winter after the leaves have fallen; just keep an eye out for the blue trail blazes. Prior to passing through a boulder field, encounter the first big, ugly red paint mark that has been slapped on trees through here. Just beyond, the path mellows and begins to drop around to the left, passing a fire ring on the right. Then the trail cuts back sharply to the left and resumes its northbound direction.

The trail winds in and out of down-sloping V-shaped drainages. Heading down, cross a tiny stream with a giant oak tree on the right. Next, look for a downed tree that has made lemonade by growing a new trunk straight up out of the old downed trunk. The very rocky trail climbs, soon passing through a wide boulder field. It is difficult to navigate through here, so look ahead for a blaze and walk toward it. Sounds of rushing water come from the right.

Continue up and pass through a patch of pines, heading southwest toward another area of downed trees. The trail resumes its northerly course and sounds of flowing water become audible once again. Approach the small stream flowing left to right, and cross at a right angle. The water pools nicely and is cold and clear. Cross another branch of this small stream, and then bear right. The trail then flattens, passing a fire ring, campsite, and homemade stone benches to the left. Reach a sign, which points right to the Blue Mountain Shelter.

Walk down about 500 feet, approaching the shelter from behind. The wooden shelter sits on relatively level ground scattered with rock and is steeply roofed with wood shingles. It is open in the front. A picnic table and fire ring will be your amenities at this rustic but well-made "hotel." Inside, there's ample plank space for ten sleeping bags with another half-dozen up top in the dark loft. The primary disappointment you will experience if you spend the night here involves mice. Be sure to hang your food bags high and far away from the shelter. And just in case you're afraid of the dark, on one of the wooden benches someone has written, "This shelter is spooked."

Return to the sign. At the Y, head left past the campsite, which will be on your right, and retrace your steps back to the parking area.

▶ NEARBY ACTIVITIES

Up the hill, about half a mile from the Cheaha Trailhead, is Cheaha State Park Campground/Registration and Store. Turn in on the right. The store is stocked with snacks, energy drinks, basic camping supplies, Pinhoti Trail maps, and other sundries. It is open 8 a.m.–5 p.m. Up the hill from the store is the Cheaha State Park Lodge and Restaurant. The breakfast and lunch buffets here are tasty, and great views can be had from the window-side tables. For more information, call (800) ALA-PARK, or visit www.alapark.com.

The Talladega Superspeedway is visible from I-20. It seats 143,000 race fans and thousands more in the 215-acre infield. Attractions include the Talladega/Texaco Walk of Fame inside Davey Allison Memorial Park and the International Motorsports Hall of Fame; call (256) 362-RACE, or visit www.talladegasuperspeedway.com for more information.

Get a bite to eat on the way back at one of the restaurants in Oxford or Anniston. If you want some catfish, hold on until Exit 162. Head off of I-20 onto US 78. The Ark is about half a mile on the right. Call (205) 338-7420 for more information.

PINHOTI TRAIL: CAVE CREEK LOOP

▶ IN BRIEF

This elongated loop hike gently undulates along ridge lines through a mixed hardwood/pine forest. Some rocky, steep portions offer a wonderful variety to the scenery and in some instances afford terrific views of surrounding countryside.

▶ DESCRIPTION

The morning I left for this hike, I noticed that someone had stolen two rocking chairs from our front porch during the night. I was really ticked off. I was still thinking about the thief as I approached the trail, but the sight of the misty woods immediately put my unruly thoughts to rest.

From the parking lot, approach the rock-wall entrance, which displays imprints of leaves from trees you'll see along way. Follow the trail into the woods and stay to the right. A map board soon comes into view. Here you can check your bearings and fill out an information card, which will let park officials know that you are on the trail. Whenever you head into the wild, it's always a good idea to let someone know where you're going and when

▶ DIRECTIONS

Take I-20 East from Birmingham for 55 miles to Exit 191. Bear right onto US 431 South. Follow signs to Cheaha State Park. Drive 2 miles and turn right onto CR 131. In half a mile, turn left onto AL 281 South, the Talladega Scenic Drive. (You'll see two scenic overlooks on the way up: at 1.5 miles and 6.5 miles from intersection of CR 131 and AL 281, both on right.) At 11.5 miles from same intersection, turn left into "Cheaha Trailhead" parking lot. Trailhead is at the far end of the paved lot, marked by a stone entrance. The drive up I-20 is fast; be extra careful between Moody and Pell City, where an inordinate number of traffic fatalities have occurred in the past.

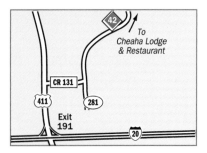

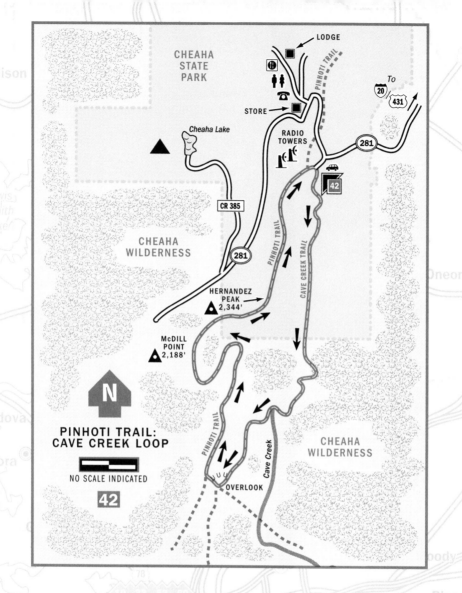

CHEAHA STATE PARK

LODGE

STORE

Cheaha Lake

RADIO TOWERS

CR 385

281

281

CHEAHA WILDERNESS

HERNANDEZ PEAK 2,344'

McDILL POINT 2,188'

N

PINHOTI TRAIL: CAVE CREEK LOOP

NO SCALE INDICATED

42

PINHOTI TRAIL

CAVE CREEK TRAIL

PINHOTI TRAIL

Cave Creek

CHEAHA WILDERNESS

OVERLOOK

To 431

281

42

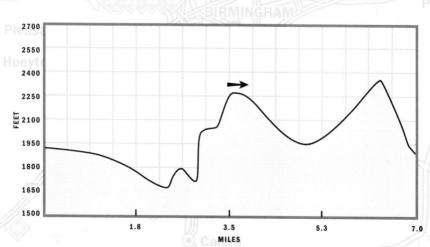

View from the Cave Creek Trail

you plan on returning home. Two days prior to my hiking, two women and two children wandered off the trail here and were missing for three days. They spent some chilly nights in the woods, but fortunately they were not seriously injured.

After dropping your registration card into the box, look for the Cave Creek Trail sign. Follow the trail as it goes left along a rooty, narrow, gravelly trail. For most of this hike, you'll follow a path about halfway between the top of the ridge and the valley below. On this clockwise loop, the ground generally slopes down to the left and up to the right. The trail is easy initially, with gentle ups and downs through numerous boulder fields. In late fall, when the trail is covered with leaves, you'll need to pay closer attention to where you're walking so that you don't get lost or stump your toes on hidden rocks.

Shortly after leaving the map board, cross a power-line swath. No blazes mark this trail, so pay close attention. It's easy to get into "the hiker's trance" and miss a turn. As you walk, look to your left for a ridge with an antenna on top, then soon pass a small fire ring on trail-left. After the fire ring, cross a narrow stream.

If you find yourself on this trail at night, like I did a couple of years ago, bits of mica in the trailbed make it faintly glow. Even in pitch dark, the trail seems to magically appear and can be followed. It's nerve wracking, though, because you can't see the rocks and may trip frequently. You can save yourself the trouble of having to rely on the trail's magical glow by carrying a flashlight.

Step over another small stream crossing (wet weather), then begin climbing gently, eventually becoming level with the distant ridge off to the left. If it's fall or winter, crunch your way through a thick layer of maple and oak leaves. About 1 mile into the hike, look for a wooden sign on your right, which reads "Cheaha Wilderness/Talladega National Forest." At this point you leave Cheaha State Park and enter the National Forest.

It's often very humid in these parts, especially in summer, and you might have sweat streaming down your face. The dampness can turn the trails in this area into mushroom highways, especially after a rain. On a nearby Pinhoti approach trail, I saw hundreds of fungi within the first 200 yards. Try a hike in August, and you might spy the prized yellow chanterelle. While the fall chill reduces the likelihood of seeing mushrooms, there is one hardy variety that likes the cold weather—the white waxy cap. You can find them along the trail even in late November.

Continuing, the trail passes through a small magnolia stand with a large rock to the left. Carefully walk out onto the rock for an unobstructed, sweeping view. The only distraction here may be a small plane droning high above the forest. Look out to the north and locate a gap with a ridge behind it. Look east, and you'll see a small clearing.

Warning! This is the crux of the hike. When you leave the overlook rock and return to the trail, be very careful—you can easily go the wrong way here. With the rock to your back, you'll have three choices. If you go left, you'll find yourself walking down a very, very steep hillside that leads deep into the forest. If you go right, you'll retrace your steps back to the map board. Take the middle path, which has a log across it. Look closely for a crudely carved "Cave Crk" with an arrow pointing ahead. This is the trail you want. Cross the log and continue forward on this connector trail, which leads to the Pinhoti Trail.

Shortly thereafter, reach an intersection. If you go left, you'll loop back around to the big rock. Instead, go straight, passing a fire ring to your right. Rocks slope up to the right as you head southwest and the trail begins to flatten. Soon pass a campsite with a built-up fire ring. Here the trail splits. Take the more distinct path to the right and begin to descend through a stand of maples. Come upon a creek to your left and a large boulder to the right. Cross the small creek, small in size—two feet across—but large in sound. The trail soon heads up and snakes toward a ridge. Watch for a big tree across the trail and enjoy level walking for a while, although there are lots of rocks in and around the path. When you encounter a morass of tangled trees and limbs across the trail, skirt the trail to the left and reach an open, gently sloping part of the trail that passes through a thin stand of small trees. Watch for a wooden post with a sign that reads "Pinhoti." This is the Pinhoti connector. Here, turn sharply to the right and follow the red blazes (the first trail blazes of the hike) north along the connector.

Continue uphill, passing through a hard garden exhibiting lots of moss-covered rocks. Once you reach the top of the ridge, the wind picks up noticeably. There are many viewing spots to your left as you gaze west over the large valley below.

The trail then drops over the ridge down to an intersection with three wooden signs. The Pinhoti proper begins here, continues around to the right, and is marked with blue blazes. Pick your way carefully through successive rock jumbles while looking for the blue blazes on the rocks. Eventually you'll spy the first Pinhoti "turkeyfoot" blaze, spray-painted white on a tree. Stay alert and don't let the hillside pull you down off the trail.

Continue forward until you see a patch of white rock high up on a ridge to your left. Along here the blazes are infrequent, and you may begin to wonder if you've lost the trail. If you're on track, the trail begins to wind down into a bowl-like area, with many bright-green, moss-covered rocks. This is where the trail jigs back to the south and then loops back north, forming a fingerlike projection on the map. It was in this area that I lost my red "Life is Good" hat. If you find it, let me know. As you walk, the wind in the trees begins to play tricks on you. I often imagine I can hear three or four people talking in the distance. (I wish I could make out what they were saying.)

Twist along the windy ridge, admiring several car-sized boulders, and soon spot your first modern Pinhoti marker. It's a metal diamond-shaped tag with "NRT" at the top and "Pinhoti" at the bottom. Next, reach a wooden sign, "Pinhoti/State Park 3." Follow the sign's lead to the left. Don't take the trail to right.

Now that you're traveling north again, reach McDill Point (2,188 ft.). A sign for McDill Overlook leads you down a quarter-mile side trail to the left. Check out the vista, then return and turn back left to continue. Here the trail becomes faint, passing through rocky areas that require you to pick a way through boulders and scramble up some short steep sections. Come to an area of overlooks to the left with nice, long views, and scan below for the Talladega Scenic Drive in the distance.

The trail continues through more boulder fields and rock gardens. Perched on top of a big rock pile, it splits briefly right and left. Go left. After the left, find a polished granite marker—"Cheaha Wilderness established January 3, 1983, Dedicated by Hon. Bill Nichols. Alabama Wilderness Coalition Chairman. R. M. Leonard. J. N. Randolph"—and then continue straight.

Again the trail through here is faint and has few blazes, leading up to the second crux of this hike. Pick your way through a rock garden and bear around to the left, looking for a brush pile and a fire-ring clearing; watch carefully for a blue blaze on a tree to your left, near the ridge's edge. Do not go right and down the steep hillside. If you do, you'll intersect a logging road. If this happens, go back up the hill and over toward the edge of the ridge and find the blue blaze on the tree.

At the blue blaze, the trail drops down through large rocks, requiring some minor downhill scrambling, with a rock wall to your right. Look for a Pinhoti tag and a blue blaze together. Here the trail flattens and forks again. Don't go right onto the logging road. Walk left and stay on the trail, soon passing through an open area with two fire rings; walk between them.

The trail bends right and crosses the logging road that you encountered just minutes before. After this crossing, the trail becomes more solid and seems much friendlier than the previous 3 miles of rocky walking. Cross the power-line swath, the same one you crossed earlier. This journey is about to end, but don't let your guard down yet. The rocks through here can be slippery.

Come to your final intersection of trails and follow the sign "Cave Creek/Parking" to the right. Down the trail to the left is the Blue Mountain Shelter, which is about 2 miles distant. From here traffic on the Scenic Drive is audible, and the map board soon appears. Hike past the map board and out to the parking lot.

▶ NEARBY ACTIVITIES

Up the hill about half a mile from the Cheaha Trailhead is Cheaha State Park Campground/Registration and Store. Turn in on the right. The store is stocked with snacks, energy drinks, basic camping supplies, Pinhoti Trail maps, and other sundries. It is open 8 a.m.–5 p.m. Up the hill from the store is the Cheaha State Park Lodge and Restaurant. The breakfast and lunch buffets here are tasty, and great views can be had from the window-side tables. For more information, call (800) ALAPARK, or visit www.alapark.com.

The Talladega Superspeedway is visible from I-20. It seats 143,000 race fans and thousands more in the 215-acre infield. Attractions include the Talladega/Texaco Walk of Fame inside Davey Allison Memorial Park and the International Motorsports Hall of Fame; for more information call (256) 362-RACE or visit www.talladegasuperspeedway.com.

On the way back, get a bite to eat at one of many restaurants in Oxford or Anniston. If you want some catfish, hold on until Exit 162. Head off I-20 to the right onto US 78. About half a mile on the right is the Ark. Call (205) 338-7420 for information.

PINHOTI TRAIL:
PINE GLEN TO SWEETWATER LAKE

▶ IN BRIEF

Follow Shoal Creek from the Pine Glen Recreation Area to its impoundment at Sweetwater Lake while experiencing the Pinhoti Trail in the northern reaches of the Talladega National Forest.

▶ DESCRIPTION

Located in the Choccolocco Wildlife Management Area (WMA), deep in the Talladega National Forest, Pine Glen is a partially cleared forest flat bounded by Shoal Creek to the north and west, FS 500 to the east, and forested hills to the south. The 31 rustic campsites here are very basic and open.

Other than the peace and quiet of the forest, Shoal Creek is the main attraction for area residents and weekend campers, who come here to frolic in the cool water. In late fall and winter months, the campground is a favorite of hunters who visit the 46,550-acre WMA. The Alabama Division of Wildlife and Freshwater Fisheries estimates that there are between 16 and 30 white-tailed deer per acre in the WMA.

You'll begin the hike where the road crosses the creek on a low cement bridge. The first 1.25 miles are level and closely follow the creek. In the next mile, the trail climbs up and away from the

▶ DIRECTIONS

From the intersection of I-20 East and I-459, travel east on I-20 for 55 miles to Exit 191/US 431. Exit and turn left on US 431 North. Drive for a mile and turn right onto US 78 East. Drive 4 miles and turn left onto AL 9 North. Continue another 4.6 miles to turn right onto Joseph Springs Motorway, which becomes gravel after half a mile. After 3.3 miles, turn left onto FS 531 (not marked here). Drive 2.6 miles and turn left at a four-way intersection onto FS 500. Drive a half-mile on FS 500 and Pine Glen will be on the left.

ⓘ KEY AT-A-GLANCE INFORMATION

LENGTH: 5 miles

CONFIGURATION: Out-and-back

DIFFICULTY: Easy

SCENERY: Choccolocco Creek, hardwood/pine forest, Sweetwater Lake

EXPOSURE: Mostly shaded

TRAFFIC: Very light during week, light on weekends

TRAIL SURFACE: Dirt forest path, occasionally rooty

HIKING TIME: 2 hours

ACCESS: Pine Glen Recreation Area day-use fee is $3

MAPS: FS Pinhoti Trail Map 2

FACILITIES: Pit toilets, water, and rustic camp sites at Pine Glen Recreation Area

SPECIAL COMMENTS: Park on the left side of the road past the entrance to Pine Glen or park in a small lot next to the pit toilets in the center of the campground. See p. 6 for a note about hunting seasons.

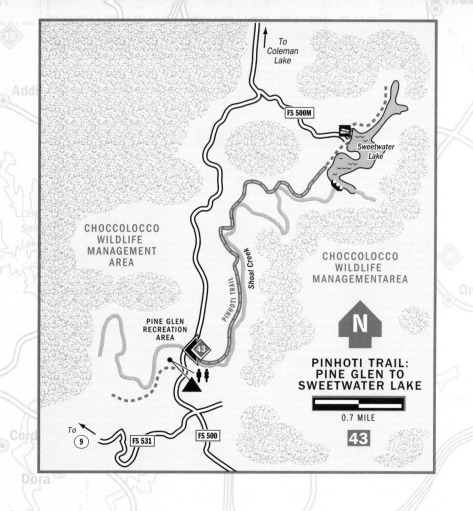

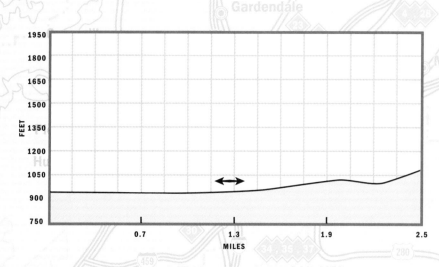

creek, following a smaller tributary. During the final half-mile of the walk out, you'll rejoin Shoal Creek and emerge into an open field above Sweetwater Lake. After exploring around the lake, return to Pine Glen along the same path.

To begin, cross the bridge and Shoal Creek to enter the forest at a hiker sign. Initially walking east/southeast against the creek's flow, cross a footbridge and bear right, walking along the bank. The creek is about 30 feet wide and averages two to three feet deep. The water is a muddy brown and runs swiftly, especially after a rain.

The ground here is flat and serves as a floodplain for the creek. The forest floor is thick with underbrush, punctuated by tall loblolly pines, red maple, white oak, red oak, beech, mountain laurel, and hickory. Soon, cross another footbridge over a feeder stream and begin to watch for the blue blazes and Pinhoti Trail diamond tags that will help keep you on the trail.

The Pinhoti, of course, is the area's premier long trail. For 104 miles, southwest to northeast, the Pinhoti runs nearly the entire length of Talladega National Forest. The Pinhoti traverses two wilderness areas, Cheaha and Dugger Mountain, and will one day link up with the Appalachian Trail via another long trail, the Benton Mackaye Trail.

Walking along the creek, you'll notice ferns and grasses that thrive in this wet area. Beech, tulip poplar, and sweetgum also enjoy the dampness. The trail swings north, past clearings off to the left, which are food plots planted to attract deer. Hunting is allowed here in deer season, so it's best to avoid this area from November 16 through January 31. See p. 6 for more information on hunting.

The ubiquitous Southern pine beetle has visited here, as evidenced by dozens of fallen and standing dead pines, all scored with 0.38-caliber bore holes. The trail, though, is generally clear of major debris, and the light gaps in the canopy have spawned a wealth of wildflowers along the trail, including bloodroot, Queen Anne's lace, and may apple. Muscadine vines and wild blackberry brambles are also common.

Half a mile in, begin to slope up above the creek. Cross a clear, pebbly feeder stream, assisted by a large root. By now, especially if it's summer, you should have a sheet of perspiration clinging to your body. The air is very humid, and if there's a low-pressure system in town, it seems you can cut the mugginess with a knife.

You may see anglers wading in the creek, casting with a rod 'n' reel for bass, or encounter them headed to or from Sweetwater Lake. You can fish here, too, but you'll need a state fishing permit. At 0.7 miles, small mats of bryophytes appear by the trail. The brilliant-green carpet looks like a tiny evergreen forest. The wood nymphs like to serve them up with black-eyed Susans, woodland butterflies, hepatica, and oak-leaf hydrangea, as well as gnats, poison ivy, and deer ticks, whether you want them or not.

At 0.9 miles, bear away from the creek as a slope builds up on your left. Go past beds of ferns, and then pass a very thick stand of young sweetgums on trail-right. Sweetgums can attain staggering heights and broad-reaching canopies. The tree is easily identified by its star-shaped leaf and prickly, round burrs.

The creek, somewhat quiet until now, picks up in volume as the flow forces itself around and through brush and boulders. Pass a small feeder stream from the left that disappears underground to re-emerge a few feet later. Pass some small mulberry trees and meander through another area rife with trailside wildflowers. The trail changes character a bit, rolling up and down along a slope indented with freshet gullies.

At 1.3 miles, 100 feet above the creek, branch off and follow a narrower tributary of Shoal Creek that flows through an attractive, narrow creek gorge. Within 0.3 miles, cross the shallow feeder on rocks, looking for minnows dancing in the sunlight. Push up the other side of the ravine, cross over a ridge, and ignore a logging road that goes right.

Wander down into a wet area with lots of seeps at 1.8 miles. The quiet here is so profound that snapping a twig under your boot sounds like a rifle shot reporting through the forest. Soon pick up Shoal Creek again on your right and cross a footbridge and another feeder. More tall, straight tulip poplars grow here, as do some very old poison ivy vines and spiky yucca plants.

The path flattens and weaves, and at 2.2 miles, begins to climb away from the creek. Catch the double-blue blazes soon afterwards, and reach a large, open grassy field. Seahorse-shaped Sweetwater Lake, an impoundment of Shoal Creek, lies ahead. An earthen dam sits off to your right. Walk through the field to get a better look at the lake, cavort in the meadow, and then return to Pine Glen along the path you've just completed.

▶ NEARBY ACTIVITIES

Built in 1994, The Frog Pond Wildlife Preserve and Observation Area makes an easy and interesting outdoor finale to the day. As you're driving back out to AL 9 from Pine Glen, 0.2 miles before you reach AL 9, look for a long narrow gravel parking area on your right. There will be a green sign about 100 feet distant that you can see from the road. Pull in, park, and walk toward the sign, which indicates that you're headed toward the Frog Pond. Walk in a short way and turn left onto a wide woodland trail (right before a piled berm of dirt). Follow the trail to the pond, where you'll find a boardwalk and an observation tower that you can sit in to spot wildlife—or just listen to the frogs. The small, marshy preserve is a joint project between Jacksonville State University and the Alabama Forestry Commission. There are no facilities here. The entire walk is 0.3 miles.

PULPIT ROCK TRAIL

▶ IN BRIEF

Take a dip downhill through impressive stands of mountain laurel to a cliff-top area with multiple long-distance views to the west.

▶ DESCRIPTION

Originally built by skilled CCC laborers, the stone cabins you'll see at the trailhead are ideally situated within easy walking distance of several Cheaha State Park trails. And if you like to go vertical, the cabins make a great base camp for a weekend of climbing on the cliffs at Pulpit Rock.

Head down the very steep and rocky trail to the south/southwest, passing through a healthy hardwood forest. Meander by van-sized chunks of quartzite scattered on the slope and slip through slicks of gorgeous mountain laurel, which is at its pink finest in spring.

▶ DIRECTIONS

Take I-20 East from Birmingham for 55 miles to Exit 191. Bear right onto US 431 South. Follow the signs to Cheaha State Park. Drive 2 miles and turn right onto CR 131. In half a mile, turn left onto AL 281 South, the Talladega Scenic Drive. There are two scenic overlooks on the way up, both on the right: at 1.5 miles and 6.5 miles from the intersection of CR 131 and AL 281, both on right. At 11.5 miles from same intersection, pass the parking lot signed "Cheaha Trailhead" on the left. Continue on AL 281 to the top of mountain and turn right into Cheaha State Park. Drive through the automatic gate (deposit $2 per person day-use fee in the honor box). Continue uphill for 1 mile and bear left at a sign for Bald Rock Lodge. Pass a campground entrance on the left to arrive at the Pulpit Rock Trail parking area, which is a small pull-out on the right. The red-blazed trail begins near the stone cabins.

ⓘ KEY AT-A-GLANCE INFORMATION

LENGTH: 1 mile

CONFIGURATION: Out-and-back

DIFFICULTY: Easy/moderate

SCENERY: Scads of mountain laurel, great long views from atop a wooded, boulder-strewn cliff averaging 80 feet high

EXPOSURE: Minimal

TRAFFIC: Light, heavier in spring and summer

TRAIL SURFACE: Rocky, rooty dirt path

HIKING TIME: 45 minutes

ACCESS: Park gate opens at sunrise, closes nightly at 9 p.m.

MAPS: FS Pinhoti Trail, Map 4; state park map—both available in park's country store

FACILITIES: Rest rooms, country store, restaurant on-site

SPECIAL COMMENTS: This is an area where folks come to rappel and climb a 70-100-foot cliff face, which is located at the end of the trail.

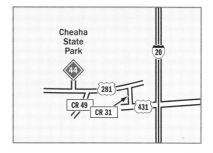

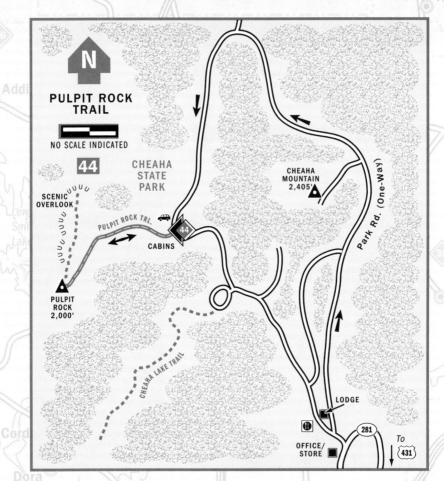

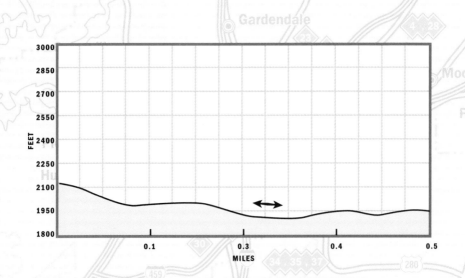

Bear right, heading north/northwest, and descend into an area of stately Virginia pines. Here the trail begins to level as it rolls through a boulder garden filled with large rocks. The trail then shifts to the west/southwest and begins a short uphill climb through more mountain laurel. Even without its blossoms, mountain laurel's twisting, wrist-thin trunks and its shiny, dark-green leaves give it an elegant air.

The trail soon flattens, heading south/southwest. Look for plentiful chestnut oaks along the trail. Continue, shortly approaching and paralleling a bluff of quartzite ledges and boulders, with open views to the west. Where the red blazes peter out, you'll be positioned to step very carefully out onto a point of rock known as Pulpit Rock. Jutting out and over the precipice below, climbers rappel and climb here. If you peer carefully over the edge, you can see a few bolts that climbers have placed for protection, a duct-taped pine that serves as an anchor, and rocks that have been duct taped to protect ropes against their cutting friction. If you want to climb or rappel here, you need to sign in at the country store located near the park entrance. The cliff is 70 to 100 feet above the forest below, so be extremely careful. It's true that the ground catches everything, but it won't save you if you slip and fall.

Even though you're not here to climb, there are plenty of long views to soak in. Looking left to the southwest, you can spot the waters of Cheaha Lake far below. Looking to the northwest, the city of Oxford, bisected by I-20, sparkles in the distance. This is a peaceful spot to relax if there's no one else around. To return to the trailhead, just follow the red blazes back to the parking area.

▶ NEARBY ACTIVITIES

Take the long walking tour of the park and make the Pulpit Trail a stop along the way. Begin by parking at the country store and walking uphill past the gate. Stay right to follow the paved road, which loops through the park. At 0.6 miles, turn left and visit the Bunker Observation Tower. The tower was constructed from local stone by CCC workers circa 1935–1937 and has been recently refurbished. Enter the tower, ascend the metal stairs to the top observation platform, and enjoy panoramic 360 degree views. Walk back out to the main road and turn left. At 1.2 miles, turn right and walk down to the Bald Rock Boardwalk Trail and out 0.8 miles to another spectacular vista. Walk back to the main road, bear right, and pass a chapel on the left. Continue straight alongside the road and pass a campground area on the left. At 1.7 miles, the Pulpit Rock Trail appears on your right. Follow its red blazes down and back for another mile of trailsmithing. Next, continue along the road to the Wildflower Garden Trail, which is bisected by the road after half a mile. Continue downhill (chalets will be on the left, and cabins on the right at 1.9 miles) and follow the road until, at 2.2 miles, the park restaurant appears on your right. Unless it's mealtime, return to your car parked at the country store, which will be visible straight ahead. The total for the road walk and all trails is 5 miles.

The park's country store is stocked with snacks, energy drinks, basic camping supplies, Pinhoti Trail maps, and other sundries. It is open 8 a.m.–5 p.m. and doubles as the campground registration office. For more information call (800) ALA-PARK or visit www.alapark.com.

The Talladega Superspeedway is visible from I-20. It seats 143,000 race fans and thousands more in the 215-acre infield. Attractions include the Talladega/Texaco Walk of Fame inside Davey Allison Memorial Park and the International Motorsports Hall of Fame; call (256) 362-RACE or visit www.talladegasuperspeedway.com for more information.

Get a bite to eat on the way back at one of many restaurants in Oxford or Anniston. If you want some catfish, hold on until Exit 162. Head off of I-20 onto US 78. The Ark is about half a mile on the right. Call (205) 338-7420 for more information.

RUFFNER MOUNTAIN:
BUCKEYE TRAIL

If you have only an hour to spare but need a vigorous walk, the Buckeye Trail is a good choice. Along its sometimes-steep length, watch for old-growth chestnut oaks, which tower above the small, sapling-sized buckeye trees for which the trail is named.

▶ DESCRIPTION

You don't have to be from Ohio to enjoy the red buckeyes common along this trail. This tree is most easily identified in spring, when its bright-red flowers bloom. Its leaves are also fairly distinct: the compound leaf is composed of a cluster of five dark-green leaflets, with distinct ribbing on each leaflet. The fruit is a seamed husk with a smooth nut inside. As a medicinal, the red buckeye had many uses among native peoples and settlers. A

▶ DIRECTIONS

From I-20 East, exit onto Oporto-Madrid Boulevard. Turn left onto Oporto-Madrid. Turn right at a light onto Rugby Avenue. Rugby veers to left; turn right onto 81st Street South. Road ends and enters steep, narrow road to Ruffner Mountain Nature Center. Drive through a small parking area and continue to the left between the pavilion and the Nature Center. Park in the large lot in front of you.

Alternate directions: From First Avenue North, turn onto 83rd Street North (left if going toward Birmingham, right if going away from Birmingham). A Ruffner Mountain Nature Preserve sign is visible on the corner. Continue to 4th Avenue South; a small sign indicates Ruffner is 1 mile ahead. Bear to the right onto Rugby Avenue. Turn left onto 81st Street South at the Ruffner sign. The nature preserve is at the top of the hill, past the gate.

KEY AT-A-GLANCE INFORMATION

LENGTH: 1.6 miles

CONFIGURATION: Out and back

DIFFICULTY: Easy/moderate

SCENERY: Artesian spring, wooded ravines, scenic overlook

EXPOSURE: Minimal

TRAFFIC: Light in winter/weekdays

TRAIL SURFACE: Rooty, rocky dirt trail, wide dirt path, some boggy areas near artesian well

HIKING TIME: 1.5 hours

ACCESS: Ruffner Mountain is open on Tuesday through Saturday, 9 a.m.–5 p.m.; Sunday, 1–5 p.m.; closed Monday

MAPS: Ruffner Mountain trail map, available at the Nature Center (free).

FACILITIES: Clean rest rooms, water fountain, drink vending machine, covered pavilion, picnic tables, small amphitheater

SPECIAL COMMENTS: None

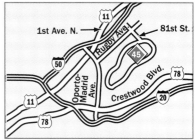

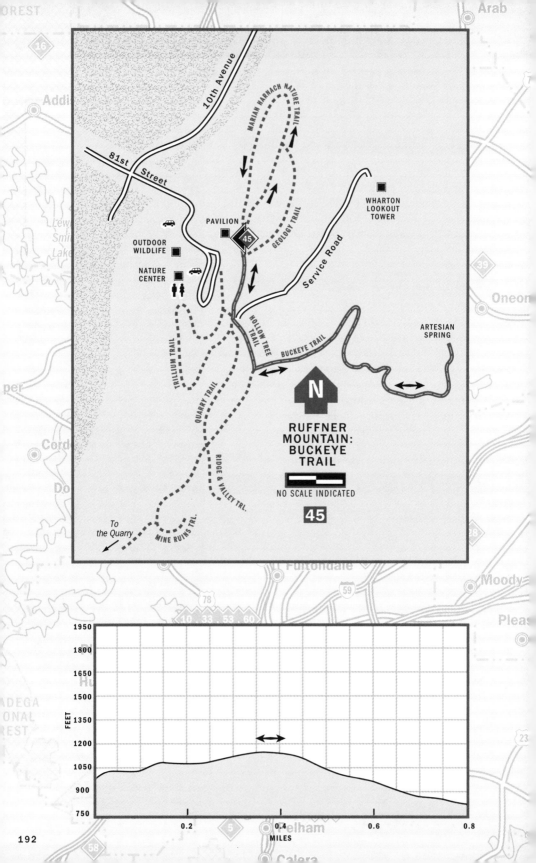

RUFFNER
MOUNTAIN:
BUCKEYE
TRAIL

NO SCALE INDICATED

45

brew from crushed twigs was used to stupefy fish and bring them to the surface. A soap and bleaching product was made from the red buckeye's gummy roots.

To start the hike, take the sidewalk uphill from the parking lot and follow the sign to the Geology Trail. The dirt trail ascends to a fork. The Geology Trail goes left; the Quarry Trail heads right. Stay right and continue uphill. In summer, keep an eye out for yellow jackets. Cross a narrow blacktop service road to an information kiosk on your right. Continue up and bear left onto the Hollow Tree Trail, which will bring you to the Buckeye Trail at 0.3 miles. After viewing the remains of a 150-year-old tulip poplar, pass a bench and an ore test pit on your right, bear left, and then continue up to reach a level, wide gravel road—the start of the Buckeye Trail. Turn left onto the gravel road and watch for the purple blazes.

As you head east/northeast, notice that Ruffner's red soil is easily visible in cut banks to your left. The road bears left, gently ascending, but follow the Buckeye Trail as it veers down and right onto a woodland path that heads roughly east/southeast. In late winter you'll see fat robins scooting through the leaves and red cardinals flitting from bush to bush.

Where the trail appears to go straight ahead but is blocked with brush, go right. The buckeyes are easy to spot, but what you can't see as you meander down is the vast room-and-pillar mine network that runs beneath you. There are still a few open slope-mine entrances to this underground puzzle, but you'll have to take a guided tour with one of Ruffner's naturalists to get any closer to the hazardous but fascinating maze.

Ramble downhill, heading generally southwest, but expect to change direction frequently. Where the ravine slopes down from right to left, take a sharp left and canter down a few rusty, dusty steps and bear back to the right into a level area. There are numerous downed trees in this area, but none that blocks the trail.

As you twist up over a rise, look for an interpretive sign on your left, with information about a dead rock chestnut oak, 150 years old, that stands a few feet away. Winding down, notice a ravine to your left. This is the area of Ruffner's old Mine Site No. 2. Not so far away, but nearly impossible to find in the mimosa jungles, are towering, massive relics of Ruffner's iron-ore mining days.

Snake around, roughly west and down, passing specimens of wild and domestic hydrangea and ground-hugging forest ferns.

At roughly 1 mile into the hike, turn right off of the trail to a marked scenic overlook. Immediately below is a small valley filled with young pine. In the distance, I-20 is visible, running beneath a limestone cut that rises behind it. Turn back, go right on the Buckeye Trail to continue, and view a live 90-foot rock chestnut oak that began growing around 1800.

As you continue down, stands of invasive privet choke areas of the bottomland that you're entering. If you keep a sharp lookout, you may spot a gleaming section of rail from the defunct Mineral Railroad that once carried ore from the mines to nearby Sloss Furnaces.

Bypass a side trail on your left and continue around to the right, soon reaching a wide dirt road. Here, turn left and hike northeast toward the artesian spring, passing through a scrubby area rife with more mimosa and privet.

Where the trail forks, bear right and immediately see a portable toilet and a picnic table, which has been placed here for the use of hikers and Ruffner employees working out in the bush. Turn immediately left to continue on a grassy trail through more brush. This bottomland is the site of a proposed wetland project that Ruffner plans to pursue. The artesian spring you'll see shortly will be the source of water for the proposed wetland area.

At the next trail fork, go left and you'll begin to hear the sound of running water. Pass a birdhouse on your left and reach a small pool of cold, clear water that runs continuously from a capped pipe that used to feed water to mine workers living nearby. On the top of the pipe is an old valve made by Stockham, a former Birmingham steel products employer. The inviting water runs into a boggy area filled with blackberry brambles. Ruffner naturalist Marty Schulman says the water has tested positive for slight traces of arsenic, but is otherwise unpolluted.

To return to the parking area, retrace your steps to the picnic table and portable toilet; turn left onto the dirt road; take your first right onto the purple-blazed Buckeye Trail, and backtrack from there.

▶ NEARBY ACTIVITIES

After the hike, step back inside the Nature Center to view animal exhibits that include indigenous turtles, fish, and frogs. Be sure to look in on the timber rattler and the copperhead that share a large aquarium. On the back porch, take a moment to view a disabled barred owl that has found a permanent home at Ruffner. There is also a small collection of fossils, arrowheads, and mining ephemera. Outside, other animal exhibits include a great horned owl, a red-tailed hawk, and other birds and mammals that have been injured and are on the mend.

For a bite to eat, head back down Oporto-Madrid and turn onto Crestwood Boulevard/US 78, where numerous restaurants of all ilks are located. For a good pizza, turn right and head up to the Festival Center, which is on the left just above Hooters, then locate Alfredo's in the far back of the Festival Center shopping complex.

RUFFNER MOUNTAIN:
GEOLOGY TRAIL

Follow this short loop through Ruffner Mountain's eastern section and examine the effect millions of years of geologic development has had on the area.

▶ DESCRIPTION

From the mid-nineteenth century to the mid-twentieth century, much of Ruffner Mountain was mined for iron ore and limestone—two ingredients critical to casting iron. This hike's focus, however, is on the effect that geologic forces made on the area in the millions of years prior. The first leg of this hike follows the beginning section of the Marian Harnach Nature Trail, accessed by walking past the covered pavilion. See p. 198 for more on this section.

This short, educational trail heads into a brushy area to begin the counterclockwise loop.

▶ DIRECTIONS

From I-20 East, exit onto Oporto-Madrid Boulevard. Turn left onto Oporto Madrid. Turn right at a light onto Rugby Avenue. After Rugby veers to the left, turn right onto 81st Street South. The road ends and enters a steep, narrow private road to Ruffner Mountain Nature Center. Drive through a small parking area and continue to the left between the pavilion and the Nature Center. Park in the large lot in front of you.

Alternate directions: From 1st Avenue North, turn onto 83rd Street North (left if going toward Birmingham, right if coming from Birmingham). A Ruffner Mountain Nature Preserve sign is visible on the corner. Continue to 4th Avenue South; a small sign indicates Ruffner is 1 mile ahead. Bear to the right onto Rugby Avenue. Turn left onto 81st Street South at the Ruffner sign, and the nature preserve is at the top of the hill, past the gate.

KEY AT-A-GLANCE INFORMATION

LENGTH: 0.5 miles

CONFIGURATION: Loop

DIFFICULTY: Easy

SCENERY: Sandstone floaters, limestone outcrops, Turtle Rock

EXPOSURE: Mostly shaded

TRAFFIC: Light

TRAIL SURFACE: Rooty dirt path

HIKING TIME: 30 minutes

ACCESS: Ruffner Mountain is open Tuesday through Saturday, 9 a.m.–5 p.m., and Sunday, 1–5 p.m. (closed Monday)

MAPS: Ruffner Mountain Trail Map, available free at the Nature Center

FACILITIES: Rest rooms, water fountain, drink vending machine, covered pavilion, picnic tables, small amphitheater

SPECIAL COMMENTS: Pick up a copy of the "Geology Trail" guide at the Nature Center. The trail is marked at intervals with numbered posts that correspond to entries in the guide.

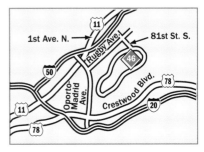

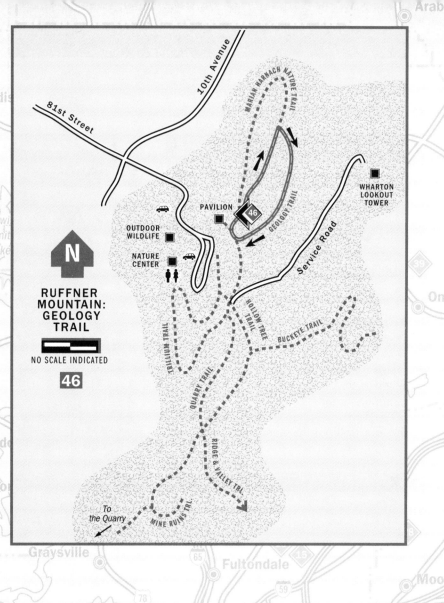

N

RUFFNER
MOUNTAIN:
GEOLOGY
TRAIL

NO SCALE INDICATED

46

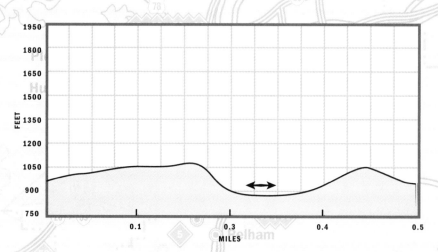

Leave the dirt trail and walk onto an old cement sidewalk. At the fork in the trail, go right and follow a slight incline. Many of the vines in this area are poison ivy, so refrain from touching them. Reach the intersection with the Geology Trail, turn right, and head uphill on stairs made of stone. Look over your left shoulder for a glimpse of a large, white water tank, a reminder of how tightly the nature preserve is woven into the city's fabric. Heading toward East Lake from downtown Birmingham, this water tank is visible from First Avenue North as you cross the viaduct next to Sloss Furnaces National Historic Landmark. Iron ore mined at Ruffner traveled by rail just a few miles to these furnaces, where it was made into pig iron.

Walk beneath a very large downed tree that spans the trail. On the left are the obscured remains of an old mining test pit dug by prospectors looking for iron ore. To see numerous examples of ore pits and other evidence of the extensive iron-ore mining that occurred here in the late nineteenth century, take a walk on the nearby Quarry Trail (p. 207).

Continue ahead to locate two large boulders, sandstone on the right, limestone on the left. The trail booklet notes that the sandstone boulder is called a "float." Its original position was higher up on the mountain, but through time, the processes of erosion and gravity have "floated" this stone down to a lower elevation.

Ascend on a series of log- and stone-reinforced steps. Head up and around to the right to locate post no. 8 for a short lesson in soil ecology. The trail through here is fairly level, as you reach a bench on your right and a large stone to your left. The stone is Turtle Rock, a car-sized limestone boulder estimated to be 450 million years old. Look closely at the large rock and see if you can locate any fossils of small marine animals embedded in it.

The trail then descends from Turtle Rock into a wide, flat area. Continue forward to post no. 5, located where the trail joins an old roadbed. Many of these old logging and mining roads crisscross the mountain, remnants of life and work from over 100 years ago.

The trail continues, passing a large limestone outcrop on your left, then angles down gently, crossing a small wet-weather stream spanned by a narrow plank and handrail. Post no. 3, with a brief lesson in erosion, is located here.

Pass another rock outcropping to your left and shortly arrive at post no. 2. Take the lead from the trail handbook and feel the grainy surface of this sandstone rock. The trail will begin to descend and soon reach post no. 1. In addition to sandstone, limestone is an important rock and very common to Ruffner Mountain. Millions of years ago, this area lay beneath a salty sea. The limestone here formed from calcium carbonate that "settled out" of the water. The remains of a massive limestone quarry lie at the end of Ruffner's Quarry Trail, probably the most popular trail at Ruffner.

Look for a signpost, turn right, and head back to the pavilion to complete this short, rocky, and informative trail.

▶ NEARBY ACTIVITIES

After the hike, step inside the Nature Center to view animal exhibits that include indigenous turtles, fish, and frogs.

RUFFNER MOUNTAIN:
MARIAN HARNACH NATURE TRAIL

KEY AT-A-GLANCE INFORMATION

LENGTH: 0.6 miles

CONFIGURATION: Loop

DIFFICULTY: Easy

SCENERY: Oak-hickory forest

EXPOSURE: Mostly shaded

TRAFFIC: Light most days

TRAIL SURFACE: Rooty dirt path with scattered rocks

HIKING TIME: 30 minutes

ACCESS: Ruffner Mountain is open Tuesday through Saturday, 9 a.m.–5 p.m., and Sunday, 1–5 p.m. (closed Monday)

MAPS: Ruffner Mountain Trail Map, available free at the Nature Center

FACILITIES: Nice rest rooms, water fountain, drink vending machine, covered pavilion, picnic tables, small amphitheater

SPECIAL COMMENTS: Pick up a copy of the "Marian Harnach Nature Trail" guide at the Nature Center. The trail is marked at intervals with numbered posts that correspond to entries in the guide.

IN BRIEF

Hike this short loop for a meandering, educational tour that highlights Ruffner Mountain's forest ecology. The trail is a simple example of how plants, animals, and human history interact.

DESCRIPTION

Walk straight through the covered pavilion and into the brush to start the Marian Harnach Nature Trail, which loops in a counterclockwise direction. This trail was named after a long-time Ruffner Mountain supporter and volunteer. Soon, leave the dirt trail and walk onto an old cement sidewalk, built in the 1930s in anticipation of housing development that never materialized. Reach a fork in the trail, go right, and then look to your right for an old, stone house foundation. The former home supposedly belonged to a bootlegger named Murphy.

DIRECTIONS

From I-20 East, exit onto Oporto-Madrid Boulevard. Turn left onto Oporto-Madrid. Turn right at a light onto Rugby Avenue. After Rugby veers to the left, turn right onto 81st Street South. The road ends and enters a steep, narrow private road to Ruffner Mountain Nature Center. Drive through a small parking area and continue to the left between the pavilion and the Nature Center.

Alternate directions: From 1st Avenue North, turn onto 83rd Street North (left if going toward Birmingham, right if coming from Birmingham). A Ruffner Mountain Nature Preserve sign is visible on the corner. Continue to 4th Avenue South; a small sign indicates Ruffner is 1 mile ahead. Bear to the right onto Rugby Avenue. Turn left onto 81st Street South at the Ruffner sign, and the nature preserve is at the top of the hill, past the gate. Park in the large lot in front of you.

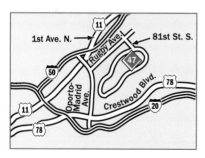

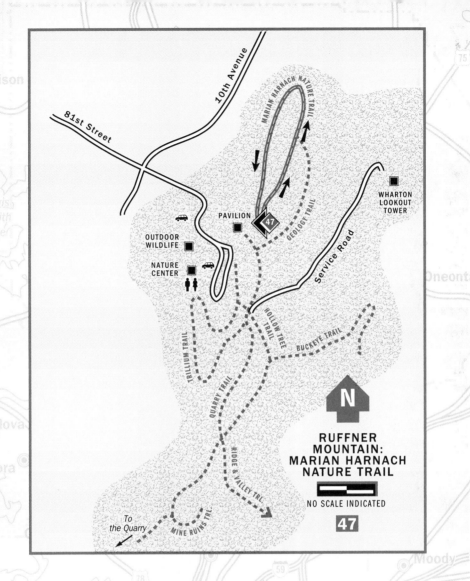

RUFFNER
MOUNTAIN:
MARIAN HARNACH
NATURE TRAIL

NO SCALE INDICATED

47

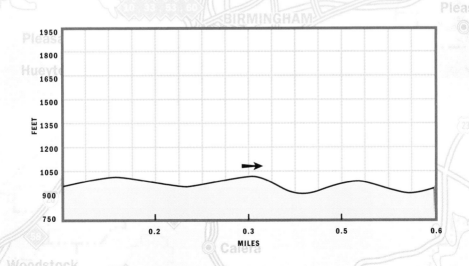

Just past the foundation, watch for a hollow tree rotting on the ground to your right. A standing hollow tree makes great shelter for raccoons and opossums. When it falls, like this one, the decaying wood attracts a variety of smaller critters like beetles. The dead tree will also attract fungi that colonize and assist in its decomposition back into the soil and air. After bearing around to the left, notice the giant vines that hang from the taller trees. Some are as thick as a person's forearm. After stopping to admire a large piece of sandstone, continue along the trail as it eases its climb to a slight incline. The trail booklet notes that sandstone in this area is a reminder of the vast ocean that once covered the state.

The oak-hickory forest here is thick with an understory of brush, vines, small trees, and briars. Many of the vines in this area are of the "don't touch" variety, specifically poison ivy. A single stem that grows outward from the climbing and spreading vine hosts a cluster of three green, serrated leaves. Where the vine clings to larger plants such as trees, brown hairy roots can be seen. The plant also produces small clusters of bright red berries. The toxin in the oily leaves produces a severe itching, and painful rash in most people, which appears as raised, reddened lines on the skin. Wash any body parts exposed to poison ivy with cool, soapy water. Remember the naturalist's maxim, "Leaves of three, leave 'em be."

As the trail booklet notes, observe areas where trees have fallen, allowing sunlight to penetrate freely to the forest floor. These light gaps, which spur growth of new plants and trees, are an important aspect of forest regeneration.

Reach a sign for the Geology Trail, which goes to the right, and continue straight. Cross a marshy spot on two raised wooden boardwalks; watch and listen for small birds flitting in the brush to your left. Continue walking and duck under a large tree that has fallen across the trail. Through here, look for instances of plants that live entirely off of humid air. Known as epiphytes, you may see examples that include the resurrection fern and a variety of lichens.

In late fall and winter, a carpet of leaves covers the trail. You should be able, though, to always make out the path. To make your own relaxation tape, carry a small tape recorder with you as you pass through and over the leaves. The crunching and swishing of boots through leaves can be hypnotizing. As a corollary, keep an eye open for rocks that the leaves may hide for the toe of your boot or shoe to discover. Continue walking as the trail soon descends four wooden steps with a handrail. Past the stairs, the trail continues its descent.

The trail curves back to the left, then descends again. A wooden handrail is located to the right. Cross over a small wooden footbridge, with another handrail on the left. Cross a small wet-weather stream and ascend uphill sharply on stone steps. Along here the trail is very rooty, and the coppery iron-rich soil is exposed. The rich, rusty dirt is tenacious and will deeply stain clothing, especially a pair of white socks.

Look for the trail to pass between two benches—a nice place to stop, rest, and listen to the sounds of the forest. The trail booklet advises listening for the song of the eastern towhee, a small, sparrow-like bird. It's call sounds like, "Drink your tea! Drink your tea!"

Next, the trail passes through an area of forest rich in plants that produce nuts and fruits, including acorns, berries, and persimmons, which are a valuable food source for resident wildlife. Even the berries of the dogwood provide sustenance for animals such as opossums and raccoons.

As the trail descends briefly, look out to your right about 30 feet and feast your eyes on a very large oak. According to the trail booklet, this is a white oak that has been standing here for 150 years. In the fall, the oak sheds thousands of bitter, nutritious acorns. The acorns excite the squirrels, but for the human palate the tannic acid makes them a distant second to an energy bar. Pick up the cement sidewalk again here, following it to the trail fork and out to the trailhead where you started.

▶ NEARBY ACTIVITIES

After the hike, step inside the Nature Center to view animal exhibits that include indigenous turtles, fish, and frogs. Be sure to look in on the timber rattler and the copperhead that share a large aquarium. On the "back porch," take a moment to view a disabled barred owl that has found a permanent home at Ruffner. There is also a small collection of fossils, arrowheads, and mining paraphernalia. Outside, other animal exhibits include a great horned owl, a red-tailed hawk, and other birds and mammals that have been injured and are on the mend.

For a change of scenery, jump in your car and head over to nearby East Lake Park for an easy 1-mile walk around 45-acre East Lake (p. 65).

RUFFNER MOUNTAIN: MINES HIKE

KEY AT-A-GLANCE INFORMATION

LENGTH: 3 miles (varies widely according to the day's hike)

CONFIGURATION: Loop

DIFFICULTY: Moderate/difficult

SCENERY: Rock crusher, tipple, sealed mines, glimpses into an open slope mine

EXPOSURE: Mostly shaded

TRAFFIC: Light, but varies with the size of your group

TRAIL SURFACE: Rooty, dirt path with scattered rocks

HIKING TIME: 5 hours (varies with group size)

ACCESS: This guided hike is scheduled irregularly. Ruffner Mountain is open Tuesday–Saturday, 9 a.m.–5 p.m., and Sunday, 1–5 p.m. (closed Monday).

MAPS: Ruffner Mountain Trail Map, available free at the Nature Center. Information packet is supplied with the hike.

FACILITIES: Nice rest rooms, water fountain, drink vending machine, covered pavilion, picnic tables, small amphitheater

SPECIAL COMMENTS: Meet the hike leader at the Nature Center at the appointed time. There, you can pay your fee and receive your Mine Hike information packet. Call the center at (205) 833-8264 or visit www.ruffnermountain.org to find out dates for this guided hike.

▶ IN BRIEF

This guided hike investigates some of Ruffner Mountain's iron ore heritage. After wandering through a mix of various hardwoods and pines, you'll discover many artifacts from Birmingham's industrial past.

▶ DESCRIPTION

If you have followed some of the other hikes in this book, there's a strong possibility that one of them introduced you to Birmingham's relationship to iron ore and the industry surrounding it. The city's development was due in large part to the presence of three important resources needed to make iron: limestone, iron ore, and coal. Ruffner Mountain was one of the primary producers of iron ore and limestone.

While a guided hike might preclude a certain amount of the spontaneity enjoyed on self-guided hikes, this one is worthwhile because it

▶ DIRECTIONS

From I-20 East, exit onto Oporto-Madrid Boulevard. Turn left onto Oporto-Madrid. Turn right at a traffic light onto Rugby Avenue. After Rugby veers to the left, turn right onto 81st Street South. The road ends and enters a steep, narrow, private road to Ruffner Mountain Nature Center. Drive through a small parking area and continue to the left between the pavilion and the Nature Center.

Alternate directions: From 1st Avenue North, turn onto 83rd Street North (left if going toward Birmingham, right coming from Birmingham). A Ruffner Mountain Nature Preserve sign is visible on the corner. Continue to 4th Avenue South; a small sign indicates Ruffner is 1 mile ahead. Bear to the right onto Rugby Avenue. Turn left onto 81st Street South at the Ruffner sign and the nature preserve is at the top of the hill, past the gate.

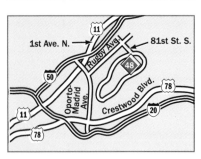

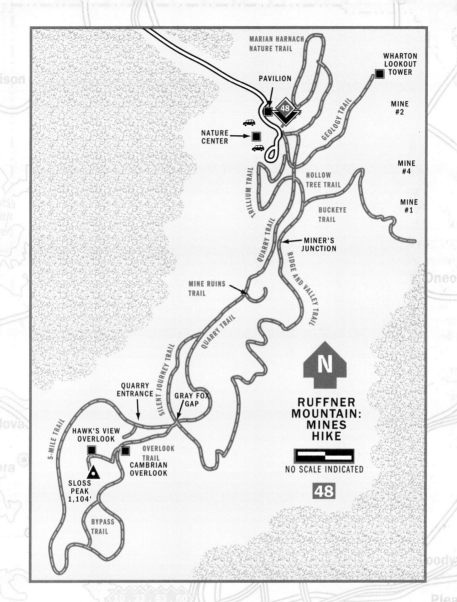

MARIAN HARNACH
NATURE TRAIL

WHARTON
LOOKOUT
TOWER

PAVILION

48

GEOLOGY TRAIL

MINE
#2

NATURE
CENTER

HOLLOW
TREE TRAIL

MINE
#4

TRILLIUM TRAIL

BUCKEYE
TRAIL

MINE
#1

QUARRY TRAIL

MINER'S
JUNCTION

MINE RUINS
TRAIL

RIDGE AND VALLEY TRAIL

QUARRY TRAIL

N

RUFFNER
MOUNTAIN:
MINES
HIKE

QUARRY
ENTRANCE

SILENT JOURNEY TRAIL

GRAY FOX
GAP

NO SCALE INDICATED

48

5-MILE TRAIL

HAWK'S VIEW
OVERLOOK

OVERLOOK
TRAIL
CAMBRIAN
OVERLOOK

SLOSS
PEAK
1,104'

BYPASS
TRAIL

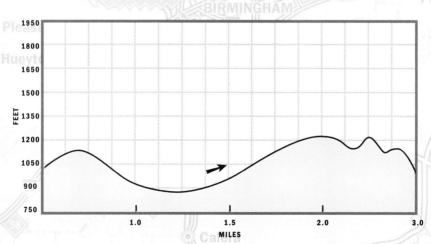

affords access to historical sites not normally available to the general public. When visiting Ruffner, it is important to keep in mind that, due to the extensive amount of mining that occurred here, it is generally not a good idea to leave the trail and strike out on your own without a guide.

With your guide, leave the Nature Center, heading up to the main ridge via the Hollow Tree Trail, where you can see the remains of a giant hollow-trunked tulip poplar. The trail next intersects Ruffner's newest trail, the Buckeye Trail, named for the abundance of small red buckeye trees that grow here. Leave the Buckeye Trail and pass by, or through—depending on that day's route—Mine Site Number 1. Although Mine Site Number 2 is the most complete site, Number 1 features several drift mine openings, a sheave pillar used to raise and lower ore cars by gravity, a hoist foundation, a motor foundation, and a crusher foundation.

Continue, heading east, and arrive at an artesian well that releases a steady flow of cold, clear water. Take your lunch at a nearby picnic table, alfresco, and imagine what the area will look like when Ruffner creates a 1.5-acre wetland here. Part of Ruffner's planned expansion, the park will impound flow from the artesian well and runoff from the mountain to create the wetland. There is a portable toilet located here, so make use of it if you are shy about woodland relief.

After lunch, you'll wend your way through the area of Mine Site Number 4. Visible from the trail are the remains of a WWII-era ore concentration facility, one of two on the mountain. To increase the concentration of pure ore in a load and decrease junk rock, various methods were used. The example at this point in the hike is a rotary kiln. Iron ore arrived at the concentrator from the mine via conveyor belt. Ore dumped into the electrified rotary kiln "roasted" and, in the process, converted the ore from hematite to magnetite. Magnets then drew off the magnetite, separating it from junk rock.

From Number 4, head to the most intact mine, Mine Site Number 2, which provides a comprehensive picture of the evolution of iron-ore mining on Ruffner. Situated in a line running downhill to the southwest, the surface features of Number 2 consist of a hoist, a mine portal, a scale for weighing ore cars, a tipple for separating and sending ore to the crusher, and the massive iron crusher itself. Downhill from the crusher are remains of the heavy media plant, a shop and office, and a crater left from a massive detonation of 20 tons of mining explosives stored nearby. The explosion occurred on July 25, 1971, and blew the heavy media facility to pieces, leaving only its foundation.

MINE SITE NUMBER 2

The most northeast of five ore mines that operated on Ruffner, Mine Site Number 2 is a case study in the evolution of iron ore mining in Birmingham. Owned by Sloss Iron and Steel Co. (later Sloss-Sheffield Steel and Iron Co.), Number 2 first yielded surface ore using strip-mining methods. When the exposed ore was depleted, miners followed the seam as it dipped beneath the surface. Using drift mines, miners drove straight into ravine slopes, sometimes working their way through to the other side of the ravine. The early drift mine openings are located high up on the ravine ridge. Heading southwest, the ore seam continued to drop, so drift mine openings were placed lower and lower on the ravine sides. Eventually the seam ran beneath the ravine, necessitating a third approach: slope mining.

By 1910, all of the surface ore and drift ore at Number 2 had been removed, and the slope mine was opened. For the next 43 years, ore from Number 2 came from beneath the mountain via the slope mine and its extensive maze of hewn underground rooms.

The most dramatic relic at Number 2 is the crusher. To get an idea of the entire process, from beginning to end, head to the top of the slope about 450 feet northeast of the crusher. Located here are the remains of the hoist house, which raised loaded ore cars from the mine and lowered them to the scale. Replacing a steam-powered predecessor, an 800-hp electric hoist manufactured by Birmingham's Hardy-Tynes was installed in 1939.

About 175 feet below the hoist is the opening to the slope mine. With your back to the hoist, standing at the mine entrance, the ground slopes down from left to right, with a retaining wall on the left. In addition to running southwest toward Mine Site 4, following Ruffner Mountain, the slope mine gently angles beneath the surface and continues nearly a mile east/southeast all the way to the Norris freight yards in Irondale. The mine entrance has been filled in, but the mantle to the portal is still visible. The date the slope was opened—1910—is still visible in the stonework. Down the slope on the other side of the ravine to your left is the man-way entrance, where miners entered. Although not visible from here, a compressor facility located over the ridge to your left piped compressed air to the mine. Practically all of the mining machinery was powered pneumatically.

After an ore car emerged from the mine, pulled by the hoist uphill, it was then coasted slowly downhill on tracks. The car traveled about 200 feet from the mine to its first stop at the scale, where it was weighed. After weighing, the car rolled onto the tipple and the ore dropped into a chute.

The tipple is an impressive structure, although not on par with the crusher. Head down to the base of the tipple and see two chutes coming down from above. The chute on the left took the junk rock; the chute on the right sent ore-bearing rock on to a conveyor belt that carried it to the crusher downhill. A solid structure of cement, stone, iron, and timbers, the tipple has lost most of its woodwork, but the stonework remains in fairly good shape. The iron chutes and other iron parts, though, are slowly deteriorating.

Although Ruffner values its industrial artifacts, rust and flaking of the metal objects is persistent and will eventually lead to their demise. The park's primary preservation strategy is to keep the stonework intact to dissuade plants from taking root in the masonry, thus maintaining the integrity of the tipple and crusher foundations.

Walk down toward the imposing crusher. Made by a firm in Cudahy, Wisconsin, the McCully Gyratory Crusher functions like a giant coffee grinder. Instead of beans from Columbia, though, this crusher ground chunks of iron-ore bearing rock that emerged from the ground just 200 feet away. Driven by a motor, first steam and then electric, the grinding head of the crusher was turned by a shaft from the adjacent motor room. Perched on a steep hillside atop its massive concrete base, the crusher is an otherworldly sight to behold.

Some junk rock was split off in the tipple, but an ore concentrator 175 feet downhill from the crusher removed even more non-iron-bearing rock. Ideally, as much junk rock as possible was removed before the ore was loaded onto the nearby Birmingham Mineral Railroad for the short journey alongside First Avenue North to Sloss Furnaces. In the early 1950s, Sloss attempted a new type of concentration (beneficiation) at the Number 2 mine. Using a heavy media concentrator, ore arrived from the crusher via conveyor belt and passed through a secondary crusher, which reduced the 6-to-8-inch diameter ore to three-quarter-inch chunks. These small pieces were then floated, allowing the heavier ore to collect on the bottom, with junk on top. According to folks at Ruffner, Sloss was successful in raising the ore content from 33 percent to 38 percent, but it was not wildly successful. Eventually, pressure from new discoveries of richer ores in South America, a gradual diminishing of Birmingham's ore quality, and mineshaft encounters with the water table led to the mines' closing on June 1, 1953.

Although there are a few more artifacts to see on the way back, after viewing the Number 2 site from top to bottom, the walk back is a time to wind down and enjoy the forest. After passing an air compressor facility, circle back around southwest for a pleasant ridge line walk along a trail/service road, which passes the high point of Ruffner (1,246 feet), back to the Nature Center.

▶ NEARBY ACTIVITIES

After the hike, step inside the Nature Center to view animal exhibits that include indigenous turtles, fish, and frogs. Be sure to look in on the timber rattler and the copperhead that share a large aquarium.

RUFFNER MOUNTAIN: QUARRY TRAIL

▶ IN BRIEF

Take a pleasant walk to an abandoned limestone quarry along Ruffner's main trail. Along the way, visit several overlooks offering good views of Ruffner Mountain, as well as a rock structure, which was part of a hoisting system used to transport iron-ore cars up and down the mountain.

▶ DESCRIPTION

Before you get started, walk across the parking lot to the Nature Center and pick up a map and a "Quarry Trail" guide. The numbered entries in this handbook, which illuminates the history and scenery of the trail, correspond to wooden posts you will see along the way. While this route is a little long for young children, if you bring a child-carrier backpack, as my wife and I did on our visit, you should be fine.

▶ DIRECTIONS

From I-20 East, exit onto Oporto-Madrid Boulevard. Turn left onto Oporto-Madrid. Turn right at a light onto Rugby Avenue. After Rugby veers left, turn right onto 81st Street South. The road ends at a steep, narrow road to Ruffner Mountain Nature Center. Drive through a small parking area and continue to the left between the pavilion and the Nature Center. Park in the large lot in front of you.

Alternate directions: From First Avenue North, turn onto 83rd Street North (left if going toward Birmingham, right if leaving). A Ruffner Mountain Nature Preserve sign is visible on the corner. Continue to 4th Avenue South; a small sign indicates Ruffner is 1 mile ahead. Bear to the right onto Rugby Avenue. Turn left onto 81st Street South at the Ruffner sign and the nature preserve is at the top of the hill, past the gate.

KEY AT-A-GLANCE INFORMATION

LENGTH: 4.2 miles

CONFIGURATION: Balloon with a very long string

DIFFICULTY: Moderate

SCENERY: Hardwood forest, limestone/sandstone formations, iron-ore pits, quarry overlooks

EXPOSURE: Mostly shady, exposed in quarry

TRAFFIC: Light during week; heaviest on sunny weekends

TRAIL SURFACE: Rocky, rooty dirt path

HIKING TIME: 1.5 hours

ACCESS: Ruffner Mountain is open Tuesday through Saturday, 9 a.m.–5 p.m.; Sunday, 1–5 p.m.; closed Monday

MAPS: Ruffner Mountain trail map, available at the Nature Center (free).

FACILITIES: Nice rest rooms, water fountain, drink vending machine, covered pavilion, picnic tables, small amphitheater

SPECIAL COMMENTS: Pick up a copy of the "Quarry Trail" guide at the Nature Center. The trail is marked at intervals with numbered posts that correspond to entries in the guide.

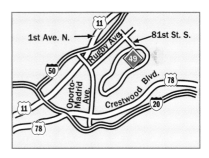

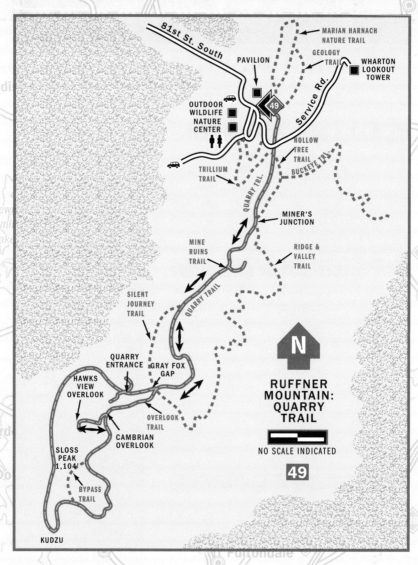

MARIAN HARNACH
NATURE TRAIL

81st St. South

PAVILION

GEOLOGY
TRAIL

WHARTON
LOOKOUT
TOWER

49

Service Rd.

OUTDOOR
WILDLIFE
NATURE
CENTER

HOLLOW
TREE
TRAIL

BUCKEYE TRL.

TRILLIUM
TRAIL

QUARRY TRL.

MINER'S
JUNCTION

MINE
RUINS
TRAIL

RIDGE &
VALLEY
TRAIL

SILENT
JOURNEY
TRAIL

QUARRY TRAIL

QUARRY
ENTRANCE

GRAY FOX
GAP

HAWKS
VIEW
OVERLOOK

OVERLOOK
TRAIL

CAMBRIAN
OVERLOOK

SLOSS
PEAK
1,104

BYPASS
TRAIL

KUDZU

N

RUFFNER
MOUNTAIN:
QUARRY
TRAIL

NO SCALE INDICATED

49

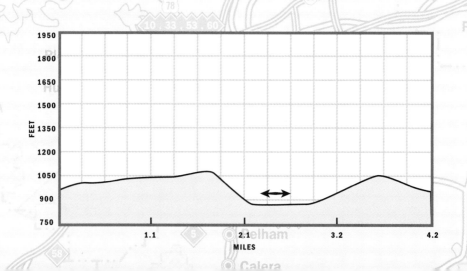

1950				
1800				
1650				
1500				
1350				
1200				
1050				
900				
750				

FEET

1.1   2.1   3.2   4.2
MILES

From the parking lot, take the sidewalk uphill and follow the sign to the Geology Trail. The dirt trail ascends to a fork. The Geology Trail goes left; stay right and continue uphill. In summer, keep an eye out for yellow jackets.

Cross a narrow blacktop service road to an information kiosk on your right. Continue straight ahead, following the Quarry Trail, which is clearly marked here. Along the way, ignore the numerous short trails that lead off to the right and left, The path climbs on stone-and-log terrace steps, steep in spots, but no scrambling is required.

The trail passes through a mixed hardwood forest dominated by middle-aged oaks and maples. In spring and summer, wildflowers are abundant, but numerous signs discourage hikers from picking them.

At an elevation of 1,105 feet, reach the posted Miners Junction, where the Hollow Tree Trail and the Ridge Valley Trail intersect the Quarry Trail. Continue straight on the Quarry Trail, which is flat as you walk along the ridge. About 15 minutes in, the Mine Ruins Trail appears on your left near a bench. Turn left onto the Mine Ruins Trail and immediately spot an old mine sluice lined with iron-ore-rich rocks. Just a few hundred feet down, you'll see a stone structure. According to the "Quarry Trail" handbook, the structure was part of the hoisting system used to ferry iron-ore cars up and down the mountain. Return to the Quarry Trail and turn left to resume the hike.

During this and other trail segments, notice the path, which at times is a coppery, muddy, orange color, evidence of the heavy iron oxide content of the soil. At Dogwood Fork, approach a bench and the intersection with the Silent Journey Trail, which leaves to the right. Stay forward on the Quarry Trail, walk across a couple of logs placed across the trail, and follow the arrow pointing left to descend in an easterly direction. You'll notice many downed pines throughout the area. Some have been blown over by strong winds, but most have been cut down due to pine-beetle damage. Watch for a large hole off to your left, indicating former mining activity. Once you're up on top of the ridge, you should have a nice breeze. Here, though, in the lee of the mountain, the air is still and warmer than up on top.

The trail continues, heading south. Pass two double-trunked oaks on your right. Pass through an area with rocks on either side and walk down stone steps placed in the trail. Ahead are two wooden "benches" that look more like boot scrapers. Here, at Grey Fox Gap, the path forks. A trail goes right, but go left to promptly arrive at a cluster of signs. Here, leave the Quarry Trail and hike left up to the rim of the mine on the Overlook Trail.

At the top of the climb, the wind picks up, providing a chilling gust in winter or a refreshing breeze in summer. The quarry will come into view ahead as you descend to a T-intersection. Turn left and immediately back right to the Cambrian Overlook. The Quarry is circular in shape and crisscrossed with trails along the bottom, at about 60 feet below the overlook. In the distance, you can vaguely see Birmingham International Airport and traffic moving along I-59. Walk back down to the Overlook Trail and turn right. The Overlook Trail continues on to Hawks' View Overlook and Sloss Peak, both accessed via a spur trail. After hitting both of these high, scenic spots, return to the main trail and turn back to the right onto the Five Mile Trail. While they are absent early on, keep an eye out for the yellow blazes marking this trail. Follow Five Mile Trail as it goes left and skirts around the quarry back to the Quarry Trail at Grey Fox Gap.

The Five Mile Trail narrows along a mild incline to reach the Bypass Trail on the right. Taking this will lop off about a half-mile from the Five Mile Trail. Otherwise, continue on the Five Mile Trail. Numerous mine pits and depressions are visible to your right and left. Soon, the Bypass Trail will rejoin the Five Mile Trail from the right.

Pass through an area of numerous downed pines, watching on trail-left for a square cement-sided cistern. No one is positive about its former function, but, according to Ruffner naturalist Marty Schulman, it was probably used in conjunction with mining on the mountain. Soon, enter a clearing framed with kudzu, where the trail veers to the right. Along this section, traffic noise is audible, as are the sounds of life from surrounding neighborhoods. Glimpses of homes and traffic along Oporto-Madrid Boulevard are visible to the left.

At one point, you can leave the Five Mile Trail and venture into the quarry through some tall rocks on a path to your right. Otherwise, stay on the trail and circle around to the main entrance to the quarry. There, turn right to enter the quarry and explore the trails and rocks. Camping, climbing, and rappelling are prohibited, so leave your ropes and tent at home. Kids enjoy running amok in the quarry interior, so don't leave them at home.

Exit the quarry and turn right onto what is now the Quarry Trail, which will lead you back to the Nature Center. If in doubt on the way back, always follow the signs for the Nature Center.

▶ NEARBY ACTIVITIES

After the hike, step inside the Nature Center to view animal exhibits that include indigenous turtles, fish, and frogs. Be sure to look in on the timber rattler and the copperhead that share a large aquarium. On the "back porch," take a moment to view a disabled barred owl that has found a permanent home at Ruffner. There is also a small collection of fossils, arrowheads, and mining paraphernalia. Outside, animal exhibits feature a great horned owl, a red-tailed hawk, and other birds and mammals that have been injured and are on the mend.

For a bite to eat, head back down Oporto-Madrid and turn onto Crestwood Boulevard/US 78, where restaurants of every ilk are located. For a good pizza, turn right and head up to the Festival Center, which is on the left just above Hooters. Locate Alfredo's in the far back of the shopping complex.

For a change of scenery, jump in your car and head over to nearby East Lake Park for an easy 1-mile walk around 45-acre East Lake (p. 65).

RUFFNER MOUNTAIN:
RIDGE AND VALLEY COMBO

▶ IN BRIEF

Begin this hike on the popular Quarry Trail, then put your feet onto Ruffner's most demanding trail: the snakelike Ridge and Valley Trail. This trail accumulates over 1,000 feet of elevation change as it drops, climbs, and winds through the forest. Top off this challenging section with a sloping climb back to the Quarry Trail via the 0.3-mile Silent Journey Trail. Overall, this is a great workout.

▶ DESCRIPTION

From the parking lot, take the sidewalk uphill and follow the sign to the Geology Trail. Where the dirt trail ascends to a fork, the Geology Trail goes left and the Quarry Trail heads right. Bear right and continue uphill. In summer, keep an eye out for yellow jackets.

After crossing a narrow blacktop service road to an information kiosk on your right, continue

▶ DIRECTIONS

From I-20 East, exit onto Oporto-Madrid Boulevard. Turn left onto Oporto-Madrid. Turn right at a light onto Rugby Avenue. After Rugby veers to the left, turn right onto 81st Street South. The road ends and enters a steep, narrow private road to Ruffner Mountain Nature Center. Drive through a small parking area and continue to the left between the pavilion and the Nature Center. Park in the large lot in front of you.

Alternate directions: From 1st Avenue North, turn onto 83rd Street North (left if going toward Birmingham, right if coming from Birmingham). A Ruffner Mountain Nature Preserve sign is visible on the corner. Continue to 4th Avenue South; a small sign indicates Ruffner is 1 mile ahead. Bear to the right onto Rugby Avenue. Turn left onto 81st Street South at the Ruffner sign, and the nature preserve is at the top of the hill, past the gate.

ⓘ KEY AT-A-GLANCE INFORMATION

LENGTH: 2.5 miles

CONFIGURATION: Balloon

DIFFICULTY: Moderate/difficult

SCENERY: Mixed-hardwood forest, mining excavation sites, tiny streams, small V-shaped valleys

EXPOSURE: Mostly shaded

TRAFFIC: Light on Ridge and Valley Trail, moderate on Silent Journey Trail, heavier on Quarry Trail

TRAIL SURFACE: Dirt with roots and rocks

HIKING TIME: 1.5 hours

ACCESS: Ruffner Mountain is open Tuesday through Saturday, 9 a.m.–5 p.m., and Sunday, 1–5 p.m. (closed Monday)

MAPS: Ruffner Mountain Trail Map, available at the Nature Center (free).

FACILITIES: Rest rooms, water fountain, drink vending machine, covered pavilion, picnic tables, small amphitheater

SPECIAL COMMENTS: Three trails make up this balloon-shaped hike: the Quarry Trail, Ridge and Valley Trail, and Silent Journey Trail, with a return on the Quarry Trail

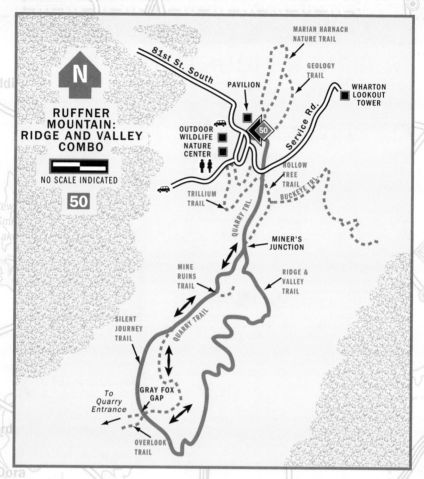

N

RUFFNER
MOUNTAIN:
RIDGE AND VALLEY
COMBO

NO SCALE INDICATED

50

81st St. South

MARIAN HARNACH
NATURE TRAIL

GEOLOGY
TRAIL

PAVILION

WHARTON
LOOKOUT
TOWER

Service Rd.

OUTDOOR
WILDLIFE
NATURE CENTER

HOLLOW
TREE
TRAIL

TRILLIUM
TRAIL

QUARRY TRL.

BUCKEYE TRL.

MINER'S
JUNCTION

MINE
RUINS
TRAIL

RIDGE &
VALLEY
TRAIL

SILENT
JOURNEY
TRAIL

QUARRY TRAIL

To
Quarry
Entrance

GRAY FOX
GAP

OVERLOOK
TRAIL

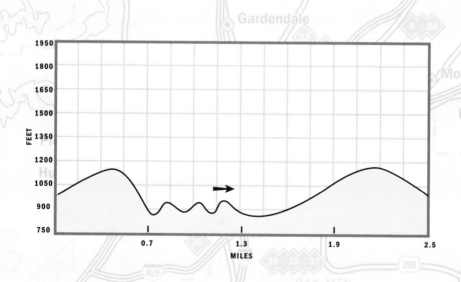

following the Quarry Trail, which is clearly marked. The path heads uphill, with footing help from stone-and-log terracing.

Reach the posted Miners Junction, elevation 1,105 feet, where the Hollow Tree Trail and the Ridge and Valley Trail intersect the Quarry Trail. Turn left onto the orange-blazed Ridge and Valley Trail, a narrow dirt path that initially descends down and to the right, heading roughly south. This path is well marked with orange blazes on trees. Look for remnants of mine excavation to the left as you pass through a mix of maples and oaks. Birds are a common sight (and sound) here, including robins and the occasional mockingbird.

The trail meanders down through an area of pines, then into an area of pines mixed with hardwoods. Typifying its rambling nature, the trail goes left, heads roughly east, levels out, bears right heading south, and then cambers back to the east once more.

Next, the trail begins one of its many steep descents, this one to a tiny stream flowing downhill on your right. Continue, passing through a rocky area, as the trail seems to roam with a mind of its own. Soon, reach some exposed sandstone blocks on your left as you continue downhill. Step up a few steep steps and turn right, heading downhill to the southeast past a very tall, leaning pine on your left.

Descend steeply to and cross over a boardwalk that spans a wet-weather drainage. Step up some stone steps, reaching a hummock of land with a drainage on either side. Notice numerous mulberry trees through here and the occasional Christmas fern. Bear around right as the trail dips down and ascends steeply. Cross a small bridge as you head due south, then turn back right over a log and up more stone steps.

Heading northwest now, pass through an area of tall hardwoods, then descend past a double-trunked oak. Continue hiking upward, roughly heading south, winding and dipping. Cross what looks like an old logging road and bear back to the right, heading west. Even in cool weather, you should have a nice line of sweat on your forehead by now.

The trail becomes difficult to follow through here, so pay closer attention to the blazes. Tromp uphill, still heading west. Look down at the soil along this stretch of path. It's a distinct rust/orange color—golden in the eyes of an iron maker. Bear right and climb steeply only to jib back to the left, heading west. See a rust-colored rock seam exposed on your right. Now head up past more exposed rock, then dip down to the left.

Look for a mining test pit on your right and then an area of large rocks, also on the right. Pass a large, singular block of moss-covered sedimentary rock and soon begin to descend steeply, heading south with a 40-foot drop to the right.

The path is very steep as you descend to a series of stone steps. Curve left and reach the bottom of a small valley, which now parallels the trail on your right. Reach another gathering of small mulberry trees, jog to the right down to a point between two slopes, then bear left. Reach a three-foot-wide stream that may be dry, cross it, and continue up and over a small ridge to see what looks like a cave entrance surrounded by blocks of sandstone embedded into the hillside—most likely the entrance to an old slope mine.

Hike uphill, now heading up the other side of the small valley, roughly heading west. Soon, you will begin a very steep and steady climb. Pass boulders to your left and hike up through what appears to be a manmade cut in the hillside. Near the top of this cut, go left and continue up.

Step onto an old logging/mining road and turn left. This is a tricky portion of the trail (you'll be tempted to go right, but go left). The path is wide as it descends eastward. Pick up the orange blazes again, which will not appear until about 100 feet after the last turn. You may hear a train blowing off in the distance, a reminder of Ruffner's urban surroundings.

The trail levels out, making its way south through an area of pleasant woodsy walking. It then veers around to the southwest and begins to descend, soon heading roughly north. Lined with stone blocks for a short distance, the trail continues to meander, this time south with a small valley appearing to your right.

Pass through six orange blazes clustered together, turn right, and drop down to the valley floor. Begin to ascend, passing onto the second hummock with drainage cuts on either side. The cut/stream to your left may be running. The cut to your right will probably be dry, unless it has recently rained.

Heading roughly north, descend to and cross a small footbridge, and then continue straight up along a rocky section. Climb steeply, passing stacks of sandstone blocks on the left. Pass a big boulder pile on trail-left, then duck under a large hanging vine and continue west uphill.

The trail snakes in tight turns up the hillside, appearing to pass through an invisible labyrinth. A short portion of level trail then dips downhill, heading southeast until the path levels again. Watch for a tree with an orange X on it. Do not turn toward the tree, but continue along a steady meandering uphill track.

Pass through an area of downed trees, primarily on the downslope to your left. Heading south now over a relatively flat, undulating path, the trail offers more pleasant, easy walking. Look for another old mining test pit to your left and then cross an old logging road. Near the boundary of the Ruffner Mountain Nature Preserve, cross over the ridge and head down once again into another V-shaped valley.

The path parallels the ridge and then turns back downward to the south/southwest until it reaches the valley bottom. With a small creek in front of you, turn right and soon turn left to cross the creek and tramp uphill. Wind along, continuing uphill, through yet another patch of small mulberry trees. Ascend a few steps and follow the arrow to the right on a wide, level path. Continue walking, heading roughly north, past rock piles along the way. The trail bears left across an old logging/mining road. Dip down, then ascend up some stone steps. Approach and ascend 15 log steps to reach Gray Fox Gap, which is also where the Quarry Trail ends. Stop here to rest on the bench if you like.

At the Gray Fox Gap sign, turn left onto an unmarked trail. Look for a turquoise green blaze as you enter. This is the 0.3-mile Silent Journey Trail, which will bring you back to the Quarry Trail, which you will then take back to the parking area.

The trail begins level and flat, with a slope up from left to right, heading north. The trail begins to climb easily in a nearly straight line. Look for a double-trunked oak on trail-left, a small pit on trail-left, and then a second double-trunker, also on the left. Pass a standout magnolia tree, with bright, waxy, green leaves, up on trail-right. Continue climbing easily until you reach the Quarry Trail. Turn left onto the Quarry Trail and follow the signs back to the Nature Center.

▶ NEARBY ACTIVITIES

After the hike, step back inside the Nature Center to view animal exhibits that include indigenous turtles, fish, and frogs. Be sure to look in on the timber rattler and the copperhead that share a large aquarium. On the "back porch," take a moment to view a disabled barred owl that has found a permanent home at Ruffner. There is also a small collection of fossils, arrowheads, and mining paraphernalia. Outside, other animal exhibits include a great horned owl, a red-tailed hawk, and other birds and mammals that have been injured and are on the mend.

For a bite to eat, head back down Oporto-Madrid and turn onto Crestwood Boulevard/US 78, where restaurants of every ilk are located. For a good pizza, turn right and head up to the Festival Center, which is on the left just above Hooters. Locate Alfredo's in the far back of the Festival Center shopping complex.

RUFFNER MOUNTAIN:
TRILLIUM/HOLLOW TREE TRAIL

KEY AT-A-GLANCE INFORMATION

LENGTH: 1.2 miles

CONFIGURATION: Figure-eight

DIFFICULTY: Easy

SCENERY: Wildflowers in spring, mushrooms in fall, a giant hollow tree

EXPOSURE: Mostly shaded

TRAFFIC: Light

TRAIL SURFACE: Rooty dirt path

HIKING TIME: 1 hour

ACCESS: Ruffner Mountain is open Tuesday through Saturday, 9 a.m.–5 p.m.; Sunday, 1–5 p.m.; closed Monday

MAPS: Ruffner Mountain trail map, available free at the Nature Center

FACILITIES: Nice rest rooms, water fountain, drink vending machine, covered pavilion, picnic tables, small amphitheater

SPECIAL COMMENTS: This trail combines the Trillium Trail (0.5-mile loop), the Hollow Tree Trail (0.4-mile), and a 0.4-mile portion of the Quarry Trail.

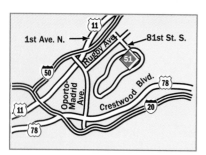

IN BRIEF

The first half of this hike offers a nice change from most of the ridge hikes at Ruffner, leading visitors through a pastoral valley and several culverts. The second half of the hike heads back up to a ridge, passing by the remains of Ruffner's famous Hollow Tree.

DESCRIPTION

From the parking lot, take the sidewalk uphill, then follow the sign to the Geology Trail. Take the dirt trail and ascend to a fork. The Geology Trail goes left; follow the Quarry Trail right and continue uphill. Cross a narrow blacktop service road to reach an information kiosk on your right. Turn right onto the Trillium Trail (the Quarry Trail continues straight). If it's not springtime, imagine an abundance of wildflowers here, including maroon trilliums. Also, if it's not springtime, you can pretend to not pick the flowers.

DIRECTIONS

From I-20 East, exit onto Oporto-Madrid Boulevard. Turn left onto Oporto-Madrid. Turn right at a light onto Rugby Avenue. After Rugby veers left, turn right onto 81st Street South. The road ends at a steep, narrow road to Ruffner Mountain Nature Center. Drive through a small parking area and continue to the left between the pavilion and the Nature Center. Park in the large lot in front of you.

Alternate directions: From First Avenue North, turn onto 83rd Street North (left if going toward Birmingham, right if leaving). A Ruffner Mountain Nature Preserve sign is visible on the corner. Continue to 4th Avenue South; a small sign indicates Ruffner is 1 mile ahead. Bear to the right onto Rugby Avenue. Turn left onto 81st Street South at the Ruffner sign and the nature preserve is at the top of the hill, past the gate.

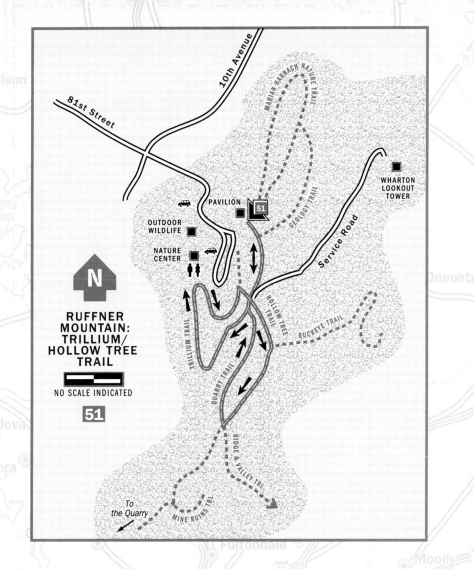

N

RUFFNER
MOUNTAIN:
TRILLIUM/
HOLLOW TREE
TRAIL

NO SCALE INDICATED

51

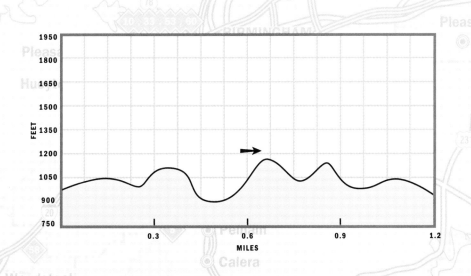

Continue forward, noticing frequent wood ferns and small scrub trees such as sourwood. The sourwood leaf is identifiable by tiny hairs that bristle up and down the stem of the green leaf. The true test is to take a nibble and feel your mouth pucker. Taller trees such as maples, tulip poplar, and oaks tower overhead, as do mulberries, with their irregularly lobed leaves.

Reach a point where the trail looks like it might want to run away to the right, but go left and up the stone steps to stay on the trail. Soon, the trail begins to descend, heading left over logs and rocks in the path. The trail is short and easy here, but be wary of the many rocks that could trigger a fall or twist an ankle. Pass a large boulder to your right as you walk down a short series of stone steps. Sandstone "drift" rocks are common in this area. Hike the nearby Geology Trail (p. 195) to find out what a drift stone is.

Continue through an area of tangled, downed trees that seem to reach out to snag your clothes. This portion of the trail is very near to a residential area, and although you can't see the houses, you may hear the faint whine of a lawnmower in the distance.

The trail curves back to the right and then levels and straightens briefly. Enter an area where there is a large gap in the canopy. Look to your left here to see a bird-house. The trail then begins to descend through half-a-dozen large pines. In one of the few places on Ruffner where this occurs, pine needles mat the forest floor. Drop down to a small wet-weather drainage and cross a footbridge made of railroad ties. You may hear the drone of a small plane passing overhead, taking off or landing at nearby Birmingham International Airport.

Descend to a rock-filled culvert, cross a plank bridge with a low handrail, and immediately head up, climbing briefly. This hike, which explores a hillside, has a much different feel than the longer and more popular Quarry Trail. The mood here is of wandering rather than of going somewhere.

Follow the trail as it continues to curve back to the right. A small shortcut to the left leads to the parking lot. Continue forward past four pines clustered together and then step over a big chunk of sandstone. Note a small magnolia tree to your left growing beside a giant oak. The trail climbs and crosses steps made of stones and logs, then curves back to the left. The parking lot becomes visible to your left as you reach the paved service road.

Turn right and walk up the paved road to access the Hollow Tree Trail. Stop at the information kiosk to read about the 150-year-old tulip tree (yellow poplar) that is the trail's namesake. The Hollow Tree stood for many years, allowing several people at a time to stand inside and look up through its trunk to the sky. In December of 1999, the 80-foot tree suffered fire damage but continued to stand. Another fire in March of 2002 led to the tree's demise and a controlled felling. Portions of the hollow trunk are on display below the main parking area.

Locate the sign to the Hollow Tree Trail, turn left, grab the handrail, and ascend. Straight up the trail, about 200 feet, are the remains of the storied hollow tree. A ten-foot portion of the hollow, charred trunk remains standing on trail-left. On trail-right lay sawn sections of the old tree. Step up into the trunk, like many others have done, and have your picture taken for posterity.

Continue forward and shortly come to a large water-filled ore pit. A bench sits to your right as well. Follow the trail up the rooty path, noting another pit to your left. Continue past a cluster of signs and turn right onto a gravel double-track road with a power line overhead. The road climbs up to the left, where two large antennae and a small brick building come into view. The trail then heads right as a footpath.

The trail here descends but only slightly. Look for a large pit off to the right as you continue to descend. Thread your way through some large downed trees and several small pits to the left and right. The trail then snakes down to a trail intersection. Look for a sign cluster on your left. Head back to the parking lot by taking a sharp right back onto the Quarry Trail.

▶ NEARBY ACTIVITIES

After the hike, step inside the Nature Center to view animal exhibits that include indigenous turtles, fish, and frogs. Be sure to look in on the timber rattler and the copperhead that share a large aquarium. On the "back porch," take a moment to view a disabled barred owl that has found a permanent home at Ruffner. There is also a small collection of fossils, arrowheads, and mining paraphernalia. Outside, animal exhibits feature a great horned owl, a red-tailed hawk, and other birds and mammals that have been injured and are on the mend.

For a bite to eat, head back down Oporto-Madrid and turn onto Crestwood Boulevard/US 78, where restaurants of every ilk are located. For a good pizza, turn right and head up to the Festival Center, which is on the left just above Hooters. Locate Alfredo's in the far back of the shopping complex.

For a change of scenery, jump in your car and head over to nearby East Lake Park for an easy 1-mile walk around 45-acre East Lake (p. 65).

SIPSEY RIVER TRAIL

IN BRIEF

This relatively flat but rugged trail traces the Sipsey River. The forest is thick, crowding the trail and subduing the light in spring and summer.

DESCRIPTION

The Sipsey Fork of the Black Warrior River begins in the Sipsey Wilderness, at the confluence of Hubbard and Thompson Creeks, and is a National Park Service–designated Wild and Scenic River (36.4 miles wild, 25 miles scenic). On its way to Smith Lake, the river flows through the Sipsey Wilderness and is joined by Borden Creek near Winston CR 60. The Sipsey Fork resumes its flow beyond the Lewis Smith Dam, at the southernmost reach of Smith Lake, and continues to flow south to meet Mulberry Fork, which, along with Locust Fork, creates the Black Warrior.

The Sipsey Wilderness is in the northwest section of Bankhead National Forest and is the largest federally designated wilderness area east of the Mississippi River. Known as the Black Warrior National Forest from 1936 to 1942, Congress renamed the forest in 1942 to honor William B. Bankhead and designated the Sipsey Wilderness Area in 1975. Acreage is estimated at 24,922 and the area ranges in elevation from 580 to 1,000 feet.

DIRECTIONS

From Birmingham, take I-65 North 46.5 miles to Cullman, Exit 308 a (rest area is located at 40 miles). Exit and turn left onto US 278 West. Drive 37 miles and turn right onto CR 33 (don't turn right on CR 33 at 31 miles). Follow CR 33 for 12.5 miles and turn left onto CR 6. Drive 3.7 miles on CR 6, which changes to CR 60, and turn left into a Bankhead National Forest day-use parking area. The sign here reads "Sipsey River Picnic/Campground." Park and walk toward the map board, which is beside the trailhead, to pay your fee.

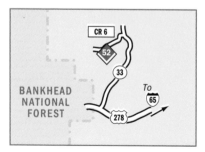

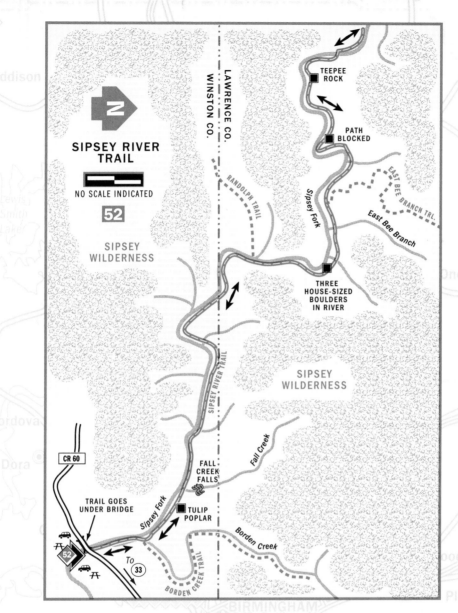

SIPSEY RIVER TRAIL

NO SCALE INDICATED

52

SIPSEY
WILDERNESS

LAWRENCE CO.
WINSTON CO.

TEEPEE
ROCK

PATH
BLOCKED

Sipsey Fork

RANDOLPH TRAIL

EAST BEE BRANCH TRL.

East Bee Branch

THREE
HOUSE-SIZED
BOULDERS
IN RIVER

SIPSEY
WILDERNESS

SIPSEY RIVER TRAIL

Fall Creek

CR 60

TRAIL GOES
UNDER BRIDGE

Sipsey Fork

FALL
CREEK
FALLS

TULIP
POPLAR

Borden Creek

BORDEN CREEK TRAIL

52

To
33

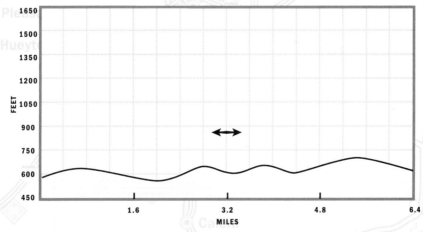

Designated as Trail 209 by the Forest Service, follow the trail marked 200/209 downhill from the map board and beneath a bridge that spans the Sipsey Fork. Heading north, walk along a shady dirt path beneath a mix of pines, maples, river birch, beech, tulip poplar, American holly, and other trees. The river to your left is shallow, about 20 feet wide, and has a sandy bottom. A peculiar wet-basement odor often permeates the forest here. It seems to emanate from the nearly noiseless river, which only occasionally offers the slightest riffling sounds. The odor is not unpleasant, just ever present.

Begin to cross feeder streams, dipping down and popping up their signature steep and slick slopes. Occasionally you can cross these numerous feeders on a downed tree. At 0.4 miles on trail-right, a thin waterfall pours off a 30-foot ledge. Look for purple spiderwort and bright-yellow black-eyed Susans in the cove surrounding the falls. In June, look for the white blooms of the oak-leaf hydrangea, Alabama's official wildflower. Although usually obscured by the thick woods, rocky sandstone bluffs on both sides of the river create a wide, boxy lane for the Sipsey fork.

In addition to numerous campsites along the trail, downed trees are frequently visible. Many have had sections removed, allowing the trail to pass through the debris, but you'll have to either scratch across or jag around many fallen trees along the way. Two primary forces bring the trees down, high winds and the Southern pine beetle. The United States Forest Services notes that 8,000 acres of pines have been killed by the beetle in the Sipsey Wilderness since the year 2000.

At 0.6 miles, approach a wide camping area where Borden Creek joins the Sipsey from the north. Often you'll find hikers standing here looking for the trail. The trail that continues around right follows Borden Creek. Standing at the confluence of the Sipsey and Borden Creek, look across Borden Creek to the far side and you'll see a steep bank that is slightly notched where the Sipsey River Trail continues.

The opportunity to wade is always fun. Unless there's been flooding, the water level of Borden Creek is less than knee-deep year-round and pleasantly cool. I just walked across with my boots on and squished along for the rest of the day. Climbing up the opposite bank, which is slick, you may have to grab at some roots to facilitate your exit. Bear left, following the Sipsey, and head northwest through a dense understory that includes hemlock and big-leaf magnolias.

For the next 6 miles you'll be walking against the river's flow along a relatively flat path that meanders occasionally between the river and the bluffs, crossing numerous feeder-stream culverts. With only the echo of songbirds audible, the forest is very quiet. It is also quite dim at times and can be oppressive as the trailside vegetation presses in. This is a trail that feels you. Overhead, the canopy is occasionally so thick that a kind of twilight descends. I love it, but I can imagine that the combination of quiet, the sense of enclosure, and the dimness might send a few people into a claustrophobic fit.

At 1 mile, reach a culvert, with a cove of boulders to the right, and dip down and up. After you pop up on the other side, see a massive tulip poplar on your right, the lower limbs (which are 50 feet up) themselves look like large trees growing out sideways from the massive trunk.

Just around the corner, reach the tumbling waterfall of Falls Creek Falls, a scenic, five-foot-wide curtain of water that drops 30 feet, boils over rocks, and then runs slowly into the Sipsey below. On your return hike, this is a great place to rest and maybe even take a cold, outdoor shower. For the next mile, walk past hawthorns, pignut hickory, hemlock, a variety of ferns and mosses, wild blackberry vines overhanging the trail, and bamboo.

Until you cross the Sipsey at mile 6.3, you'll repeat the pattern of crossing feeder culverts—some wet, some dry—that lead into rocky coves. The shallow river will accompany you the entire way, often deepening where the watercourse bends. You might expect mosquitoes to be a problem in such a wet area, but they aren't. Most of the water here is flowing and thus prevents mosquito breeding, which requires still pools.

At 2.8 miles, after losing sight of it for awhile, the bluff to your right reasserts itself. If you ever lose the trail through here, head left toward the river to pick it up again. Pass many scenic overhangs, and at 3 miles walk back up into a cove to see a small 20-foot falls.

At 3.5 miles, a barely readable marker post indicates that Trail 202 (Randolph Trail) begins across the river to your left. Right about here I surprised a wild turkey, which responded by exploding through the canopy like a slowly fired cannonball.

At 4.5 miles, approach another carved post that is difficult to read. This marks the East Bee Branch Falls Trail (Trail 204), which leads to the state's oldest tree, a tulip poplar. The tree is over 500 years old and 150 feet tall with a circumference of 21 feet. The out-and-back spur to see the tree is about 4 miles. Continuing, pass an old beech with a large gall on a lower branch. Take the opportunity, when you can, to venture down to sandy bars that occasionally line the riverbank. You'll see a variety of minnows and maybe even glimpse the rare musk turtle. While you're down there, look for animal tracks in the sand.

Around 5 miles in, where a campsite sits out on a point, the trail bears right to a spot where you can cross a brook on a fat log. Pass through a sawn, fallen beech, encounter mammoth boulders, and then reach two huge fallen beech trees that block the path. They may have been cleared by the time you get there. If not, scramble around them and cross another rocky culvert. Nearing 6 miles, pass a square 20x20-foot block of sandstone and then a rock teepee.

At 6.2 miles, a worn trail marker indicates that the Sipsey River Trail (209) crosses the river and continues on the other side. This makes a good turnaround, especially if you've had a late start on the trail. Otherwise, drop down to the river and wade across about 30 feet through gently-flowing, knee-deep water. The footing is good, but the exit is a slippery, scrambling affair. Once over, don't go straight as some maps indicate, but bear to the right, following the Sipsey, which now flows down to your right.

Walking on a very sandy trail, you'll pass many campsites along the way to the turnaround at the Needle's Eye, the only whitewater you'll see on the entire hike. Forced into a channel against the far bank, the water backs up here to create a Class 1–2 rapid at mile 6.4. From here, retrace your path back to the Sipsey River Picnic Grounds parking area.

SLOSS FURNACES TRAIL

KEY AT-A-GLANCE INFORMATION

LENGTH: 1 mile

CONFIGURATION: Out-and-back with loop

DIFFICULTY: Easy, requires climbing a short flight of stairs

SCENERY: Two mammoth iron furnaces along with the brute industrial accoutrements needed to make pig iron

EXPOSURE: Alternates between open and shaded

TRAFFIC: Light during the week; days when Sloss hosts special events may be crowded

TRAIL SURFACE: Pavement, wooden sidewalk, short dirt trail, grassy field

HIKING TIME: 1.5 hours

ACCESS: Free (donations accepted); open Tuesday–Saturday, 10 a.m.–4 p.m., and Sunday, noon–4 p.m.

MAPS: Available at visitor center

FACILITIES: Rest rooms, water, phone, gift shop at visitor center

SPECIAL COMMENTS: Bring your camera for some spectacular industrial shots.

IN BRIEF

A National Historic Landmark, Sloss Furnaces offers an ideal urban stroll through a spectacular example of Birmingham's iron-producing past. Circle the base of a goliath restored furnace, pass in the shadow of towering blast stoves, and thread your way between giant smoke stacks. End your walk with a short loop hike in a field lined with curious iron sculptures.

DESCRIPTION

Looking over at Sloss Furnaces as you drive across the First Avenue viaduct into downtown Birmingham, this bastion of industry represents both the roots and wings of the Magic City. Without the vast iron ore, coal, and limestone deposits located in and around Birmingham, today this city might well be nothing more than a place to buy gas between Montgomery and Huntsville.

Donated to the city in 1971 by the Jim Walter Corporation, Sloss Furnaces is an official city museum, as well as a National Historic Landmark. On the grounds of Sloss, the Historical Society is housed in the Duncan House, which was relocated here from nearby Tarrant City. As you walk toward the viaduct, pass a row of shotgun houses built for furnace workers and the Historical Society on your left. You may want to stop in and purchase one of their excellent publications.

DIRECTIONS

From 1st Avenue North, heading north from downtown, cross the viaduct (you'll see Sloss below on your right). After crossing, turn left onto 34th Street. Turn left onto 2nd Avenue North; an entrance to the Sloss complex stands at the end of the street. If the gate is closed, turn left and look on your right for an open entrance. Otherwise, enter a large gravel lot from 2nd Avenue North. Park and walk under the overpass.

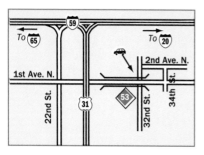

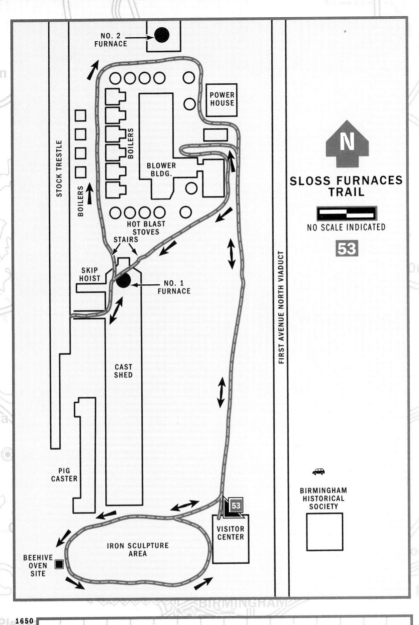

NO. 2
FURNACE

POWER
HOUSE

STOCK TRESTLE

BOILERS

BOILERS

BLOWER
BLDG.

HOT BLAST
STOVES

STAIRS

SKIP
HOIST

NO. 1
FURNACE

FIRST AVENUE NORTH VIADUCT

N

SLOSS FURNACES
TRAIL

NO SCALE INDICATED

53

CAST
SHED

PIG
CASTER

BIRMINGHAM
HISTORICAL
SOCIETY

53

VISITOR
CENTER

IRON SCULPTURE
AREA

BEEHIVE
OVEN
SITE

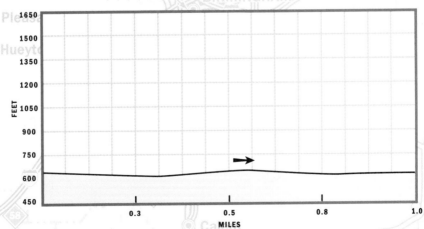

Blast Furnace No. 1 is to the right.

Continue straight, passing beneath the viaduct, and follow a sidewalk into the gift shop. Here, you can pick up a self-guided tour brochure, sign the guest book, and exit through the gift shop into a small courtyard with benches and a wrought-iron gate to your right.

The tour follows the path of the raw materials used in the furnace (air, iron ore, coke, and limestone), then tracks the path of pig iron after it left the furnace. Interpretive signs along the walk illuminate the various buildings and structures that you see on the tour.

As you walk with the long No. 1 Casting Shed to your left, traffic click-clacks by on the elevated First Avenue viaduct to your right. Pass between some iron crane buckets and a rusting crane as you head west. Pass a water fountain on the right and a line of magnolias and pines. As you follow a fence, look for yellow arrows on the sidewalk and turn left into a walkway that leads into the Blower Building complex. Through a fenced opening, view machinery that pumped air through the hot blast stoves and into the furnace to assist the ore-smelting process. Eight steam-engine air compressors from the early 1900s each stand 30 feet tall. The compressors turned flywheels are 20 feet in diameter. In 1949, two turbo-blowers replaced the old steam-driven compressors.

Turn back, walk out, and bear right to the paved plaza surrounding the Sloss water tower. On the way, pass six towering, hot blast stoves on your right. The towers heated the air pumped from the blower building to 1,400 degrees. The blast stoves are lined with fire brick called checkers. Waste gas from the furnace heated the air inside the blast stoves, which giant pipes carried to the furnace.

Pass beneath the water tower to a set of stairs that leads up to Furnace No. 1. Freshly painted in 2002, the coffee-colored blast furnace is accented with green ductwork and yellow railings. For a blast furnace, this one looks pretty sharp.

To take in the sights in the order that iron was made, pass by the furnace and walk out onto a metal walkway to the right to see the stock trestle. This is where raw materials for iron (iron ore, limestone, coke) arrived by rail from nearby sources such as the mines of Ruffner Mountain, which Sloss owned. Walk out to end of the walkway. From here you can visualize how the raw materials were brought in by train, dumped into carts below the trestle, and then dumped into another railcar beneath that which carried it to the bins on the skip hoist. The skip hoist (a steep conveyor belt) rises at an angle in front of you to the top of the furnace. A steam-powered pulley system pulled the skip cars up the incline to change the ore, limestone, and coke into the furnace's hungry mouth at the top. The interpretive sign indicates that a typical charge consisted of two skips of coke (6,200 pounds) and two skips of ore (10,000 pounds), with 1,500 pounds limestone added to the second skip of ore.

There has been talk of a ghost at Sloss since 1927. According to lore, Theophilus Calvin Jowers fell into a blast furnace at Alice Furnaces in 1887. When Alice furnaces closed in 1927, the ghost moved to Sloss and has been a regular presence ever since.

Walk back to the imposing base of the No. 1 Furnace. Originally built between 1881–1883, the furnace was replaced in the 1920s by this one, which is quite the beast, especially up close. I suppose if I fell in one of these, any other place (even Hell) would seem cool by comparison.

Look beyond the furnace into its casting shed, which has been transformed into one of the coolest concert halls on Earth. An especially outstanding (and deafening) musical event held here in 2001, conducted by internationally acclaimed cellist Craig Hultgren, was dubbed "Iron Music." Other concerts are held here regularly with artists ranging from the Birmingham Symphony Orchestra to Marilyn Manson.

Back at the furnace, after the raw materials tumbled into the furnace top, melted, and combined, three main products resulted: molten slag, molten iron, and furnace gas. The iron and slag flowed out separately through notches at the furnace bottom (the gas was channeled away to power boilers). The slag flowed into pits, and the iron flowed through a curved trough called a runner into ladle cars below the furnace. The ladle cars then rolled out to the pig caster, where the molten iron flowed into a system of runners that filled molds passing by on a conveyor belt. After being sprayed with cooling water, and reaching the end of the conveyor, the molds flipped over, dumping the iron "pigs" into railroad cars for transport to mills.

With the furnace on your right, walk down a set of steep stairs past a small brick building on the left. Known as the Pyrometer House, it housed temperature-measuring instruments and provided shelter for workmen whenever the furnace threatened to blow.

With the water tank to the right and imaginary trains charging by to the left, walk beneath 20-foot-diameter pipes above a plank walkway to the boilers, which created the steam necessary to power the blowers, skip hoist, furnace charging mechanism, and plant generator. The boilers primary fuel was waste gas from the blast furnace. Four newer boilers stand on the left, with six older boilers on the right. With occasional sprigs of grass growing up through the masonry and iron, the scene looks like an abandoned city, built entirely of pipes, iron, and bricks.

At the end of the plank walkway, turn right onto a paved walkway and pass the No. 2 Furnace and its companion casting shed on your left. This furnace is as massive and imposing as No. 1, but lacks its fresh paint. The casting shed beyond No. 2 is a frequent site of blacksmithing exhibitions.

As you pass through this amazing architecture, there are numerous opportunities to meander among the works, but please don't climb on them; it's dangerous as well as destructive. At the end of the sidewalk, see an old crane and First Avenue North straight ahead. Bear right and pass the Power House on the left, which generated electric power for the plant. This is the end of the self-guided tour.

To walk the loop portion of this trail, return to the visitor center, pass behind it to the right, and walk toward the nearest iron sculpture (*Exiles* by Buchen Goodwin). Pass a settling pond and approach a small patch of woods and a sign that reads "Beehive Oven." Turn left onto a dirt path, passing through a scrubby area to a covered excavation site. The dig is the site of an old bank of beehive ovens. Prior to the coke processing methods used today, coke was made from coal inside beehive-shaped ovens lined with fire brick. The ovens were hazardous, spewing black smoke into the air day and night.

A modern version of the coke oven can be seen at the ABC plant in nearby Tarrant City. Superheated in an oxygenless vertical tower, coal is refined into high-grade carbon, which is used in the production of steel. Although the process is just as dirty today as it was 200 years ago, a major focus of modern coke production is the capture of the various toxic byproducts such as benzene and carbon monoxide, which the beehive ovens freely spilled into the air.

Continue past the beehive ovens, walking east, and turn left at the fence. Walking in a counterclockwise loop, visit all of the sculptures (which range from whimsical to sinister) on your walk around the settling pond. For a more detailed account of the role Sloss Furnaces played in the rise of Birmingham as an industrial center, read Marjorie White's *The Birmingham District: An Industrial History and Guide*, published by the Birmingham Historical Society.

▶ **NEARBY ACTIVITIES**

To make a complete iron day of it, continue your hike at nearby Ruffner Mountain where you can see and touch the rich red ore and the limestone that fed Sloss's furnaces. See the Quarry Trail on p. 207.

MUNNY SOKOL PARK LOOP

▶ IN BRIEF

Carved by mountain bikers, the trails of Munny Sokol Park make the most of a boggy bottomland. It's buggy in these woods and eerily beautiful.

▶ DESCRIPTION

The single-track at Munny Sokol Park is a popular destination for mountain bikers, but also makes a great addition to an area hiker's trail portfolio. From overhead, the trails must look like someone threw a handful of spaghetti on the ground. This makes great technical riding possible on fairly level ground. For a hiker, however, this can be problematic, since the usual idea is to make a defined loop or walk from point A to point B. Hikers may choose to wander with abandon along the reported 8 to 10 miles of snaking trail, or follow a loop such as the one detailed on the trail map.

Now deceased, Morris "Munny" Sokol served the city of Tuscaloosa for many years as a civic leader. In 1973 he was named president of the Chamber of Commerce. From 1970 to 1975, Sokol served as chairman of the Tuscaloosa

▶ DIRECTIONS

From the intersection of I-459 South and I-65, take I-459 South for 16 miles and merge with I-59 South/I-20 West. Drive another 32 miles and take Exit 73 onto US 82/McFarland Boulevard. Bear right, drive 5 miles, and turn right at the Munny Sokol Park sign onto CR 47/Watermelon Road. Drive 2 miles and turn right onto an unmarked road that passes between two large brick pillars. There will be no sign for the park here. Pass a ball field and take the first left onto another unmarked road. Drive 0.3 miles and look for two red farm buildings on the left. Just beyond the buildings is a gravel parking area fronted by a couple of large water oaks. Park there to begin the hike.

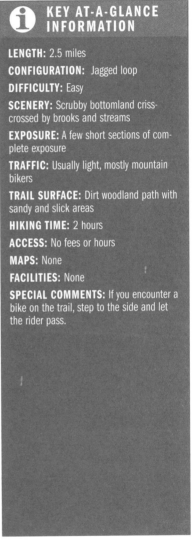

ⓘ KEY AT-A-GLANCE INFORMATION

LENGTH: 2.5 miles

CONFIGURATION: Jagged loop

DIFFICULTY: Easy

SCENERY: Scrubby bottomland criss-crossed by brooks and streams

EXPOSURE: A few short sections of complete exposure

TRAFFIC: Usually light, mostly mountain bikers

TRAIL SURFACE: Dirt woodland path with sandy and slick areas

HIKING TIME: 2 hours

ACCESS: No fees or hours

MAPS: None

FACILITIES: None

SPECIAL COMMENTS: If you encounter a bike on the trail, step to the side and let the rider pass.

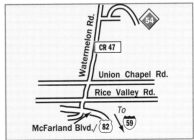

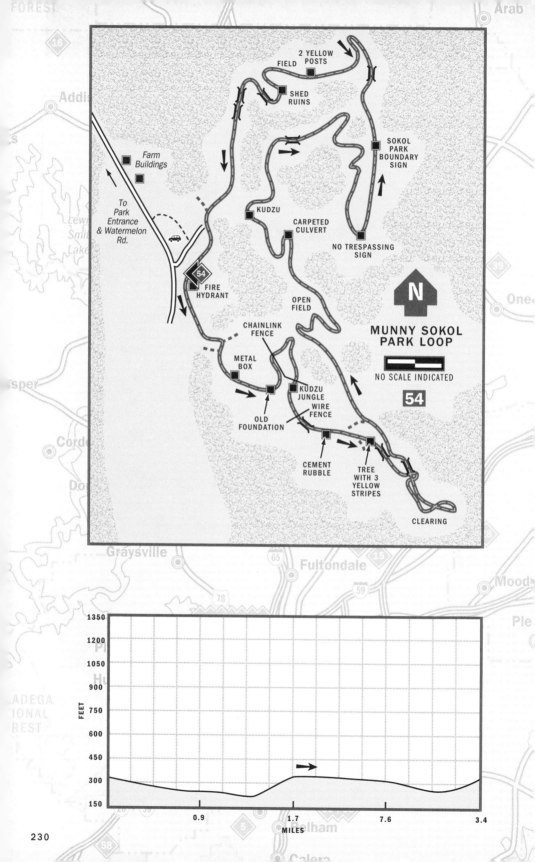

MUNNY SOKOL
PARK LOOP

NO SCALE INDICATED

54

County Parks and Recreation Authority. In appreciation to Sokol for making Tuscaloosa a better place to live, the city purchased land north of the Black Warrior River that is now Munny Sokol Park.

Head southeast from the parking lot toward an unmarked three-way intersection. Across the road you'll see a narrow trail that begins by a red fire hydrant. With ball fields off to your right, take the slim, level single-track through a grassy field to begin the hike.

At the first fork, go right to enter the scruffy woods and hit a wider path that again bears right at a T-intersection. There is no official trail, but there are numerous, yellow trail signs fixed to trees and posts. You'll immediately see plenty of fat-tire tracks, but on my hike I saw no one, other than a few gray squirrels and a chipmunk. This trail has so many twists and turns that it would be ridiculous to dictate every move you'll have to make. The hike I've outlined here is just one of many possible configurations. To navigate the route as described, use the trail map, which is marked with all of the footbridges, yellow trails signs, and odd features such as cement rubble.

Pass a large metal box on trail-left and with crows likely cawing overhead, also pass the foundation of an old house. Walking easily through a wooly understory along a corkscrew path, meet up with a chain-link fence on your right. The trail will bear right; pass through the chain-link fence and continue downhill.

A smooth dirt track here crosses over an old pipe in the trail. With the fence running on your left through a flat area, the trail veers left. Pass through another break in the fence into an open area best described as a kudzu jungle. Cross the first of many footbridges in the park, heading east up a mild grade.

Despite the gruff nature of these bottomland acres, the scenery and solitude make for a very peaceful trek. Hardwoods you'll see include red oak, red maple, sweetgum, sourwood, water oak, and tulip poplar. Pass a pile of cement rubble on trail-right and at a Y, bear right and downhill. Look for a large American holly tree and wild muscadine vines hanging from the trees. In summer, you should be able to see clusters of green muscadine grapes on the vines.

Near a cedar tree, the trail forks again; go straight instead of right, and then at a tree painted with three yellow stripes, bear left. When you cross a brook on a footbridge, you'll be 0.65 miles into the walk. Curve left and cross the stream again. The path is very muddy, but the stream is crystal clear as it flows over a bed of pretty amber pebbles. Look for a water-loving beech by the creek and negotiate yet another wooden footbridge followed by an unsteady plank crossing over a marshy spot.

Pass a clearing to your right that is evidence of the encroachment of new construction near the trail, and at the next intersection, turn left to shortly cross another footbridge. Mark your progress by looking for a pair of very tall, robust cedar trees, one on either side of the trail. Encounter and follow a dilapidated barbed wire fence and bear right at a yellow trail sign (YTS).

It seems like every time I get out in the woods, I have at least one snake encounter, usually with a nonpoisonous species. The slick fellow I met here was a lustrous black king snake, about three-and-a-half feet long. It quivered its tail mimicking a rattlesnake, darting its black tongue, before rapidly sliding into the brush.

Take the next trail, a wide sandy path that comes in from the right. Across the open field here, you'll be able to see the parking lot where you parked. Although it seems like you've squeezed out a couple of miles at this point, you're only 1 mile in. At a fork bear right, back into woods where lots of small sweat bees and mosquitoes will worry the devil out of you if you stop moving. It's always good to do a cursory tick check on exposed arms and legs every now and then.

Reach a small area of downed trees, and go left passing above a steep ravine down to your right. Look off trail-right for a massive water oak with branches as wide as it is tall. Pass over a rolling section of trail, pass a YTS, and at the next intersection bear left at another YTS. Here you'll encounter an odd site. The small, but steep, culvert in front of you is layered with cheap, green outdoor carpet. It should give that rear wheel a little extra bite and even assisted me to pop up the ascending slope without slipping. What'll they think of next?

Continue straight, passing a large red oak and some wrist-thick poison ivy. Look left for another field of kudzu and a macadam road. Take a hairpin left at a tall white oak, slink into a clearing, and bear right to cross a clear brook alive with minnows. Remnants of an old bridge support are visible to the left. The path is briefly a two-lane track, but soon whittles back to single-track and re-enters the cover of woods.

After taking a right, cross another small stream on a small bridge to reach a very sandy path. I looked down here to see a granddaddy longlegs waddling along, clutching some sort of prey in its mouth. I'd never seen that before. Many ferns and devilwood bushes line the trail here. At the next intersection, go left with a YTS. Now 1.6 miles into the trail, the forest floor is very flat and covered with a tangle of natural debris. Here I saw something else that I had never seen before— a tree with a big, nasty, slug-filled gall. Ugh.

Pass a closed-off area on your right and notice a "No Trespassing" sign beyond the yellow caution tape. Follow a posted wire fence on your right and reach a wooden sign that reads "Sokol Park Property Line." At the next YTS, at a Y, go right and then straight until you cross a wooden footbridge over a wet-weather drainage. If it's summer, you'll find juicy wild blackberries growing through here.

You may begin to hear a loud whining sound in the near distance. It sounds like a mosquito from hell, but it's just a model airplane buzzing at the nearby City of Tuscaloosa model airplane field. Cross over a hummock and take a hairpin left. Down to your right, you'll see a yellow metal gate. At a YTS, drop off into a gully and then wander into a clearing with two yellow posts to your right. Bear left and walk a line between a field to your right and the forest to your left. After you slip back into the shade, take the next left at a YTS and pass an old shed that has collapsed.

In a thick tangle of scrub, veer right and cross a plank bridge spanning a tiny stream. Cross another stream via footbridge, and then clomp over a long plank that bridges a boggy spot. Go straight at a YTS to near the end of the trail. Throughout the hike you'll notice evidence of regular trail maintenance. Pitch in while you're here. If you see a limb in the trail, stop and throw it to the side. At a clearing, the trail will T into a dirt road. Go left here and the parking area will be straight ahead.

▶ NEARBY ACTIVITIES

On the way down, stop at the Mercedes plant near Vance and take the industrial tour. Visit www.mbusi.com for all of the information, including dress code and visitor restrictions (children under 12 years of age are not permitted to take the tour). You must reserve a spot by calling (888) 286-8762 or (205) 507-2252. There is a tour fee ($4–5), but the visitor center and museum are free. The one-and-a-half-hour factory tours are given Monday–Friday in the morning at 9, 9:15, 11, and 11:15, and in the afternoon at 1 and 1:15. Visitor Center/Museum hours are Monday–Friday, 9 a.m.–5 p.m. and the first Saturday of month,10 a.m.–3 p.m.

SUMATANGA MOUNTAIN LOOP

KEY AT-A-GLANCE INFORMATION

LENGTH: 4 miles

CONFIGURATION: Loop

DIFFICULTY: Moderate/difficult

SCENERY: Lush, sloping hardwood forest; Lake Sumatanga; ridge top overlooks of the lake and valley; small wildlife such as turtles, turkey vultures, and snakes

EXPOSURE: Mostly shaded

TRAFFIC: Very light

TRAIL SURFACE: Old, rocky, rutted logging road; steep dirt/rock trail

HIKING TIME: 2.5 hours

ACCESS: The area closes at sundown.

MAPS: None

FACILITIES: Rest rooms, water at picnic pavilions; fenced playground

SPECIAL COMMENTS: Fishing is allowed in the lake, except on Sunday. There is a $1 honor-system fee. Camp Sumatanga is a Christian retreat center. No illegal drugs, alcohol, or pets are allowed.

IN BRIEF

Starting alongside scenic Lake Sumatanga, this hike explores a portion of the steeply sloping northern side of Chandler Mountain. The path is rocky and very steep in places.

DESCRIPTION

Camp Sumatanga retreat is owned and operated by the Methodist Church. While the facilities and surrounding land are used primarily by registered guests, the trails are open to the general public during the day. This gorgeously shaggy hike satisfies a real need for a walk on the wild side. Used far less than the more popular Red Trail (p. 238), this trail exudes a real sense of remoteness.

Beginning by the lake, the trail climbs up the steep side of Chandler Mountain and eventually picks up a southwesterly course about halfway up the forested slope, roughly paralleling the ridge above. You'll work your way back down to the lake on a section of the steep Mountain Trail, follow a small creek that empties into the lake, and then follow the lakeshore back to the dam.

From your car, walk across the earthen dam with the lake to the right and the long ridge line

DIRECTIONS

From the intersection of I-459 and I-59, travel north on I-59 for 30 miles. Take the Ashville/US 231 exit and turn left onto US 231. Drive 3.3 miles and turn right at the large Horse Pens 40 sign onto CR 35. Pass CR 42 and, at 3.4 miles from US 231, turn right onto CR 44/Sumatanga Road at a large Camp Sumatanga sign. After another 1.4 miles, enter the camp. Drive past the retreat center and cabin areas (all of which are for registered guests only) and soon reach the lake on your right. Drive along the lake to the dam on your right. Park on the side of the road, being careful not to block the dam access road.

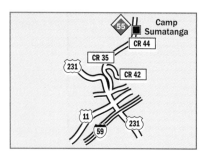

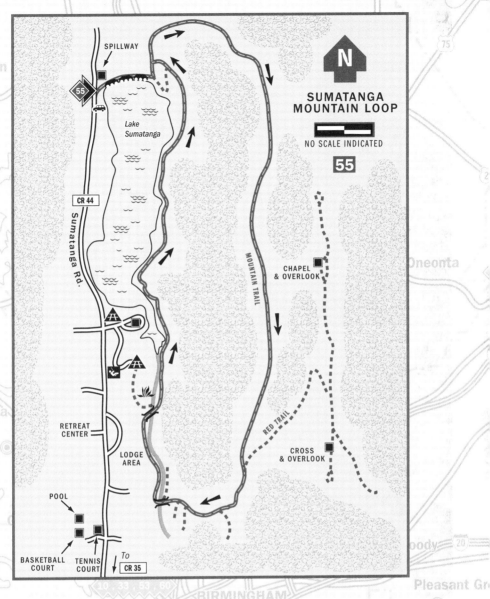

SUMATANGA
MOUNTAIN LOOP

NO SCALE INDICATED

55

SPILLWAY

55

Lake
Sumatanga

CR 44

Sumatanga Rd.

RETREAT
CENTER

LODGE
AREA

POOL

BASKETBALL
COURT

TENNIS
COURT

To
CR 35

MOUNTAIN TRAIL

RED TRAIL

CHAPEL
& OVERLOOK

CROSS
& OVERLOOK

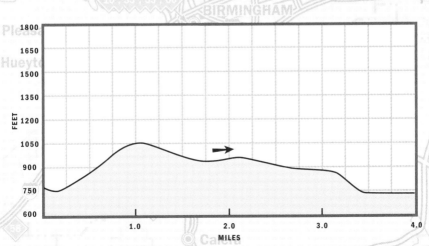

Lake Sumatanga

of flat-topped Chandler Mountain looming ahead. At a wooden sign that reads "Lake Trail," turn left onto a wide grassy path lined with red maple, hickory, hawthorn, oak-leaf hydrangea, wild blackberries, honeysuckle, and tulip poplar. A thick understory of small trees and brush occasionally extends into the trail, but never obliterates it.

Reach a trail intersection and briefly go straight and down. The trail bears right to the east, and begins a slight uphill track that can be muddy after a rain. Meander uphill along a trail that acts as a water channel when it rains.

At a little over 0.1 mile, bear right, picking up the southwesterly course that indicates you're now traversing the slope about halfway between the ridge top above and the lake below. Take a sharp left to head steeply uphill, south/southeast. The wind blowing above the trees here, which are taller and older than those a few hundred feet below, sounds like water flowing in the distance.

At 0.4 miles into the hike, as the trail levels and resumes a southwest course, pass boulders resting alongside the trail. You'll see an abundance of oak-leaf hydrangea scattered up and down the slope. The official state wildflower of Alabama, the oak-leaf hydrangea is a wild version of the ornamental hydrangea found in the yards of many area homes. In spring, look for spears of white, four-petaled flowers amid large, lobed oak-like leaves.

The trail is wide through here and appears to be an old logging road. You'll encounter a huge tree across the trail that may push you off the trail briefly as you negotiate around it. There is a healthy crop of poison ivy throughout this forest, along with briars, so you may want to wear a pair of long pants on this hike.

The trail levels at 0.6 miles, bears right and heads downhill. Soon, though, the trail bears back left, again to the southwest. Prior to reaching a T at 1 mile, walk through an outcrop of trailer-sized boulders, and then watch the bottom drop out as the trail descends. At the T, turn left and south to make up for your recent downturn with an invigorating climb.

You'll enjoy the black-eyed Susans growing here and there, but you may not be so fond of the gnats, yellow jackets, and mosquitoes that buzz your brow for a taste of your blood or sweat. Where the trail levels at 1.3 miles, pass beneath a dead tree that is home to a gaggle of nimble granddaddy longlegs.

The trail thins occasionally but is still easy to follow. In general, the trail is at its most overgrown along level stretches. At 1.7 miles, reach a crossroads; go right onto the Mountain Trail, and walk (leaning back) steeply downhill. Follow the red arrows on a well-worn but rocky path. While walking here, you may, as I did, hear a loud thrumming sound and spy the darting forms of hummingbirds flitting among the hickory, sassafras, poplar, and chestnut oak trees.

When you encounter a blue water tank in an open area, bear right back into the woods and just keep on trucking down, down, down. Beginning at 2.2 miles, you'll pass two trails coming in from your left as well as two strangely placed, red fire hydrants.

At an intersection, passing a nature trail to your right, bear left, cross a small stream, and pass a sign that reads "Mountain Trail, Chapel 1 Mile." Cross a wooden footbridge over a wide creek and enter an area behind the camp's retreat center. Take the path to your right and follow the creek as it flows northeast toward Lake Sumatanga. Through here you'll encounter tall pines and moisture-loving beech trees.

Pass a small stone bench up to your left, while scrambling up and over large boulders. Stay with the creek and you won't lose the trail. At 2.7 miles, go right across another wooden footbridge, turn left, and, with the creek on your left, follow the creek until it enters a slough that leads into the lake. You may hear the pounding of the heavy-hitting pileated woodpecker hammering here as you pass majestic beeches. On a slightly slippery trail, with the creek slogging slowly ten feet below, trace the slough and push your way through small slicks of mountain laurel that overhang the trail.

Around 3.2 miles, the path opens onto a weedy dirt track leading into a clearing. From here, the walking is easy and pleasant as you track the lake north/northeast back to the dam. At a T, turn left and find the Lake Trail sign on your left at 4 miles. From here, walk back to your vehicle.

▶ NEARBY ACTIVITIES

If it's summertime, you may want to include a trip to the top of flat-topped Chandler Mountain and take a look at the acres of tomato fields. Buy a basket of the famously tasty produce at one of the packing houses or pay a small fee to pick your own. To access the top of Chandler Mountain, drive back toward US 231 and turn left onto CR 42.

SUMATANGA RED TRAIL

KEY AT-A-GLANCE INFORMATION

LENGTH: 2.4 miles

CONFIGURATION: Out-and-back

DIFFICULTY: Moderate/difficult

SCENERY: Lush, sloping hardwood forest; Lake Sumatanga; overlooks of the lake and valley from a ridge top chapel and a cross; very steep trail sections

EXPOSURE: Mostly shaded, except on top of the ridge

TRAFFIC: Light/moderate

TRAIL SURFACE: Well-defined rocky path

HIKING TIME: 1.5 hours

ACCESS: The area closes at sundown.

MAPS: None

FACILITIES: Rest rooms, water at picnic pavilions; fenced playground

SPECIAL COMMENTS: Fishing is allowed in the lake, except on Sunday. There is a $1 honor-system fee. Camp Sumatanga is a Christian retreat center. No alcohol or pets are allowed.

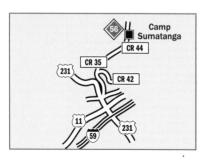

IN BRIEF

Take a direct and very steep path to reach two scenic overlooks atop Chandler Mountain, where you can rest first at a large cross and then at an open mountaintop chapel.

DESCRIPTION

Set amid 1,700 acres of wild Alabama woodland, Camp Sumatanga is truly a retreat. Although miles of trail crisscross the slope of Chandler Mountain above the camp's retreat center and cabins, the red-blazed Mountain Trail is the path that most people walk. A mile straight up, and a mile straight down, the only relief from gravity that you have on this strenuous hike is the ridge top visit to two scenic overlooks, one marked by a cross, the other by a chapel.

With the pavilion in front of you, turn right and walk toward the woods, passing a swampy area (a big, weedy frog pond) to your left and a playground to your right. Reach a path into the woods, cross a brook, and then bear left into an open area. Trace the frog pond to a wooden footbridge, but don't cross it. Instead go right, heading west against the flow of a lazy creek on your left.

DIRECTIONS

From the intersection of I-459 and I-59, travel north on I-59 for 30 miles. Take the Ashville/US 231 exit and turn left onto US 231. Drive 3.3 miles and turn right at the large Horse Pens 40 sign onto CR 35. Pass CR 42 and, at 3.4 miles from US 231, turn right onto CR 44/Sumatanga Road at a large Camp Sumatanga sign. After another 1.4 miles, enter the camp. Drive past the retreat center and cabin areas (all of which are for registered guests only) and soon reach the lake on your right. Turn right onto Bud Floyd Circle. With a pavilion on your left, bear right on a gravel road toward the pavilion to your right. Park here.

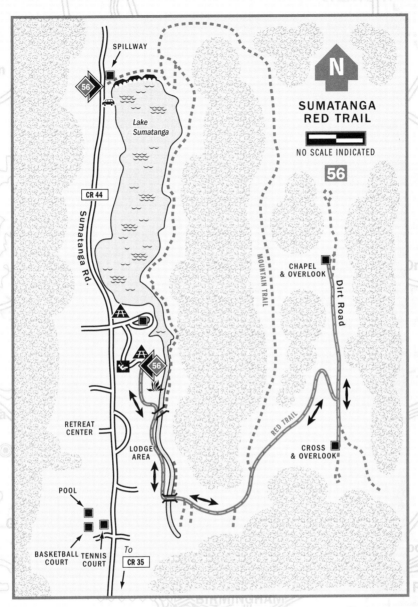

SPILLWAY

Lake
Sumatanga

CR 44

Sumatanga Rd.

MOUNTAIN TRAIL

CHAPEL
& OVERLOOK

Dirt Road

RED TRAIL

RETREAT
CENTER

LODGE
AREA

CROSS
& OVERLOOK

POOL

BASKETBALL
COURT

TENNIS
COURT

To
CR 35

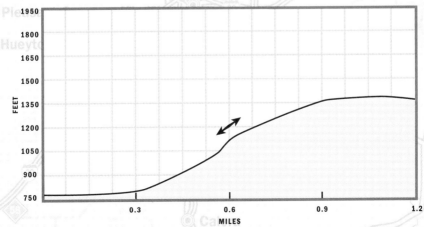

FEET				
1950				
1800				
1650				
1500				
1350				
1200				
1050				
900				
750				

0.3   0.6   0.9   1.2

MILES

The Red Trail seems like a staircase at times.

The narrow path winds among tall pines, beeches, and a mix of other Southern hardwoods. Pass a stone bench perched on the slope to your right, with the camp's retreat area beyond. When you reach the second wooden footbridge, turn left, cross the creek, and immediately begin uphill. Where the trail forks, bear left. Pass a sign that reads "Mountain Trail, Chapel 1 Mile" and follow its red arrow-shaped blazes. From a satellite view, the Mountain Trail works its way up at a slight angle to the very steep slope of Chandler Mountain.

A flat-topped mountain, 9 miles long by 2 miles wide, thrust straight up approximately 750 feet above the surrounding area, Chandler Mountain is famous for its tomato fields and the natural boulder horse enclosures at nearby Horse Pens 40 (p. 87).

Hiking slowly up the Mountain Trail, you'll feel as if you're leaning into the mountainside. Climbing to the southeast on stair-like tiers through a rocky corridor, pass a trail on your right as well as the first of two conspicuous red fire hydrants. Bordered by scattered oak-leaf hydrangeas, the path can be slippery and provides poor footing to a slick-soled boot.

Continue up, passing through a mixed hardwood forest alive with poplars, maples, and hawthorns. After you pass the second fire hydrant on your right, the trail seems to get even steeper. Just when it seems it can't get any steeper, you thankfully emerge into a small, level clearing, facing a large blue water tank. At this point, you're just about halfway up the slope. Bear left to pick up the trail again and continue your ascent. Meander a bit and then gear down for another lean up about 100 feet of super-steep trail. Pause for a breath as the path levels in an area thick with pignut hickories. This is one of those hikes on which you're tempted to sit down in the shade and think about fast food.

Walking east, reach a trail coming in from your right; continue with the red arrows here and go straight, sloping down left and then up right. Switchback to your right, heading southwest, then bear left into a clearing on top of the ridge. A short trail to your left leads to an old-fashioned, but functional, outhouse.

Walk through the clearing to the dirt road and go right to visit the cross. After about 0.2 miles, the 20-foot-high, steel-girder cross appears on your right. There's a nice overlook here onto the valley below and the ridges of Blount Mountain beyond, but the lake is not visible.

With black turkey vultures soaring above, face the road, turn left, and walk half a mile to the Creel Memorial Chapel. An open, stone and timber, A-frame building, the chapel looks northwest out over the scenic valley below, including 55-acre Lake Sumatanga. This is one of the best scenic views in North Alabama.

Return to the clearing, locate the Mountain Trail, and brace your thighs for a pull down the mountain. There will be spots where you'll either have to hold back or let yourself run carefully in a quick zigzag down the trail. On one really precipitous section, I found myself running nearly out-of-control. It's fun if your legs can stand it and you don't mind risking trail rash. My own downward jaunt, however, was stopped short by a large black snake (probably a black racer, or a whip snake) lying coiled directly in the middle of a sunny spot in the path. I managed to pull up and get a picture before it detected me and shot off into the brush, as if someone were cracking a black whip.

▶ NEARBY ACTIVITIES

If it's summertime, you may want to include a trip to the top of flat-topped Chandler Mountain and take a look at the acres of tomato fields. Buy a basket of the famous produce at one of the packing houses or pay a small fee to pick your own. To access the top of Chandler Mountain, drive back toward US 231 and turn left onto CR 42.

SWANN BRIDGE TRAIL

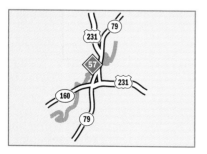

IN BRIEF

The trail beyond Swann Bridge is a bit rough and overgrown, but the river scenes, towering rock face, and small falls are worth the extra effort.

DESCRIPTION

Finding a trail like this is very satisfying. I just stopped by the covered bridge out of curiosity, and after a little exploring discovered a wooly but scenic path that follows Locust Fork.

Built in 1933, the Swann Covered Bridge is still in use today. Only one vehicle can cross at a time, and you're likely to find sightseers traversing its length, so drive across slowly. As you creep through the long wooden tunnel, the beams and planks groan and moan, but overall the bridge feels solid. The bridge is elevated about 50 feet above the Locust Fork of the Black Warrior River on two massive stone pillars.

On the other side, park, walk down to the river, and bear left for a short out-and-back to a popular swim beach. Walking upriver, northeast, along a sandy two-wheel track, you'll pass through a shady area where campers and boaters park. If you elect to do the same, just make sure your ride can make it back up the steep dirt incline. Numerous trails branch off here and there, but stick with the path that is closest to the river.

Walking through the cool woods, you'll glimpse the river through the trees while passing

DIRECTIONS

From I-20/59, take the Tallapoosa Street Exit onto AL 79 North through Tarrant City. Drive 35 miles and look for a small Swann Covered Bridge sign on the left. Turn left onto the unmarked road, which is Swann Bridge Road. Drive 1 mile, cross the covered bridge slowly, and park along the side of the road. Follow the dirt road down to the river beneath the bridge to begin the hike.

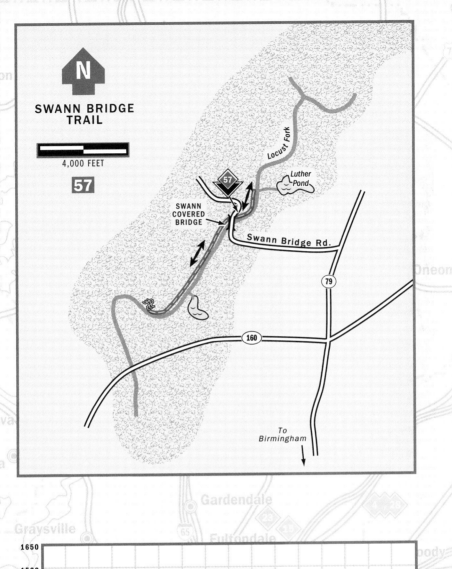

SWANN BRIDGE TRAIL

4,000 FEET

57

Locust Fork

Luther Pond

SWANN COVERED BRIDGE

Swann Bridge Rd.

79

160

To Birmingham

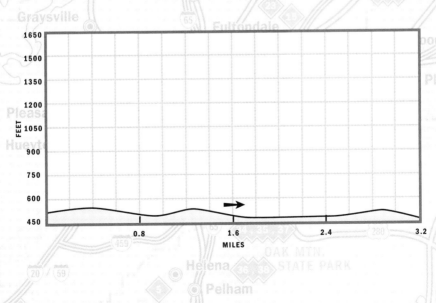

FEET		
1650		
1500		
1350		
1200		
1050		
900		
750		
600		
450		

0.8   1.6   2.4   3.2
MILES

through a flat and scrubby river gorge. Across the river a bluff of sandstone rises 100 feet above the water, which is filled with large boulders. At 0.15 miles, a great view of the rock wall opens up alongside a nice swimming hole.

Continue into a sandy area where the river deepens. Here, at 0.35 miles, you'll find a large open area and a swim beach. The trail slips back into the woods, and a steep rocky slope develops on your left. When the trail peters out and you're forced to boulder-hop at around 0.4 miles, turn around and begin the trek to the falls. On your way, look for loblolly pine, tulip poplar, hickory, red maple, black maple, sweet-gum, water oak, cedar, and lots of oak-leaf hydrangea.

Pass beneath the bridge, following the river west along a sandy, rooty, and rocky path. The flat and slow river drifts by on your left, while a steep hillside rises to your right. The river averages about 50 feet across, but occasionally widens or gets squeezed into a narrower channel such as the one at 0.8 miles into the hike.

A short tenth of a mile later, the trail gives way to rocks, and you must scramble along the riverbank. You'll pass another sandy area and a couple of rope swings as you head southwest. Among the brush you'll glimpse a variety of wildflowers, including morning glory. At 1 mile, the river narrows on your left and the dirt trail picks up again as it weaves in and out of the shade.

Pass some tulip poplars, another small beach, and a finger of boulders that juts from this side of the river, forcing the water to channel to the far side. Here, the trail meanders away from the river about 50 feet and soon crosses a small feeder stream, heading southwest. Scramble up the stream bank and bear back left to pick up the trail, brushy with weeds and wildflowers that attract yellow and blue swallowtails.

At 1.1 mile, where the river channels through a river-wide boulder field before running deep and still again, the path becomes clear and sandy. At 1.25 miles, do some more trailless rock hopping, but soon pick up the path again over to the right as you pass a small flood-channel island to your left. You'll find attractive Christmas ferns through here, but be aware that poison ivy is prevalent as well.

After the river is cut off from view briefly, pass by some beech trees and then a dripping rock ledge located at 1.5 miles on trail-right. Characteristic of a brushy, little-used trail, the foliage will press in and embrace you with scratchy arms. At 1.7 miles, cross over a piece of land that becomes an island during high water, and then pass across a dry, rocky channel.

Soon, with a roar of water developing in the distance, reach the scenic-falls area, bear left, and come up to a vantage point that allows you to look down the falls from behind. Stretched across the riverbed is an eight-foot-high shelf of rock that is broken on the near side. The water pours through here down a steep stair-stepping, rock falls. This spot, the turnaround for the hike, is a great picnic venue.

▶ NEARBY ACTIVITIES

In Locust Fork and just beyond, you'll find food at Jack's, Country Kitchen, and Wayne's Barbecue. If you enjoy watching movies in the great outdoors, try the Cheyenne Drive In. The theater is located on AL 79 just beyond the town of Locust Fork. Call (205) 559-8033 for movie information.

TANNEHILL IRONWORKS TRAIL

This hike passes the park's main attraction, the massive Tannehill blast furnaces, then crosses Roupes Creek and winds counterclockwise through a mixed hardwood-pine forest. Along the way, view a slave cemetery and pass through an area that housed slaves who were forced to work in area mines.

▶ **DESCRIPTION**

Visited on a sunny weekday, Tannehill State Park is a sleepy, peaceful place. With only a handful of campers and a small scattering of day visitors, the parking lots will be empty and the trail will likely be your own. Weekends might be a little busier, especially if you come on Trade Days, usually the third weekend of each month. However, once you leave the main area surrounding the visitor center and historic buildings, you should meet with relatively few, if any, other people. It's possible to push a stroller along the entire loop, but you'll need one with at least 12-inch wheels (such as a Baby Jogger). The rocks and pebbles in the trail contain a large quantity of small ore pieces and what looks like bits of coal.

▶ **DIRECTIONS**

From Birmingham take I-459 south to Exit 1. Turn left onto Eastern Valley Road (CR 18) and follow it for 7.5 miles to the park entrance, which is on the left.

Alternate directions: From Birmingham, take I-59 south. About 25 miles from downtown Birmingham, take Exit 100 and follow the signs to Tannehill State Park. Turn left onto AL 216 East. In 0.5 miles, turn right onto Tannehill Parkway and follow signs. Enter the park; pay your admission. During the off season, the honor system may be in operation. As you enter the park, the visitor center will be right in front of you. Park in this area.

ℹ **KEY AT-A-GLANCE INFORMATION**

LENGTH: 3 miles

CONFIGURATION: Loop

DIFFICULTY: Easy

SCENERY: Tannehill blast furnaces, Roupes Creek, Mill Creek, hardwood forest, slave cemetery

EXPOSURE: Mostly shade

TRAFFIC: Light during cold weather, moderate during Trade Days

TRAIL SURFACE: Wide dirt path, rutted in places, along the Iron Road; wide gravelly path along Slave Quarters Road

HIKING TIME: 2 hours, depending on time spent at the furnaces and other attractions along the way

ACCESS: The park is open year-round, except on Christmas Day. Admission is $2 per adult, $1 for ages 6–11; children under 6 are admitted free.

MAPS: Tannehill Trail Map available at the park's visitor center and country store

FACILITIES: Rest rooms, phone, vending, country store

SPECIAL COMMENTS: The park becomes crowded on Trade Days. Held on the third weekend of each month March–November, Trade Days features arts-and-crafts exhibits and a giant swap meet.

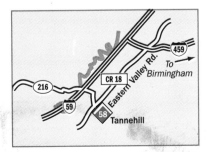

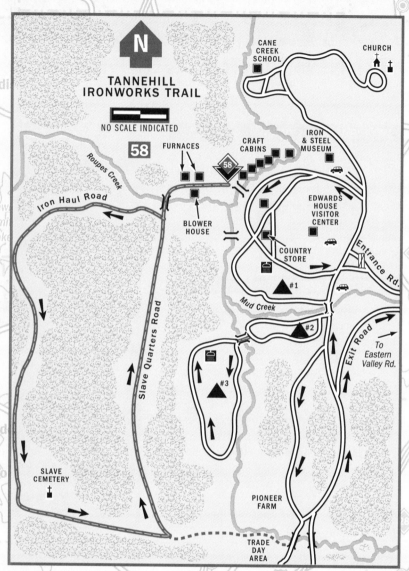

TANNEHILL
IRONWORKS TRAIL

NO SCALE INDICATED

58

FURNACES

CANE CREEK SCHOOL

CHURCH

CRAFT CABINS

IRON & STEEL MUSEUM

58

EDWARDS HOUSE VISITOR CENTER

Roupes Creek

Iron Haul Road

BLOWER HOUSE

Slave Quarters Road

COUNTRY STORE

#1

Mud Creek

#2

Entrance Rd.

Exit Road

To Eastern Valley Rd.

#3

SLAVE CEMETERY

PIONEER FARM

TRADE DAY AREA

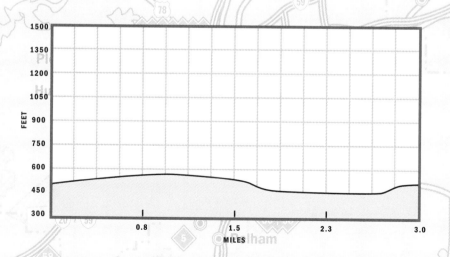

FEET				

1500
1350
1200
1050
900
750
600
450
300

0.8　　1.5　　2.3　　3.0

MILES

To reach the trailhead from the visitor center, walk toward the country store and pass behind it through an open picnic area with a gazebo and rest rooms. Walk toward a footbridge and, after crossing a small stream, turn left onto Plank Road, which leads past a row of old cabins on the left, including the Tannehill Craft Center. The center is open weekends March through November.

Pass a wrought-iron bridge on your left and veer right and up a short set of cement steps. As you leave the campground area behind, turn left onto a wide dirt road. Below you and to the left, 20-foot-wide Roupes Creek runs several feet deep in places. Pass an old dam site on right; the dam was carried away by flood in 1866. You've reached the trailhead at the massive quarried-stone furnace with its blower house.

The Roupes Valley Ironworks Steam Engine House, located on your right, provided steam power to the furnace works. The building on your left is a reconstructed blower house. The water-powered blower blasted air through blowing tubes into the furnace, raising the temperature high enough to smelt the combination of charcoal, iron ore, and limestone that yielded pig iron. A canal, extending 285 feet to Roupes Creek, channeled water through the blower house. In operation from 1855 through 1865, the furnaces produced more than 20 tons of iron a day. During the Civil War, the iron produced at Tannehill made its way into Confederate cannonballs, musket shot, and even pots and pans. To view the complex from above, take the winding set of wooden stairs up to the top of the furnace.

To begin the loop, head back down the steps, turn right, pass the Snead House on your right, and head toward an iron bridge (Folsom Bridge) off to the left. Cross over Roupes Creek, pausing on the bridge to take in great views up and down the scenic channel.

After crossing over, bear right onto Iron Haul Road. Head south and uphill along a wide dirt path; Roupes Creek tags along briefly. The land slopes up from right to left and is home to a mixed forest that includes beech, pine, maple, and oak. Perhaps the strangest "tree" you'll see along this hike is the devil's walking stick, a slender tree covered with spines, prickles, and barbs.

As the trail levels and bends to the left, notice a sign that marks this trail as a National Boy Scouts of America Hiking Trail. The trail winds as it moves south/southwest, descends toward the southeast, then levels out, bearing to the northeast. Cross a tiny stream and enter an area that can be muddy in wet weather. Roupes Creek will reappear briefly to the right, but immediately flows away to the east.

The trail continues to roll, passing through another boggy area, then winds as it approaches a stand of pine 30 feet in height. Here the trail drops around to the left and re-enters the mixed hardwood/pine forest where young pines flank the trail. Rutted in places, the trail passes over a small creek, which then flows with the trail.

Reach a distinct clearing on your right, then pass a large piece of sandstone. Bear around to the left, east/northeast, and pass a low swampy area on trail-right. Numerous cedars grow through here. After passing an old stack of beams on the right, soon reach an open area to the right. Stay on the trail, though, to descend, heading north and then southeast in a winding motion. Pass another pile of beams on trail-left, roll up and downhill, and approach an unmarked junction, approximately 1.7 miles into the hike. Don't go right, which leads to a dumping ground, but go left to head northeast. Shortly, the path seems to bear left again, but stay straight as you pass through a very brushy area scattered with scraggly hardwoods.

At about 2 miles, approach a sign pointing to the slave cemetery. Turn left to reach the cemetery. The square-shaped burial ground is roughly 100 feet on each side and scattered with simple sandstone markers; it dates from the 1850s. According to an interpretive sign onsite, the cemetery was associated with the Oglesby Plantation and reportedly holds the remains of more than 400 slaves who picked and processed cotton, as well as those who worked in the Tannehill Ironworks. Sadly there is only one marked stone in the entire cemetery. The stone simply reads "Josh Stroup 1862."

Continue out the other side of cemetery and follow the trail to a T-intersection with the Old Bucksville Stage Road. Turn left, heading northwest. The trail here is wide, with brightly oxidized orange rocks in the bed. The gently rolling trail is also muddy in places and contains bits of heavy, dense, black rock. As the trail levels and passes through an area of pines, ignore a right turn. Instead continue straight, heading roughly north.

Break the flat pace briefly with a long uphill walk (you'll see an occasional red blaze through here), and then descend in a northerly direction. Soon reach an intersection with Slave Quarters Road, where the trail bears left. Approach, but do not pass beneath, a large iron gate that is marked "Shirley Real Trail." Pass two benches on your left and begin to encounter labeled trees, first a persimmon and then a post oak. Other trees you'll see on this segment include winged elm, slippery elm, and the spiny devil's walking stick.

This wide gravelly trail initially penetrates a brushy area, heading west with several benches placed along its length. Travel through a mix of hardwood and pine as the level trail snakes through the woods. Cross over a small stream, make a slight descent, and reach a bench and an open field on your right. The nearby interpretive sign indicates this was the site of a slave cabin, circa 1860. Although chimney bottoms mark the homes of 600 slaves who worked at furnaces, the evidence is not easily viewed from the trail. The cabins reportedly were burned by Federal Cavalry troops in 1865.

Pass a succession of benches as you travel in a westward direction. Reach an open field on the left, a butterfly garden, and pass a pond on the right that has a short pier extending into the water. Continue walking at a leisurely pace to an open area, where you'll find two benches placed back to back. Cross a footbridge over a stream to your right and head toward the arching iron bridge to cross Roupes Creek back to the furnaces. From the furnaces, return to the parking area.

To top off your hike, visit the Alabama Iron and Steel Museum, just uphill from the park's visitor center. The museum is open Monday–Friday, 9 a.m.–5 p.m.; Saturday and Sunday 10 a.m.–5 p.m. Admission is free.

▶ NEARBY ACTIVITIES

If you're hungry, Exit 108 is the place for eats. Restaurants located here include Applebee's, Santa Fe, and Cracker Barrel. Alternately, if you're driving back on I-459, the only nourishment available before you pass the Galleria shopping mall is fast food at the McCalla exit.

UNIVERSITY OF ALABAMA ARBORETUM TRAIL

KEY AT-A-GLANCE INFORMATION

LENGTH: Up to 3 miles if you see everything

CONFIGURATION: Combo

DIFFICULTY: Easy

SCENERY: Gorgeous array of melding forest environments, replete with labeled trees and wildflowers

EXPOSURE: Mostly shaded

TRAFFIC: Light, unless a school group is visiting

TRAIL SURFACE: Dirt woodland path with roots and a few rocks

HIKING TIME: 1–2 hours

ACCESS: Hours are 8 a.m.–sunset; usually open on weekends but call (205) 553-3278 to confirm a particular weekend.

MAPS: Arboretum map available at the pavilion

FACILITIES: Rest rooms, water

SPECIAL COMMENTS: On the way down, 36 miles from Birmingham, is a nice rest area—a great place to freshen up before or after the hike (there's a twin rest area on the northbound side of the interstate). At the Arboretum, visitors are asked to stay on trails and to not pick flowers or remove any other flora from the premises.

▶ IN BRIEF

This easy collection of meandering trails is the best place I know of to practice your tree- and wildflower-identification skills.

▶ DESCRIPTION

What a peaceful place this is. You can wander the 60-acre arboretum's network of trails without really paying attention to where you're going. This gives you the freedom to focus on the labeled trees, shrubs, and wildflowers. On the accompanying trail map is a suggested route that takes you throughout the park and hits all of the highlights. But the best plan is to have no plan and wander for as long as you want.

Founded in 1958 by the Department of Biology at the nearby University of Alabama, the arboretum is as much a showplace as it is a research facility. The arboretum is divided into three main areas: a native woodland (the western area) that includes the Holly, Sweet Gum, Hickory, Poplar, Post-Oak, Pine, and Sumac Trails; an

▶ DIRECTIONS

From the intersection of I-459 South and I-65, take I-459 South for 16 miles and merge with I-59 South/I-20 West. Drive another 32 miles and take Exit 73 onto US 82/McFarland Boulevard. Bear right and drive a mile to 15th Street East. Turn right onto 15th Street East and follow it for 2 miles. Bear right at a sign for the arboretum and then bear back left (don't go straight into the activity center parking lot). Follow the sign onto Arboretum Way. Pass Harry Pritchett golf course on your right and at another arboretum sign bear left onto a narrow dirt road. Reach a gravel lot above a small pavilion/greenhouse complex and park. Walk down to the pavilion and pick up a map.

15th St. E.

← To McFarland Blvd.

Arboretum Way

Harriet Pritchet Golf Course

Loop Rd.

59

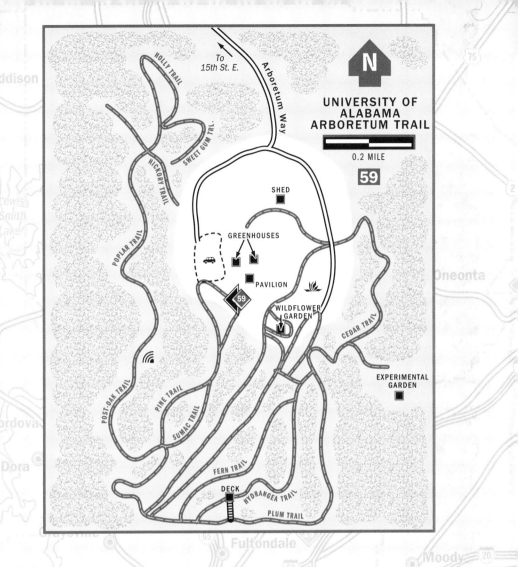

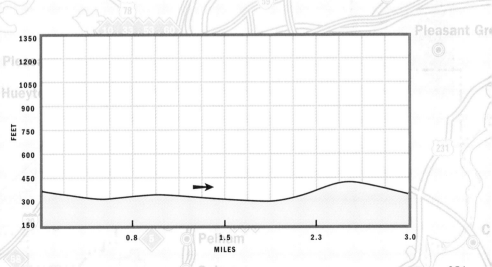

ornamental section (the southeastern part of the park); and a wildflower garden (in the center, near the pavilion).

If you're into trees, the fun begins right away. On your short walk down to the pavilion from the parking lot, pass a knobby-kneed crape myrtle, a common sweet shrub, a gorgeous Japanese flowering cherry with prickly bark and a super-wide canopy, and a persimmon tree. To begin the walk shown on the map, bear right at the pavilion and head toward a yellow arrow that reads, "Trail." Heading south on the Sumac Trail, you'll encounter a nice selection of interesting, less-familiar trees, including a cork amurtree, thriving among more commonly known red and white oaks, sweetgum, Eastern hemlock, and holly. Stands of oak-leaf hydrangea and flitting butterflies add to the charm.

If you're new to the tree-naming game, don't try to learn everything in a single visit. Four important hardwoods to learn, found all across our area, are the white oak (with silvery, flaky bark), red oak (dark, knobby bark), tulip poplar (tall, straight, smooth, gray trunk), and sweetgum (star-shaped leaves and spiky balls). These are only the tip of the iceberg, but make for a good start. In addition, begin to learn to distinguish the more common pines, such as loblolly of which there are many fine specimens here.

Initially a wide woodland path, the trail is remarkably uncluttered. The arboretum's trails are intentionally unmaintained to allow forest decay and regeneration to occur naturally. Pass a post-oak—its acorns are popular food for turkey and other wild animals—noticing how its trunk would indeed make a great post. At the intersection of the Sumac and Pine Trails, continue on the Sumac Trail. There you'll see a 100-foot, straight-trunked loblolly pine that is scored with Southern-pine-beetle burrows. It appears to have weathered the onslaught thus far, unlike many other pines in the arboretum.

Reach a multiple trail intersection with a stone bench, then bear left onto the Pine Trail, passing between a sweetgum and a white oak. At 0.14 miles into the hike, the woods change from an oak-and-hickory-dominated woodland to a pine forest mixed with opportunistic trees such as sourwood. The shift indicates a disturbance, such as fire, wind, or disease, that killed off the hardwoods, allowing the pines to grab a foothold in the ensuing light gaps. Continuing left at the next intersection, look for one of many water oaks in the park. You can find giant specimens of these hardwoods growing in wetter lowland forest areas, often marking an old homeplace. The oak's bark is smooth and the small leaves are somewhat reminiscent of a propeller blade.

Clusters of large sourwood and black cherry greet you just before an intersection and small wooden bridge. Turn left, pass a Chinese chestnut, a giant magnolia that is as wide as it is tall, and towering, stately tulip poplars. The walking is easy and level here.

With the pavilion to your left, go right into the wildflower area. I'm keen to learn more about our native wildflowers, but the task is more intimidating than hounding trees. Wildflowers can appear very different at their various life stages, and to my untrained eye often look like an unremarkable weed. All of the arboretum wildflowers are labeled, including yellow trillium, Walter's violet, bluebell, white-crested iris, spiderwort, and bloodroot.

The Wildflower Trail has a number of short spur trails that you can wander. If you go straight in and left, you'll find a delicately leafed bald cypress, but you'll also hit a dead-end. From the wildflower area, work your way over to the Cedar Trail. You'll see as many people jogging as you'll see walking in the arboretum on a Sunday morning.

The Cedar Trail is narrow and crowded, with a dense understory. Trees are not labeled here, so you can test your new knowledge right away. When you reach a wet gully, cross it on a small footbridge that squeezes between two large beeches. Meandering through boggy bottomland, go left up a set of wooden stairs, noticing the abundant poison ivy along the trail.

At the top, emerge into the experimental garden area. This area is designed to appeal to children, but I thought it was informative and entertaining as well. Past a compost demonstration site on your right, you'll see a handful of small garden plots. There's a small butterfly-shaped garden filled with plants that butterflies like to visit. Kids will like the Harry Potter–esque Professor Sprout's Magical Garden, which consists of plants that have a distinct feel, such as sharp, soft, or prickly. The sign encourages visitors to touch the plants, including the incredibly soft lamb's ear. Next is a novel scratch and sniff garden filled with aromatic herbs. While you're here, try out the annalimatic sundial. Follow the directions and get a pretty accurate estimate of the time of day, just by raising your arms overhead.

Back at the Cedar Trail, turn left, follow the path to a dirt road, and turn left again. When you reach the Hydrangea Trail, take it to the left along a slope that leads down to a bog. You'll pass beneath an elevated boardwalk, walk back up to your left, and then take a short stroll to its end, where a white oak grows up through the decking. It's about 40 feet to the ground as you look out over the forest sloping down and away.

From the Plum Trail, take the Fern Trail, rife with fern growth. Look along the trail here for patches of the wildflower *hepatica*. Beyond the Hydrangea Trail, which comes in from your right, work your way around the greenhouses and up to the parking area to explore more of the native-woodland section of the arboretum.

On the Hickory Trail, watch for thick vines, some smooth and some hairy. The smooth vines are muscadine, which in late summer will be heavy with juicy and tart muscadines. The hairy vines are poison ivy. To squeeze the most out of the trails here, turn right onto the Sweetgum Trail. A sign indicates the location of an old wagon road off to the right. At the Holly Trail, cross a footbridge and circle the loop back to the Sweetgum. Pick up the rolling Poplar Trail, where I saw the largest in-ground yellow jacket nest that I have ever encountered.

The last new ground you'll cover is along the Post-Oak Trail, where you'll find wild yucca and a stone amphitheater that looks like it would be the perfect spot for an afternoon lecture (or nap). Take the Pine Trail back to the parking area to complete your ramblings. If you did not visit the greenhouses, pop in for a look.

▶ NEARBY ACTIVITIES

On the way down, stop at the Mercedes plant near Vance and take the industrial tour. Visit www.mbusi.com for all of the information, including dress code and visitor restrictions (children under 12 years of age are not permitted to take the tour).

VULCAN TRAIL

KEY AT-A-GLANCE INFORMATION

LENGTH: 2.8 miles (add 1.5 miles if you do the ramble at the end of the trail)

CONFIGURATION: Out-and-back with two supplemental out-and-backs

DIFFICULTY: Moderate

SCENERY: Old hardwoods, kudzu, sweeping views of downtown Birmingham, and soaring antennae

EXPOSURE: Half shaded, half exposed

TRAFFIC: Light

TRAIL SURFACE: Asphalt

HIKING TIME: 1¾ hours

ACCESS: Open year-round (parts of the hike on top of Red Mountain may be off limits in the future)

MAPS: None

FACILITIES: None (currently)

SPECIAL COMMENTS: People mountain bike and run on this trail as well as walk. Vulcan Park is scheduled to re-open early in 2004. The refurbished park will offer a new visitor education center and outdoor interpretive exhibits. The centerpiece, of course, will be the completely restored statue of Vulcan.

IN BRIEF

This newly minted trail follows the path of a former train track used to shuttle iron ore mined from Red Mountain for use at Birmingham's many iron ore furnaces. Wonderful views of downtown Birmingham await through the heavily wooded slopes of Red Mountain.

DESCRIPTION

The city of Birmingham might have remained a mere hamlet if not for the occurrence of three resources found in the area: coal, iron ore, and fluxing stone. These three mineral resources enabled Birmingham to become the leading producer of iron and steel in the South. The Vulcan Trail follows a stretch of the former Birmingham Mineral Railroad, a 156-mile loop that followed the Red Mountain Iron Ore seam from Ruffner Mountain to Bessemer, enabling the distribution of mined ore to the many foundries in the area.

The parking area and trailhead lie just below Vulcan Park, constructed in the 1930s to showcase Giuseppi Moretti's 56-foot iron statue of the Roman god of the forge, Vulcan. The statue was taken down in 1999 and sent to restorers in Alexander City, who refurbished the badly deteriorated statue. Vulcan was re-erected in the summer of 2003.

DIRECTIONS

From downtown Birmingham drive onto 20th Street heading south. Pass through Five Points, continue up the hill, and bear around left as 20th Street climbs Red Mountain toward Vulcan. Stay in the right lane and watch for a blinking yellow light atop the hill. Here, turn right into an unmarked gravel parking lot, which will appear at the end of the guardrail on your right, and park.

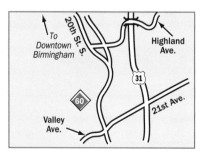

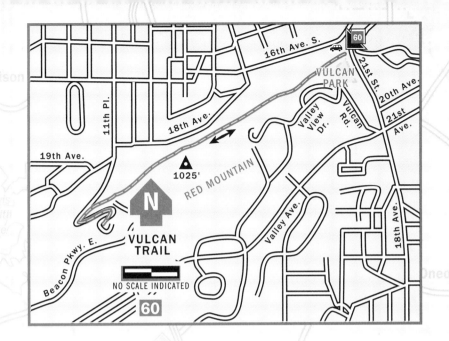

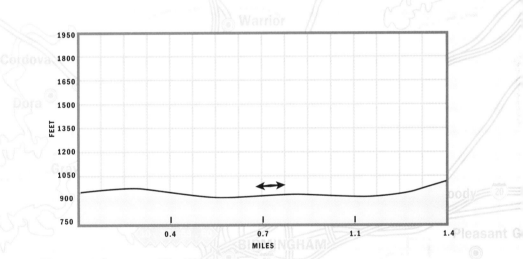

With Vulcan looming above and to your left, step onto the sidewalk at the far end of the parking lot and follow a metal handrail. Continue until the sidewalk intersects a wide paved path, then turn right, heading south/southwest. Tall, stately hardwoods abound along this hike, including oaks and maples. To your left the land slopes up acutely; to your right the land falls away sharply, towards joining residential backyards.

Eventually, the giant red neon letters of WBRC as well as a large antenna come into view. Pass through a big patch of kudzu smothering both sides of the trail. Here you can look out over downtown Birmingham, which appears periodically to the right (facing north/northwest). The BellSouth building, the abandoned City Federal building, the SouthTrust building, and other downtown landmarks are all visible. Along this stretch, the wide path civilizes a bit, changing from dirt and mud to fine gravel.

Pass another kudzu-plastered hillside on your left and look for the white curve of The Club, a longtime haunt of the city's gentry. To your right with the UAB campus in the foreground, take advantage of a power-line clearing to gain a clear downtown vista. Peering over trees drenched in kudzu and wisteria, in the distance you may be able to see flames or plumes of white smoke in Tarrant City, both byproducts of coke production at the ABC plant there. Used in the manufacture of iron and steel, coke works to remove impurities from molten ores.

Continuing southwest, The Club looms high above the trail on your left, along with two tall antennae, and downtown views pop up on your right. Soon, see a large microwave tower and get your first close-up look at someone's roof on the right.

Reach a large mortar-and-stone structure on the left that looks like it may have had steps going up through the middle. This is the remains of an old tipple base, a telling artifact that hints at the miles of honeycombed mine shafts beneath the skin of Red Mountain. Cars of iron ore were lowered by gravity from above, dumped, and then taken by conveyor over the tipple into larger train cars waiting below. This particular location was the site of the Valley View Red Ore Mine, which operated between 1904 and 1924. Ore extracted from this site went to the plant owned by Central Iron and Coke Company in Holt, Alabama.

Pass a small patch of mulberry trees along the left side of the trail. Then to your right, over the top of a square-shaped apartment complex, catch a wide, clear view of Birmingham, encompassing Legion Field in the distance. Pass some small mimosa trees on the left, then look for a large ten-foot square, stacked-stone structure on the left, most likely another tipple base.

The trail continues, passing more apartments down to the right and numerous antennae and microwave towers on the left. Reach an intersection of power lines and continue straight ahead. The sounds of birds mingle with the distant drone of traffic and the occasional airplane buzzing through the clouds.

Enter an area of very tall hardwoods where the steep downward slope to the right levels out a bit. Along this stretch, you may be able to see exposed samples of the rich, red dirt that indicates the presence of iron oxide. Pass an old, narrow paved road on your right and then turn abruptly left at a pile of aged sandstone blocks. The official Vulcan Trail ends here, but the hike continues on an old, broken, narrow paved road that switchbacks up the mountain to its top. From here, on a Sunday morning, you may hear church bells sounding in the distance.

Heading east and climbing, look down to the left to see Vulcan dropping away from you. The trail switchbacks right with a view straight onto a microwave tower. Heading roughly west, pass a big patch of kudzu, as the steep road levels slightly. Switchback to the left to see a white water tank painted with the Birmingham Water Works Board logo.

Most hikers will probably want to turn back here for a nearly 2-mile walk. The next segment is truly a wandering ramble across the top of Red Mountain. If you wish to continue, turn right and, instead of walking up to the water tank, continue on a leaf-covered dirt trail that can be muddy after a rain. The trail runs down through scrub and a small patch of pines. Exit the woods onto a sidewalk paralleling Beacon Parkway East. The Regency Summit condos are on the right

Turn left onto the sidewalk, heading due east with a pine-dominated forest on the left. After apartments appear to the right, exit the sidewalk and head up a gravel road with a large gravel parking lot to the right. Transmission antennae loom overhead. Head through the gravel lot toward the paved road in front of the Channel 21 studios. Pass TV 21 on your left as the road dips down. Antennae-anchoring cables are interspersed along this trail segment. Pass the cooling units for the TV 21 antenna on the left; a quiet, woodsy, kudzu-infiltrated area on your right.

Stay on the paved road, which begins to climb back to the left. The road enters and circles clockwise around a large, tiered, paved parking area. Keep left and head straight up. Approach the top of the lot, rife with small mimosas, and curve as you descend steeply around the outside of the parking area. Exit at the bottom to complete this short side loop.

Head uphill the way you came in, with the TV 21 cooling units on your right and the gravel parking lot straight ahead. Turn left here and descend down the paved road (Golden Crest Drive), heading southeast. Look for an antenna-anchoring cable spanning the road with a large red ball in the middle of the span. Pass the entrance to Channel 42 and then pass PAX Channel 44, both on the left. In front of PAX, a steep sidewalk begins. The sidewalk bears left as the entrance to Valley Ridge apartments appears on the left. Descend until you intersect Valley Avenue at the bottom of the hill.

Turn around and retrace your steps up the steep hill to complete this out-and-back segment. Pass PAX 44 and WIAT 42 on the right. Look up about here to see a tremendous web of antennae anchor wires above and in front of you. Pass under the red ball and return to the gravel parking lot and turn left heading north/northwest.

Walk toward the red and white microwave tower and bear left. Pass along a chain-link fence and the water tank to your right, with apartments to your left. Exit the gravel lot and regain the sidewalk that brought you here. You are now retracing your journey back to the parking lot where you left your vehicle.

At the Regency Summit condos, turn right onto the dirt road back into woods. Trudge up toward a different view of the red-and-white microwave tower in front of you. With the water tank to your right, turn left onto the old, narrow paved road that switches back down to the Vulcan Trail. At the bottom, turn right to return to the parking lot. A broken paved road continues down to the left, but stay to the right on the level path.

On a Sunday morning after your hike, try the brunch at the Mill on 20th Street next to the fountain in Five Points. For breakfast anytime of day, look for the Original Pancake House, which is located diagonally across the Five Points South intersection from the Mill. There are so many other good restaurants in this area, just look around and take your pick. If you want to kick back and refuel on caffeine, look for Starbucks or Joe Muggs, both located right off of 20th Street near the fountain.

60 Hikes
within 60 MILES

BIRMINGHAM
INCLUDING ANNISTON, GADSDEN, AND TUSCALOOSA

APPENDICES
& INDEX

APPENDIX A:
HIKING STORES

Academy Sports & Outdoors
in Homewood
251 Lakeshore Parkway
(205) 945-9998

near Trussville
1612 Gadsden Highway
(205) 661-1140

Alabama Outdoors
in Homewood
3054 Independence Drive
(205) 870-1919

in Pelham
110 Cahaba Valley Road
(205) 403-9191

in Tuscaloosa
700 Town Center W3
(205) 752-2914

in Steele
Horse Pens 40
(800) 421-8564

Backcountry Sports
in Fultondale
513 Bergan Drive
(205) 841-8495

Cahaba Outdoors, Inc.
in Cahaba Heights
4137 White Oak Drive
(205) 967-1995

Deep South Outfitters
in the Colonnade
3431 Colonnade Parkway
(205) 969-1339

Hibbett Sporting Goods
in Homewood
451 Industrial Lane
(205) 942-4292

High Country
in the Galleria
US 31 and I-459
(205) 985-3215

Homewood Sporting Goods
in Homewood
2941 18th Street South
(205) 879-2828

Mountain Brook Sporting Goods
in Mountain Brook
66 Church Street
(205) 870-3257

Rogers Trading Company
off of US 280
4639 US 280 South
(205) 408-9378

Trak Shak
in Homewood
2841 18th Street South
(205) 870-5645

Trussville Sporting Goods
in Trussville
107 Morrow Avenue
(205) 655-4124

Urban Outpost
in Birmingham
1105 Dunston Avenue
(205) 879-8850

APPENDIX B:
PLACES TO BUY MAPS

LOCATION/CITY

Alabama Outdoors
in Homewood
3054 Independence Drive
(205) 870-1919

in Pelham
110 Cahaba Valley Road
(205) 403-9191

in Tuscaloosa
700 Town Center W3
(205) 752-2914

Carto-Craft Maps
in Birmingham
738 Shades Mountain Plaza
(800) 444-4095

United States Geological Survey
(888) ASK-USGS
www.usgs.gov

APPENDIX C:
HIKING CLUBS

LOCATION/CITY

The Alabama Trails Association
P.O. Box 371162
Birmingham, AL 35237
www.alabamatrailsasso.org

The Alabama Hiking Trail Society
P.O. Box 477
Andalusia, AL 36420
www.alabamatrail.org

Appalachian Trail Club of Alabama
P.O. Box 381842
Birmingham, AL 35238
(205) 991-0534
sport.al.com/sport/atca

Sierra Club, Alabama Chapter, Cahaba Group
1330 21st Way South, Suite 110
Birmingham, AL 35205
(205) 786-0622
alabama.sierraclub.org/cahaba.html

Vulcan Trail Association
mmcs.paramedics.com/vta2.html

INDEX

INDEX

INDEX

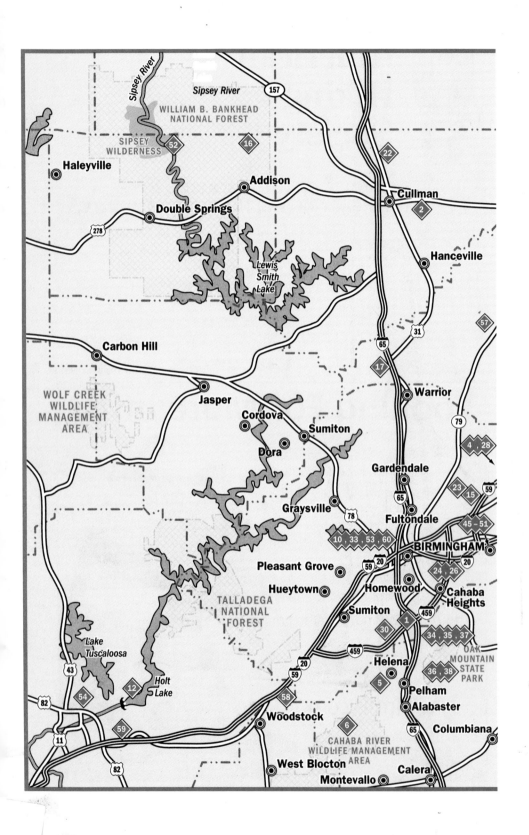